What Others Are Saying About This Book

Dr. Robert DeMaria's book Dr. Bob's Drugless Guide to Balancing Female Hormones *is a must-read for every woman. Being a menopausal woman is not easy: There are hot flashes, mood swings, and fatigue, along with the pressures and stresses of daily life. Through concise, easy-to-read chapters that explain what our bodies are really going through, Dr. Bob will walk you through practical solutions to feeling better through diet, exercise, and natural supplements. We cannot always change our circumstances—but we can change our body so that we are not overwhelmed by day-to-day challenges. This book helps you make lifestyle changes for a healthier, happier life.*

Marilyn Hickey
President and Founder, Marilyn Hickey Ministries

As a women's health and fertility naturopathic specialist, I have put this book on my MUST-READ list for every patient that comes into my practice. It is so vital to understand the truth about women's hormones. More so, it's important to appreciate the subtle dance of hormonal interrelationships and how powerful natural medicines, a whole-food diet, and stress management help to create hormonal balance for the rest of a woman's life! The realistic, achievable, and powerful hormone-balancing strategies Dr. Bob will teach you in this book will guide you to achieve the results you've dreamed of—drug-free, optimal hormonal health!

Dr. Angela Hywood, ND
Holistic Gynecological, Obstetrical & Natural Fertility Specialist

Dr. DeMaria makes a valuable contribution to the often confusing, always vital, battle of bringing balance to female hormones. Add this book to your library!

David J. Frähm, ND
President and Founder, Health*Quarters* Ministries

As a 39-year-old mother of three small children, I was experiencing problems common to many women of my age. My migraines, most notably, were being poorly treated by conventional healthcare, and they were getting worse.

Following Dr. Bob's advice, many of my symptoms have dramatically improved or resolved. After three months, I look better and feel younger. I am a true believer in Dr. Bob's approach to healing from the inside out.

P. Brethauer, MD

Dr. Bob's

DRUGLESS GUIDE TO
BALANCING
FEMALE
HORMONES

Dr. Robert DeMaria
The Drugless Doctor

Drugless Doctor LLC™
Westlake, Ohio

Dr.Bob's DRUGLESS GUIDE TO BALANCING FEMALE HORMONES
by Robert DeMaria, DC, NHD

Published by
Drugless Doctor LLC™

Gemini Tower II
2001 Crocker Road
Westlake, Ohio 44145
Phone: (440) 323-3841
Fax: (440) 323-1566
E-mail: drbob@druglessdoctor.com
Website: www.druglessdoctor.com

Library of Congress Control Number: 2007906534
ISBN: 978-0-9728907-5-5

Printed in the United States of America
10 9 8 7 6 5 4 3

DISCLAIMER
This information is provided with the understanding that the author is not liable for the misconception or misuse of information included. Every effort has been made to make this material as complete and accurate as possible. The author of this material shall have neither liability nor responsibility to any person or entity with respect to any loss, damage, or injury caused or alleged to be caused directly or indirectly by the information contained in this manuscript. The information presented herein is not intended to be a substitute for medical counseling.

Book cover design by Ariel Vergez of Vujà Dé Studios, LLC

Page design by Peri Poloni-Gabriel, Knockout Design, www.knockoutbooks.com

About Dr. Bob

Dr. Bob has been helping patients with natural, drugless care since the 1970s. Over his career, he has noticed a progressive decline in the quality of life of new patients coming into his office. Conditions that used to occur in women who were 50 and 60 are now affecting women in their 30s and 40s. The incidence of surgeries and invasive procedures has escalated to the point where nearly every new patient, young or old, has been prescribed a medication or has experienced some type of surgical intervention. These facts have motivated Dr. Bob to pursue natural, drugless answers for conditions that are occurring in epidemic proportions and continuing at an alarming rate. Hundreds of thousands of hysterectomies, cholecystectomies (gallbladder extractions), and breast cyst removals can be prevented by making appropriate lifestyle modifications.

Dr. Bob has a bachelor's degree in human biology. He is a practicing DC and has relentlessly continued with his post-graduate education, earning a natural health doctor (NHD) degree, fellow status in spinal engineering, and diplomat status in treating bone and joint conditions without medication. Dr. Bob graduated valedictorian of his class with honors. He is a recognized worldwide expert and is frequently a keynote speaker.

Dr. Bob teaches post-graduate-level, continuing-education classes in the health, business, legal, and teaching areas. He has been a college instructor, and has spoken in Europe and Canada. He has been on television internationally, and he hosts his own weekly regional TV program with his wife of over 35 years, Deb. They have two sons.

Dr. Bob has five other popular books focusing on natural health restoration, including *Dr. Bob's Guide to Stop ADHD in 18 Days, Dr. Bob's Trans Fat Survival Guide, Dr. Bob's Guide to Optimal Health, Dr. Bob's Drugless Guide to Detoxification,* and *Dr. Bob and Debbie's Guide to Sex and Romance. Dr. Bob's Drugless Guide to Balancing Female Hormones* is an accumulation of over 30 years of experience that will surely help make a difference in anyone's life.

Dr. Bob knows it is time for the public to take control of their own future regarding the state of their personal health. He experiences that it can work; he sees it happen every day. The information in this book will make a difference. All you have to do is take action. Today is your day!

Acknowledgments

The information that you will find in this book is an integral part of my clinical career. A generation of women has suffered considerably over the years due to the serious side effects of strong prescriptions. Recently, a government-sponsored study tracked the effects of hormone replacement therapy. After revealing that HRT may cause heart disease and other blood vessel challenges, the study was brought to an abrupt halt. This was very positive because quick action has saved thousands of lives.

I would like to acknowledge my female patients who have made appropriate lifestyle changes, resulting in a healthy hormonal life. Congratulations to each of you who continues to pursue optimal health naturally in spite of all the pressures of the medical community to take prescription medication.

Thank you to the editors and readers of the manuscript: Teri Forthofer; Laura Meyer; Dr. Jack Kohl; and my typist and liaison editor, Kim Plaso. I would like to thank Connie Schnorr and Sue Dowden, who helped with the final details; Chantelle Layton for her artistic assistance; and Karen Hurguy, whose drawings were used to depict the functions of the body. A special expression of gratitude goes to my friend and colleague Dr. John Madeira for sharing his familiarity with and insight into the Amish community and their lifestyle.

I would not be in a position to create the several books I have been able to generate without the unconditional support and passion from my wife, Deb. She has been a consistent motivator, knowing that we are making an impact on our generation. I would also like to thank my sons, Dominic and Anthony, who have been a joy to raise and have seen how natural healthcare can make a difference.

I would like to acknowledge all of you, the readers, who have an opportunity to improve your health without medication. Congratulations in advance as you explore the new realm of optimal health; I promise that you will not be disappointed!

Dr.Bob
The Drugless Doctor

Contents

Preface

Congratulations on choosing this natural health guide, which has the potential to positively impact your and your family's lives for generations to come. We are living in a time of great knowledge and awesome technological advances. It appears, as you look from the outside in, that if you have any type of condition that is causing your body not to function properly, all you have to do is go to your healthcare provider and you will be prescribed a pill, potion, or cream that will make everything better. When you read magazines and news articles today, you are led to believe that the healthcare industry has a handle on all situations involving sickness.

Investigation is being conducted in a variety of newer areas, including stem-cell research and experimentation affecting the makeup of gene pools. We have successfully used artificial organs and human organ transplants to lengthen the lives of many who otherwise faced premature death. I would like to applaud all the very fine physicians and scientists who passionately do their very best to help satisfy the desire of the public—to find answers to very elusive questions and concerns.

The real truth of the matter is, as a general mass of human flesh, we are not as healthy as is being portrayed on television and in news releases. It was recently reported, with the intention of reassuring us, that the dollars for cancer research were helpful and being used wisely, that there were a few thousand fewer deaths from cancer over the last couple of years.

Another publication released a statement that the amount of cancer has diminished in the last couple of years not because of new procedures but because women have made a choice on their own to reduce the amount of hormone replacement therapy they are taking. Conflicting information? Yes. Are we getting the truth from scientific circles? One of the commentators in the article suggested that even though people may be surviving the aggression of cancer, their post-cancer treatment has left them disfigured. I would also like to point out that while patients may live a season longer with a transplanted organ, they are also suffering with the side effects of anti-rejection drugs.

Considering that billions of dollars have been spent on cancer research and treatment over the last several decades, one might think that the cancer rates would be constantly on a downward trajectory. I would like to suggest that if we have the technology to increase gas mileage in a vehicle and send operational equipment to Mars, surely it's logical that we should be able to solve some of the common ailments that appear to be increasing in intensity and destruction.

This is a sobering thought, especially given the positive correlation between the reduction of synthetic hormone replacement and reduced cancers. Is the right treatment approach being pursued for female health? The government has had to step in and suggest that the years of hormone replacement therapy may be causing more harm than good. Recently, it was released that hormone replacement therapy may be safe for select age groups. It is very frustrating as a consumer to know that you might not be able to trust the information coming from drug companies, who have a lot to gain. How much of the information is motivated by profit? We are talking about the lives of individuals, not playing patty-cake kid games.

The media have been inundating us with articles that would make us think we were waiting for a flu epidemic to wipe out humanity. There are daily news releases about potentially disastrous ailments lurking to attack you and create total misery for you and your family. I would like to tell you that it is not all that bleak. I also want to be one of the first to tell you that you do have control over your current and future health. The body functions at the cellular level. That means you will get well and stay well if you feed the body real, whole food; hydrate it with pure water; exercise it on a consistent basis; give it an opportunity to rest and restore function; and maintain the spinal structure that connects brain cells to tissue cells, enabling proper nervous system function.

"But, Dr. Bob, I have not felt good my whole life; can you still help me?" This is a statement I hear regularly in my practice. Here is another: "I have had my gallbladder, colon, and uterus removed." The answer I commonly respond with is, "I have good news and I have bad news. The good news is we can support the function you have and improve it by educating you to make logical, healthy life choices. The bad news is we cannot reverse the loss of the organ."

Often, the patient expects that normal function can be restored after an organ has been removed, and this is a challenge to the healthcare provider. If the patient is willing to make a decision to work with the organ systems that remain intact, it is astonishing how the body can adapt. I am not trying to be foolish. There is a limit to what the body can do. Surgically removing female reproductive tissue is attacking the nervous system of the body. Function will be permanently changed to some degree.

I just got off the phone with a very educated woman from the East Coast asking how I could support her body; her ovaries have been removed. This is a huge dilemma. The body is designed to be self-healing and can adapt to many situations. She may be required to take some type of supportive supplement for the duration of her life. However, if she modifies her habits, feeds her body so that it can detoxify itself, and restores nervous system function through spinal corrective care, her body will adjust to the change and continue functioning. The real key is to create the environment for optimal health. She cannot continue with the same self-destructive habits she had prior to surgery, or she will not see restoration.

I have practiced since the late 1970s, so you could say I have been back and forth down the "yellow brick road" of life a few times. I was trained to think of healing from the "inside out" versus from the "outside in." And by the way, I have always been a natural doctor, long before it was popular. I was not trained with the Western medical mind-set of masking symptoms—which can actually prevent the body from getting rid of toxins, and slow and sabotage the healing process. If you follow some basic natural principles of feeding the body right and stop dumping artificial foods into it, as well as restore the nervous system, the body will do everything it can to detoxify and heal itself. Our bodies are self-healing structures.

I would like to start this adventure by inviting you to participate with me on a journey as if you were one of my patients. Not all accept care because it requires change. Many have been invited; some have walked the road for a while and have gone back to their prior patterns. Others have stood fast, making an educated decision to be the captain of their own ship.

I am really fortunate because I have treated patients for a long time. The significance of this to you is that I have a pool of women who have implemented what I have written. They do not or did not have hot flashes, tender breasts with menses, cysts in their ovaries, or breast removals or other common interventions. I have even treated patients who were diagnosed with cancer 30 years ago who chose to follow some logical suggestions, and they are alive and well and approaching 90 years of age. I know natural care works.

I would like to help you navigate this very exciting time in your life. You do not have to fear hearing the "C" word with a tear in your eye. I am going to teach you the basics; this program is not complicated or mysterious. I will give you a logical approach to engage in your daily routine. Think of this book as your map to allow you to celebrate with your inner circle of friends and family—children, grandchildren, and great-grandchildren. You are going to a new land and I am excited to have you on the trip. Get ready...because here we go.

Be Blessed

Dr. Bob DeMaria
America's Drugless Doctor

Introduction

MY ASPIRATION in writing this book is to reveal to you a potentially new set of thoughts and ideas, especially if you are just discovering the other side of medicine or if this is a renewal of your passion for natural health remedies. The reason I say "potentially new" is that you may have heard and read about drugless care but never really knew how to pursue it, and this is the first time you have reached out for something totally untested by your mind-set.

I will look at your current body signals through your—the patient's—eyes. I have repeatedly witnessed that healthcare providers get so focused on what they do that they forget patients are people just like themselves. As you read the text, with its insights into the area of human female hormone physiology, I want you to know that I am listening and talking to you from these pages as if you were in the room with me. I feel your entreaty, "Please listen to me." I know there is a natural answer. My main purpose in writing this book is to give you a breath of fresh air and HOPE. There are simple answers to your tough questions; I have been answering them in my natural practice for over 30 years.

What I want to share with you is very important for your long-term health. What I will be discussing is countercultural. The good news is there is a natural answer to your current situation. The thoughts and ideas that I would like to share are based on my extensive, clinically based evidence and experience.

Honestly, today the pharmaceutical and natural health fields offer so many concepts and ideas to treat people that navigating them can be like going through a maze. I believe from what I see, hear, and read that some of the proposed treatments are an educated guessing game. Unfortunately, people's lives are at stake.

I will keep the explanations as basic as I can. The biggest concept I can share with you is that healing comes from within, no matter who you are. Long-term optimal health will never come from a modality or treatment applied to the outside of our bodies; healing comes from the inside out.

When an idea is conceived, it is called a thought; when a thought is conceived, it is called a concept. We can only understand life to the degree that our concepts are correct. If an idea is wrong, the concept will be wrong; consequently, our understanding will be inaccurate and incomplete. You will suffer the consequences of a wrong concept in the health arena if it opposes natural principles. You won't respond long-term regardless of your economic and social achievements. I have known billionaires who have died because they followed an incorrect treatment protocol.

The real reason so many never achieve optimal health, regardless of the amount of technology, surgery, and medication they utilize, is that they were led to believe the wrong idea.

You are able to understand properly if your concepts are in alignment with your ideas, and your ideas are based upon truth. I am not sure if you have been told the truth when it relates to hormones in the female body. A number of the treatment procedures that have been prescribed for hormone replacement are also on a list of carcinogens, or substances that cause cancer. Are you aware of that? These substances are listed on the American Cancer Society's website for the whole world to see. Check out www.cancer.org; search for carcinogens, and you will get the entire list.

The chemicals listed are actually quite common. I suggest you study the list. You may be exposed to some of these carcinogens, and you really need to avoid them. The most frightening one to me is the synthetic hormone used to treat menopause. It does not make sense to me that a person would take a product known to cause CANCER.

Today the public is doing what it can to say "NO" to prescription medication. Who ever would have thought that there would be a proactive community looking for answers to their own health questions—answers that did not include a prescription? We live in a very inquisitive time. A possible challenge is, whom do you believe? Personally, I write in order to present the true facts on natural healthcare.

So, let's talk a bit about the reality of what is going on out there in the world. You see, every day I consult with patients who have been on the medical merry-go-round. They have frequently been coerced into radiation and chemotherapy when diagnosed with cancer. "This is the way we have always done it," was what one physician recently told a new patient before she came into my office.

I have also had the pleasure of treating healthcare providers and physicians. Do you know what? They have the same issues you do. There is no difference. A degree after your name does not create positive physiology. In fact, I have often seen the use of ineffective Western medicine delay the implementation of a natural treatment that would work. Healing always has to come from the inside out, not the outside in. This is a natural principle.

I have consulted with patients who had a cancer level of ZERO (on a scale of one to four) and yet were told they needed to put radiation and chemicals into their bodies. Rarely does it come up in my consultations with patients that their physicians ever discussed with them WHY they had cancer and WHAT treatment options were available. Yes, this sounds crazy, but it is true!

Not too long ago, if a physician said anything against hormone replacement therapy, he or she was ostracized and thrown out of the hospital and out of the inner circle. Today, the "hip" physicians are suggesting herbs and creams—and unfortunately antidepressants. Ever since the government released statistics on hormone replacement therapy and some of the side effects, women have been asking more questions.

Pharmaceutical companies and their representatives are ruthless in their desire to force information on physicians who are actively seeing patients. Do you ever wonder who gives physicians their information once they graduate? Do you know who pays for their continuing-education events? I have attended many medical events where there were HUGE numbers of physicians in attendance, and guess whose banners were flying in the hallway. Yes, you guessed it…the banners were those of the pharmaceutical industry, trying to woo the allopathic healthcare providers to use their products. It is not uncommon for one cholesterol-lowering prescription medication to generate over TEN BILLION dollars in ONE YEAR.

Okay, so what are we going to talk about in this book? I AM NOT GOING TO TALK ABOUT THE BENEFITS OF SOY AND BIOIDENTICAL HORMONES. You won't need to find a compounding pharmacist who formulates designer hormones for you; the best pharmacist is living inside of you. Has anyone ever told you how to wake up the pharmacist in yourself?

I have charted a course with ideas and protocols that may not be the current standard but nonetheless have been proven by a positive track record over time by natural doctors. Thirty years ago, everyone was told to use the low-fat diet, which was based on trans fat, only to find out this was wrong. Remember this very significant point: YOU CANNOT FOOL MOTHER NATURE! The early explorers were in untraveled waters more often than familiar territory, and they lived to tell about it. Imagine listening to some of their wild adventures. Well, what I will discuss is not wild, but it is delightful to read the testimonies my patients have penned for you while they have been on the journey with me. We will be focusing on the following subjects.

NATURAL POINTS TO OPTIMAL FEMALE HEALTH

- ♂ Keep the lymphatic system moving.
- ♂ Clean the machine for optimal liver function.
- ♂ Stoke the thyroid to keep the fire going.
- ♂ Support the adrenal glands—your backup hormonal system.
- ♂ Strengthen the frame and structure.
- ♂ Maintain communication between the brain and tissue cells.

ACTION STEPS

- ♂ What do I eat?
- ♂ How do I exercise?
- ♂ What tests should I have completed?
- ♂ How do I change?
- ♂ What supplements do I need?
- ♂ How do I get off my medication?

YOU ARE WHAT YOU EAT

- ♂ Shift your diet using the food transition guide.
- ♂ Eat the right fats.
- ♂ Consume only the recommended sweeteners.

I would encourage you to be open-minded; some of the information I am going to suggest may be just the opposite of what you read in the magazines and popular newsletters from which you normally get your data. I am going to focus on what you need to do if you want to have optimal health.

I will be explaining the function of certain endocrine glands, such as the adrenal glands, which are located on top of your kidneys, and the thyroid gland, found in the middle of your throat area; and organs like the liver, which is a HUGE player in the whole process. From researching journal articles and listening to my patients, I have learned that there are patterns associated with certain conditions. If you can discover your pattern and change it, you should be able to help prevent or correct a deficient or diseased state. The breast-cancer pattern is a very important pattern to understand.

I would like you to know that habits formed when you are very young affect your menstrual and female health as you get older. Addictions to sugar, fries, and chocolate at two years old can precipitate a lifetime of misery. I treat four and five generations of females. I see habits started with great-granddaughters that are the same habits strangling great-grandmothers. If you have had menstrual issues your whole life, chances are you will have hormonal challenges as you get older. That means, moms, your daughters may have the same harmful body signals you have unless they heed your advice now. I know it is not always easy. Just because people are friends or relatives does not mean they will listen. I have observed my own family members and acquaintances suffer post-surgical complications and pain syndromes because they did not want to follow my suggestions.

My wife had dysplasia (abnormal cells around her cervix) when she was 30; that was the time we decided to make lifestyle changes in order to overcome this problem. She ate ice cream nearly every day as a teen, took the pill, drank alcohol, and ate fried foods like most others raised in her era. Her dilemma motivated us as a couple to do everything we could to help *ourselves* along with our patients. Organic whole foods, weight training, aerobic activities, and stretching became a part of our daily regimen. As a result, her

---

overall health has been awesome for the last 20 years, without any significant female health problems.

I am not a gynecologist, and I am not pretending to be one. However, I do understand physiology and know that if you can make lifestyle changes, you have the potential to get better. Stopping destructive habits produces a healthy life. The challenge is connecting poor habits to poor health and providing a logical alternative and motivation to change. Patients are tired of receiving medical care that does not get to the cause of the problem. Often the side effects of medication appear to be more harmful than the benefits. I have successfully helped women who come to my office with medically diagnosed conditions that have not responded to traditional treatment protocols. I treat them without using medications and/or special, proprietary ingredients from some distant land.

It comes down to this basic plan: Get estrogen levels to normal in women not yet into menopause, feed the thyroid and ovaries the right nutrients and get them working as they are supposed to, and have the colon evacuating freely. After the onset of menopause, support the body by supporting adrenal function. If this plan is followed, everything else will fall into place. We also need to correct spinal articulations and free up the communication between brain cells and tissue cells. I know it sounds easy, and guess what: It is! Once you understand what you need to do, you will smack the palm of your hand against your head and say, "I should have done this a long time ago." I have spent a practice lifetime assessing progesterone/estrogen saliva tests, diet journals, thyroid panels, acoustic cardiogram graphs, symptom survey forms, spinal films, zinc and pH saliva screens, hair tissue mineral analyses, and countless hours of consultation with females of all ages (pre-teen, teen, 20s to 90s) and in all types of relationships (single; never married; divorced once, twice, or many times; widowed). I have seen and heard a lot.

I will do my very best to create a whole new world for you IN SIMPLE-TO-UNDERSTAND LANGUAGE. Please DO NOT CHANGE

ANYTHING immediately. This means do not go off your medication, have surgery, or add supplements until you read this entire book.

Then, I would pray for wisdom and crystal-clear thinking as to what you need to do for your own situation. Your current health is specific to you, not your neighbor, sister, mom, or best friend. You have your own unique circumstances. Yes, there are patterns; just don't do anything until you have discovered your own pattern.

Be blessed! It will get better, I promise. I have seen it happen for over 30 years, naturally...without drugs or surgery.

PART I

TEN NATURAL POINTS TO OPTIMAL FEMALE HEALTH

Chapter 1

Hormones: The Basics

Iam sure by now you have read many articles about female hormones and/or listened to many of your friends, all trying to tell you what to do. There are days you may cry because you think you are the only one with your condition (hot flashes, heavy menses, PMS, postmenstrual headaches, tender breasts, fibroids, etc.). No one seems to understand. You are mad at yourself or your spouse, best friend, neighbors, high school or college friends, sister, or even your own mother. Heaven forbid your husband comes home with "the sex twinkle" in his eye.

Your libido, which was once on fire, is waning, and if you have one more night with a hot flash, you are going to move to Alaska and wait till this desert heat is over. You are beside yourself. I know; I've been there. Not in my physical person, but with thousands of women who have been through what I just described. I have talked to women who are very frustrated and confused. They just want someone to tell them honestly what to do. I mention all this because as both a healthcare provider and a husband for over 30 years, I've seen and heard a lot. I have had conversations with many women who are tired of being led down a road they have no control over.

Hormones are a part of the many communication systems that help your body navigate through life. Think of hormones as messengers. Hormones are a part of the endocrine system, which manufactures them. There are organs, such as the uterus, with receptors that are impacted by this hormonal form of communication. Hormones are actually very potent compounds, and when they are in balance, they work awesomely. When you are under stress or overworked, and do not eat the right foods, a puzzle is created that even the most astute endocrinologist (doctor who works with the endocrine, or hormonal, system) has a challenge figuring out—and many times cannot figure out. The whole body is interdependent, which is why it is very significant when one part of the body is not functioning properly or when someone wants to have any organ or gland removed, especially an endocrine gland.

The endocrine system regulates the body's major continuous and prolonged processes:

♂ **Reproduction**

♂ **Growth and development**

♂ **Cellular metabolism and energy**

♂ **Blood balance of nutrients, electrolytes, and water**

♂ **Mobilization of body defenses against stressors (things that cause wear and tear on the body's physical and mental resources)**

The endocrine system is made up of eight different glands located strategically throughout the body.

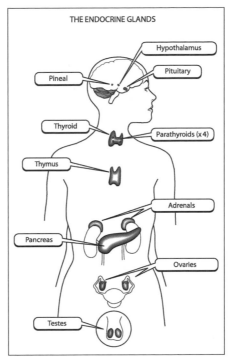

THE ENDOCRINE GLANDS

♂ Ovaries (in men, testes): produce progesterone and estrogen

♂ Adrenals (located on top of your kidneys): make sex hormones

♂ Pancreas islets (part of your pancreas): create insulin and enzymes

♂ Thyroid (located in your throat): makes thyroid hormone

♂ Parathyroids (part of your thyroid mechanism): assist in calcium function

♂ Pineal (in your brain): controls how light affects your body

♂ Pituitary: secretes many leading hormone activators

♂ Hypothalamus: is the CEO of your body

Besides these major glands, the endocrine system includes pockets of hormone-producing cells in tissues in the small intestine, heart, kidneys, and stomach. The endocrine system develops and begins producing hormones by the end of the second trimester of fetal development.

It is safe to say that the endocrine system is probably the first system impacted by nutritional imbalances and deficiencies. Viable nutrients are needed to make and replace hormones, and the metabolic functions performed by hormones are nutrient based and transferred from one place to another in our bodies. That is why I see so many patients who wonder why they do not feel good. I find they are usually eating convenience foods and are addicted to sweets, soda, and ice cream. Your body takes what you feed it and attempts to use it. Unfortunately, when fed the wrong things, your body won't allow you to function optimally.

The hypothalamus is the commander in chief of your hormonal system. I like to think of it as the maestro. Have you ever been to a major orchestral performance? The maestro can take a collection of musicians who sound great on their own and lead them to create beautiful music together. This music can create emotions that allow you to reflect on favorite times in your life. The hypothalamus connects your emotional and physical selves. It controls autonomic reflexes such as the activity of the heart and smooth muscles. It houses the body's thermostat and biological clock, which maintains the rhythm of the 24-hour sleep/wake cycle.

The pineal gland also has a role in biological timekeeping, being sensitive to retinal responses to light. The pineal gland is believed to coordinate fertility hormones and produces melatonin, the hormone known for its sleep-triggering ability.

I suggest to my patients that wearing sunglasses can affect their health by altering the ability of light rays to reach the back of the eyes. When the adrenal gland is stressed, which is very common, the pupil, or dark circle in your eye, cannot stay small or constricted, so light bothers your eyes. The adrenal gland indirectly has an impact on how the pupil operates. Wearing sunglasses inhibits the ability of the full spectrum of natural sunshine to enter the eye.

Do you sneeze when bright light hits your eyes? This may be another sign of adrenal strain. I know that the patients who enter my office with chronic health issues always have sunglasses in their purses or pockets or placed chicly on top of their heads. It is a consistent pattern and helps keep the sunglass business a multimillion-dollar industry. We will talk more about this in Chapter 8, about the adrenal glands.

The hypothalamus also initiates the female cycle by producing gonadotropin-releasing hormone (GnRH), which signals the pituitary to secrete follicle-stimulating hormone (FSH). FSH stimulates the ovaries to secrete estrogen, the sex hormone that stimulates development of breast, uterine, and ovarian tissue. It should be noted that the synthetic forms of HRT are associated with excessive cell growth that leads to cancer.

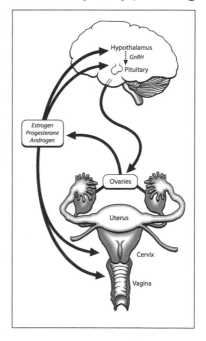

When estrogen reaches a certain level, it signals the hypothalamus to trigger the pituitary to secrete luteinizing hormone (LH). Estrogen levels then fall, while the level of LH rises and peaks (around day 14 of the 28-day cycle), stimulating ovulation, the release of an egg from its ovarian follicle. I generally have seen very few women who have completed the estrogen and progesterone saliva assessments who have a normal cycle. I have observed the peak of estrogen to be at all times of the month. A critical issue with female hormonal health is xenohormones; synthetic estrogen is everywhere and literally is the key to the whole puzzle I will unravel for you.

After ovulation, the follicle (now called the corpus luteum) is filled with cholesterol, which is converted first to pregnenolone (a hormone precursor) and then to progesterone. The newly made progesterone is used, in part, for the building up of the uterine lining. If after about 13 to 15 days the egg is not fertilized, the uterine lining is sloughed off in menstruation, when both estrogen and progesterone levels drop. Both estrogen and progesterone are necessary in the female cycle, and their BALANCE IS KEY FOR FULL HEALTH!

Many women in our culture have an imbalance of these hormones, especially insufficient levels of progesterone to counter excessive estrogen—an imbalance that is further complicated by chronic stress, liver congestion, and low levels of iodine, resulting in a poorly functioning thyroid and ovaries.

Progesterone is a hormone important to a number of bodily functions. During times of stress or conditions of chronic adrenal hyperstimulation, progesterone is capable of being converted into the stress hormone cortisol (natural cortisone, which helps take away pain and affects blood sugar stress). This explains why both men and women who go to their healthcare provider tired and in pain often find out their cholesterol is high. Their body is creating cholesterol to help handle stress and inflammation, by being a precursor for the body's natural cortisone.

 When one goes through chronic stress or severe long-term stress, the hypothalamus at first triggers an overproduction of the adrenal hormones, especially cortisol and DHEA (a hormone that helps make other hormones). This eventually leads to adrenal weakness, a state in which the exhausted adrenals cannot respond adequately. You're tired, bright light bothers your eyes, and you crave carbohydrates and salt (pickles, olives, and chips). You may also have been told that your blood pressure is low—and of course, your back goes out very easily. Does that sound like you?

The thyroid is also adversely affected by chronic stress. This gland's role includes regulating calcium metabolism and glycolysis (the breakdown of glucose for the body's energy and fuel). Under normal conditions, the fight-or-flight response from adrenal stimulation causes the thyroid to increase glucose breakdown. Again, glucose is the system's fuel.

In conditions of chronic stress, however, the thyroid is overstimulated and eventually becomes depleted. Body signals of a low thyroid include cold hands and feet; HOT FLASHES; depression; constipation; thinning hair; morning headaches; thinning outside eyebrows; widely spaced teeth; and menstrual problems, including scanty menses, sluggishness, and high cholesterol. Thyroid function is also disrupted by excessive estrogen, but this can be prevented by adequate progesterone levels. Hyperthyroid (overactive thyroid functioning) and especially hypothyroid (low thyroid functioning) have become more common. Adrenal and other hormone gland dysfunction can cause some of the above symptoms and many more, which will be discussed in more detail in Chapter 8.

One very damaging adrenal dysfunction is excessive cortisol production, which causes, among other serious problems, increased calcium mobilization from the bones—leading to osteoporosis, or loss of bone density. In a person with a healthy stress response, excessive levels of cortisol are automatically buffered. Constant stress destroys this feedback loop.

Hormonal imbalances compromise not only physical health but psychological health, manifesting as problems ranging from depression to panic disorder. One way the body tries to compensate for imbalances created and exacerbated by the demands of stress is to overproduce key hormones. Another way it tries to compensate is by converting sex hormones to stress hormones, thus further diminishing reproductive functions and the enjoyment of sexual health. This, by far, is one of the leading body signals that I see in my practice…the loss of sexual desire. If you do not have the desire or ability to engage in sexual intimacy, you probably have a severely drained system that needs to be recharged. This is very common in the dual-income family, whose members lead overcommitted lives centered around children, parents, coworkers, and extracurricular events.

It is very helpful to learn about hormonal interdependencies because they allow you to see the bigger picture. The problems commonly associated with menses or menopause are actually an indicator of a greater endocrine imbalance. For many women, the next step to understanding the bigger picture may be to look at their digestive health, including liver function and the foods that promote long-term cell efficiency.

THE PROBLEM WITH SYNTHETIC HORMONES

Hormones function much like a key mechanism with two ends on it. Let's call one end the R, or receptor, end. It fits exactly into a cell receptor and "unlocks" the metabolic door to start an action. The enzyme, or E, end fits precisely with the cellular enzymes that transform the hormone into another hormone or into a metabolite for excretion.

When a synthetic hormone enters the cell receptor, its R end is similar to the real one but not the exact fit. This jams the cell receptor or alters the action initiated. These are the reasons there are side effects from synthetic hormones. The synthetic hormone does not have the correct E end, so it cannot be properly cleared from the receptor, transformed into other hormones, or correctly metabolized and excreted. This creates more bad effects. If you want to disrupt the delicately balanced endocrine symphony, taking synthetic hormones is an excellent way to do it.

The negative effects on the body can be even more intense when the steroid system in the body is disrupted. The steroid system has its own interdependent melody that controls many functions in the body. The real issue occurs with synthetic steroid hormones produced by pharmaceutical companies. In the natural care field today, there are many who suggest the use of "sterols," natural plant-based ingredients, to make female hormones to normalize function. Soy-sourced bioidentical hormones are an example of these products. The pharmaceutical companies, on the other hand, have created a variety of items sourced from horse urine in attempting to normalize female hormonal health. The trouble with both attempts to help from the "outside in" is that neither gets to the cause of the problem. Granted, there are individuals who do respond, and I would suggest they may want to stick with what they are doing. However, I have consulted with many who, over time, begin having side effects that generally involve heavy menses, emotional swings, tender breasts, and even upper respiratory irritation.

There is a huge challenge with conventional hormone replacement therapy. No one in his or her right mind would think of taking a sophisticated jet into flight and entering alien commands into its computer control system. Yet conventional hormone replacement therapy does the equivalent. Alien (and therefore unpredictable and unknown) commands are entered into the endocrine system—or main "computer control system"—of a patient through the HRT drugs inaccurately called "hormones."

CONVENTIONAL HORMONE REPLACEMENT

Premarin® (also called conjugated estrogens) is made up of estrogen obtained from the urine of pregnant mares. This horse estrogen is the most commonly prescribed estrogen in the world. It is also the form of estrogen most commonly used in research. This means that most of what we think we know about estrogen replacement in women is actually about horse estrogen "replacement" in humans. I suggest as an experiment that you take one of those little yellow pills, add hot water to it, and sniff. Yes, you guessed it. You have reconstituted horse urine.

In our practice, we often use a combination of herbs and whole-food supplements to provide the proper nutrients—feeding the body what it needs to create the environment to produce estrogen naturally. I will be discussing in Chapter 8 how supporting adrenal function can help your body make enough estrogen for your physical and emotional needs during and after menopause. You see, when women are in their childbearing years, they have an abundance of estrogen. As the nest empties, so does the natural time frame for abundantly flowing estrogen. However, in today's society and culture, women are expected to take care of their grandchildren and great-grandchildren. This situation creates an unnatural, stressful atmosphere and is a reason we see health challenges in women who are raising their grandchildren. I see major burnout in many women due to overexpectation. I am not suggesting that you go into seclusion. I am suggesting that you may want to evaluate the level of stress being placed on your body. Many women today are the major sources of income for their families. There are many women who are single due to divorce or being widowed and have the additional burden of working 40, 50, or 60 hours per week—holding down as many as three jobs. This creates an environment for physical meltdown.

Estrogen is a steroid. Steroids are used to make natural cortisone. So, in essence, if you are stressed, are eating sugar, and are nutritionally exhausted, I can almost guarantee you will have estrogen deficiencies.

The bad side effects of Premarin® (which is for horses, not humans) include the following:

♂ **Heavy menstrual bleeding, cramping**

♂ **Breast tenderness**

- ♂ Fluid retention, edema, weight gain, increased fat storage
- ♂ Headache, migraine
- ♂ Depression, anxiety
- ♂ Glucose intolerance, insulin resistance
- ♂ Estrogen dominance
- ♂ Stimulation of the growth of fibroids
- ♂ Worsening of endometriosis
- ♂ Nausea, vomiting, cramping, bloating
- ♂ Leg cramps
- ♂ Eye problems
- ♂ High blood pressure
- ♂ Increased blood clotting tendency
- ♂ Venous thromboembolism, pulmonary embolism
- ♂ Increased risk of endometrial cancer and breast cancer
- ♂ Loss of scalp hair, growth of facial and body hair
- ♂ Gallbladder disease
- ♂ Pancreatitis

The composition of horse estrogen is vastly different from that of human estrogen.

HUMAN ESTROGEN	PREMARIN®
Estriol 60–80%	Estrone 75–80%
Estrone 10–20%	Equilin 6–15%
Estradiol 10–20%	Estradiol and others 5–19%

The metabolic breakdown products in Premarin® are biologically stronger and more active than the original horse estrogens. Various studies have shown that these breakdown products can produce DNA damage that is cancer causing. So, for example, the incidence of breast cancer increases when women take Premarin®. Like all conventional HRT, Premarin® is prescribed in standard dosages and not tailored to individual requirements. This means women are often taking much more "estrogen" than they need. It takes about eight weeks to clear Premarin® out of the body. In contrast, natural hormones are completely metabolized and cleared in 6 to 12 hours. Premarin® can easily, and usually does, throw a woman into estrogen saturation or dominance. The word *saturation* is significant because there is just plain too much in the body. Outside sources of synthetic hormones create imbalances, causing an excessive increase in sex hormone–binding globulin (SHBG)—which, in turn, blocks thyroid hormone function. You will learn more about this in Chapter 7, about the thyroid. Estrogen and stress block thyroid function. This is all starting to sound like a very interesting puzzle, isn't it?

Progestin, another human knockoff medication, is a chemical or drug imitation of progesterone, with its own set of negative side effects. Provera® (medroxyprogesterone acetate) is the most common progestin. It is also used in Prempro®, which is Premarin® and Provera in combination. Most progestins are made by taking natural progesterone and altering the chemical structure so it can be patented. Another type of progestin is made by altering a synthetic form of testosterone.

Problems with progestins include suppressed production of natural progesterone in the body. Progestins disrupt the steroid hormone pathways, which can cause both immediate and slow undermining of both adrenal and human hormone function. Since the progesterone pathway is fundamental to energy and vitality, this drug is usually a prescription for the chronic fatigue common with patients who have inflamed tissues or the named condition fibromyalgia. The list of myriad negative side effects includes the following:

♂ Depression

♂ Anxiety, nervousness

♂ Fatigue, leading to chronic fatigue over time

♂ Fluid retention and breast tenderness, weight gain

♂ Migraine

♂ Coronary artery spasm

♂ Angina, palpitations

♂ Menstrual irregularities, spotting

♂ Glucose intolerance, promotion of insulin resistance

♂ General edema

♂ Nausea

♂ Insomnia, sleepiness

♂ Skin rashes, acne

♂ Hair loss on scalp, facial hair growth

There are potentially life-threatening adverse effects of progestins. Spasms of the blood vessels around the heart are the most significant. Some other life-threatening adverse effects are

♂ Stroke

♂ Pulmonary embolism

♂ Breast cancer (implicated in causing)

Ninety percent of men who have heart attacks have atherosclerosis, or obstruction of coronary arteries, but only 30 percent of women do. The majority of heart attacks in women are caused by coronary artery spasm. In our practice, we use a B vitamin and magnesium to assist in metabolizing fat, which helps strengthen the adrenal glands to protect against heart blood vessel spasm. In Chapter 15, about tests, we also incorporate an assessment of heart sounds to determine what nutrients may be needed to promote natural function of the heart muscle.

Recently, information and statistics have been released about the link between the discontinued use of synthetic hormones and a reduction in breast cancer. There is a lot of debate on the subject. As a result of my clinical experience, I am of the opinion that you cannot put synthetic hormones into a body, knowing that the components do not match with the human counterparts, and expect nothing to happen. I would not take any synthetic hormone regardless of how safe any drug manufacturer says it is. Drug manufacturers have been wrong before, and they can be wrong again.

FACTORS THAT ALTER HORMONAL HEALTH

The physical condition of your mother and your birth order have an impact on your present hormonal health. Your birth order is important because if you are child two or three in the family order, the likelihood is that your mom had an overworked liver and fewer nutrients available to you. I really see this happen a lot in patients who were the second child. If you were kept in the hospital or had to go back because of jaundice, it is probable you had a reaction with your mom's system. The liver is affected even before you arrive into the world. A congested liver from the beginning of life can be a challenge as you become a teen.

The amount of quality whole-food oil your biological mother consumed also has an impact on your hormonal health. That does not mean you cannot modify and alter your life now. I am making a statement of possibilities. I see patients of all ages who start life off with unusual circumstances. They may have had asthma or eczema from the very beginning of their lives. Then they just seem to have a lifetime of hormonal health issues. I know that sexual hormones do not become evident until late adolescence, but your hormonal existence depends on many factors that are established very early in life. Even whether or not you were breast-fed has an impact on your hormone levels. Breast-fed children get more complete nutrients.

A body signal for liver congestion I commonly see is freckles right below the eyes and on the nose when a child is anywhere from eight to ten years old. That is when the hormones start to kick in and the liver is working overtime to process them. Freckles, from my experience, are a sign of excess copper and not enough zinc. Freckles in adults are also a signal of high copper. Patients with high copper usually have high estrogen. High estrogen typically suggests thick and pasty bile accompanied by digestive distress and bloating. Stagnant bile flow is often considered a medical reason to have the gallbladder removed. The medical community historically does not see the gallbladder as a significant gland or organ in the body. There are 500,000 removed every year. Eating half an apple daily will help you work on supporting liver function. Apples have malic acid, which will help keep your bile moving. Women who ate foods that were toxic to the liver when they were adolescents can continue their entire life with challenges, since the liver has been under never-ending overload.

Also, did you have mononucleosis when you were a teen? This is a red flag for liver stress. Mono wreaks havoc on the liver, which is one of the main organs with special cells that clean up toxic and foreign substances. The liver is important in processing all the used hormones, toxic foods, preservatives, medicines, and other outside toxins in the body.

Would you believe that if you have had a lifetime of eating fruit after meals that you could have liver stress? The fruit ferments on top of the food in your stomach. It is like having a constant drip of alcohol from the fermentation process. Your liver needs to process it. Has your life been a fog? Have you experienced poor memory? It is possible that your liver is overworked.

I have seen from my practice that when you feed the body correctly, it will be able to make its hormones specifically for your needs. You cannot fool Mother Nature.

REVIEW OF SYMPTOMS AND CAUSES OF HORMONAL PROBLEMS

The hormonal system is a communication system. There are eight organs associated with the hormonal, or endocrine, system.

☐ Stress can be the main cause of your hormonal issues by affecting the adrenal glands and the thyroid.

☐ Low blood pressure, wearing sunglasses, getting dizzy when going from a sitting to a standing position, and craving salt are signs of adrenal stress.

☐ Cold hands and feet, HOT FLASHES, constipation, thinning outside eyebrows, and morning headaches may suggest a low thyroid.

☐ Cholesterol elevations can be directly linked to inflammation-causing foods like sugar and trans fat.

☐ Cholesterol will elevate when the body is under chronic stress.

☐ Estrogen that is not balanced by progesterone can create hormonal imbalances and is the MOST COMMON CAUSE OF FEMALE HORMONAL issues prior to menopause.

☐ Xenohormones are common substances in our toxic environment that can create estrogen dominance. You will want to create a strategy that supports the liver to clear out estrogen saturation.

☐ A healthy liver is necessary to process toxic substances, including medications, synthetic hormones, and estrogen.

☐ What you eat has a bearing on your hormonal health.

☐ Processed foods, including trans fat and partially hydrogenated fat, congest the liver and lymphatic system.

NOTES _____

_____

_____

_____

_____

_____

_____

_____

_____

PATIENT TESTIMONY:

"Before making Dr. DeMaria's recommended lifestyle changes, I had been dealing with some cysts accompanied by very heavy periods and clotting. Following his advice, I eliminated sugar—the desire for it gradually went away and I occasionally used soy. I gave up dairy for the most part and added flaxseed. Pretty much completely giving up the refined carbohydrates was the most difficult change.

Being a patient of Dr. Bob's has benefited me greatly over the many years I have been going to his office. Six years ago, I was told by my OB/GYN that he would recommend laparoscopy to check one of my ovaries and possibly remove it. This was after MRIs, blood tests, and ultrasounds proved negative. Dr. Bob gave me the confidence to say "no" to this unnecessary procedure. Changing my diet to eliminate sugar and dairy and to include flaxseed oil and food supplements every day helped me greatly. Of course, the regular spinal adjustments were extremely important, as well, to keep my body running optimally. Today I still have two healthy, intact ovaries and have Dr. Bob to thank for helping me.

I feel healthier just coming to his office. The nutritional advice, adjustments, supplements, and encouragement from Dr. Bob and his staff all help. Additionally, my last menstrual period was 13 months ago. I feel great and am not bothered with any menopausal symptoms!"

Melanie McCrone

Chapter 2

Estrogen and the Liver

A machine depends on all of its parts to be working at 100 percent. If one part is not functioning up to par, the whole unit suffers. I was reading an article about the sport of rowing, or "crew." The participating athletes are, in essence, a group of very strong, high-testosterone young men working as a contiguous unit. The difference between victory and second place is passion and attitude. If one team member loses focus for one stroke, the whole team can be thrown off: That ONE paddle will cause a loss of synchronization, and the other paddles will collide. The body is a little more forgiving. It will work very hard to have another organ or system compensate for one that isn't functioning properly—for a season.

My research indicates that there are two camps out there when it comes to the liver and how it works: those who want you to buy their product to cleanse the liver/gallbladder mechanism, and those who have gone on record saying strongly that cleansing the liver does not promote improved health. I have witnessed firsthand that individuals who avoid the toxins found in food, water, and the environment have awesome results with their hormonal issues, versus those who continue to maintain toxic patterns. The latter do not respond to cleansing, even succumbing to surgical intervention.

Getting healthy is not about taking another "all natural" remedy or a prescribed medication. You do not necessarily need something else, natural or pharmacological; you really need to stop challenging liver function with what you put into your body.

Here is the key: There are two main reasons for hormonal issues before and after menopause. The first is that before menopause you have too much estrogen, and afterward you don't have enough. Your liver is the organ that processes estrogen to be recycled or eliminated from the system. If your liver is busy working on processing out sugar, dairy, and trans fat, how is it going to adequately process estrogen? The second reason is that if you are too stressed out, the liver is working to create an environment in the body to handle the stress—instead of fulfilling its job description. People often experience major sicknesses after stress. The wife of actor Christopher Reeve, who portrayed Superman in the movies, died shortly after he did—I am sure because of the enormous burden her system was under.

It is like this in your life. If you devote most of your time to one area, another area will be limited. There is an axiom, "Where your mind goes, your energy flows." Your time might be consumed with painting, golfing, or crocheting, for example, but your laundry and dirty dishes are piling up. What do you do when you need to wear something or to serve a meal on something? You must come to understand that your body needs to be in synchronization. You don't want your liver to be so busy and overworked that it cannot keep up—drowning in the waste that is gushing in to be cleaned up.

The liver has several pathways to clean up this toxic burden. One is called the P-450 system. The challenge is that in our society, the liver has to process an abundance of chemicals and debris that has become a part of our "normal lives"—not counting the extra burden you may place on your liver because of the choices you make "in moderation." The idea of eating in moderation gets more people into an overload situation than can be imagined. Think about telling a heroin addict that he or she can have "only a little." Sugar, which has been shown to have addictive properties, is one of those substances that patients like to tell me they consume "only in moderation."

As you drive down the road smelling fumes from vehicles, your liver needs to cleanse those fumes from your body or you will become a toxic dumping ground. Our bodies are also relentlessly bombarded by what is undetectable to the senses. Chemicals that enter through your skin, the water you drink, and the air you breathe need to be transformed into non-toxic substances. The daily patterns of modern life result in a continuous flow of toxins into our bodies—creating the potential for developing toxic residue. These noxious substances can generate an environment for the formation of free radicals.

Free radicals are a part of the oxidation reaction that occurs when items deteriorate. Think of free radicals as the rust you would see on a car or any metal object. Free radical production can damage fat and protein molecules in the body. It can also interfere with the genetic makeup of cells, creating the potential for cancerous cell growth. This is a major reason it is imperative that you keep exposure to toxins to a minimum.

Here is an experiment for you. Cut an apple in half with a sharp knife. Also cut a lemon, and squeeze some of the juice onto one half of the apple. Wait about 30 minutes. Look at the flesh of the two apple halves. What do you notice? The half with the lemon juice should be whiter than the half without it. The brown is oxidation. The lemon juice acts as an antioxidant, preserving the apple. You can slow down the natural oxidation, or rusting out, of your own body by eating blueberries and spinach, excellent sources of antioxidants. This basic test will motivate you to avoid processed foods, which foster the creation of free radicals—oxidizing (decaying) your body.

The endocrine glands secrete hormones that are excreted by the liver or are chemically altered to make them water soluble so that the body may expel them effectively. The steroid hormones that are altered by the liver include estrogens, cortisol, aldosterone, thyroxine, and others. The liver detoxifies these hormones or excretes them into bile. Bile is an antioxidant and a body degreaser. If the liver is not functioning properly, there may be an abundance of hormones circulating in the body at one time, leading to hormonal overactivity or toxicity. This excess of circulating hormones will tax the endocrine system and cause other toxic reactions to occur, such as too much circulating estrogen.

A part of this mechanism is the liver's ability to properly metabolize protein; this is critical to your survival. The liver takes hurtful substances and makes them less noxious, with the help of protein, and then excretes them from the body. Think of the liver as the agent by which toxins are neutralized. The liver also plays a central role in the synthesis of large amounts of cholesterol.

The liver is in charge of the metabolism and storage of carbohydrates, as well as the assimilation and storage of fat- and water-soluble vitamins. It is also critical for the storage of minerals. Now you can see why it is essential that the liver remain in optimal working condition. Artificial toxins in the body can create a demand on the liver, resulting in impaired function ("sluggish" liver). Symptoms of such toxic damage include fatigue, hormonal imbalance, increased fat stores, headaches, and blurred vision, all associated with multiple health challenges.

The liver is responsible for more enzyme reactions than can be listed in this book. I want to make it clear that the liver is a very important part of the restoration of optimal female endocrine health. It is essential that you mentally absorb this information. For you to get to the root cause of premenopausal estrogen saturation or dominance, your liver needs a source of whole-food B vitamins to properly process estrogen. This is very VITAL. What I have witnessed is that there is a widespread deficiency of B vitamins in our society. One of the factors that creates a B-vitamin deficiency is ingesting foods that are a poor source of B vitamins in the first place and then compounding the problem by eating products sourced from refined grains. Before becoming animal feed, refined grains have their very precious B vitamins processed out. Animals eat the grains, and when we consume the animals, we are not getting enough vitamin B. Another factor is eating anti–B vitamin foods, with sugar being the primary villain. Sugar depletes the body of B vitamins, and so does stress. Common symptoms of B-complex deficiency syndrome (BCDS) include the following:

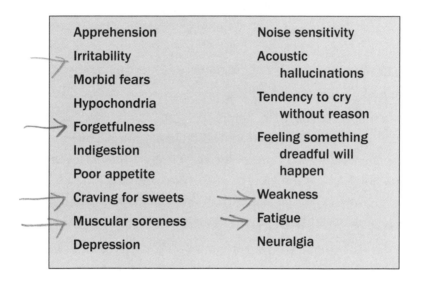

Apprehension	Noise sensitivity
Irritability	Acoustic hallucinations
Morbid fears	
Hypochondria	Tendency to cry without reason
Forgetfulness	
Indigestion	Feeling something dreadful will happen
Poor appetite	
Craving for sweets	Weakness
Muscular soreness	Fatigue
Depression	Neuralgia

How many symptoms do you have? By far, the most common one I see, nearly every day and in all ages and both genders, is crying without any reason. I also commonly see a fear of impending doom. If you suffer from six or more of these symptoms, my recommendation would be for you to first minimize the amount of refined grains you consume, reduce your sugar intake, and do what you can to minimize stress in your life.

I would like to add one last point. Do mosquitoes seem to think you are one big piece of cake? Individuals come into the office and say, "Dr. Bob, look at my arms and legs. The mosquitoes were out last night and I was the only one they wanted." These people are deficient in whole-food B vitamins. There is something about having enough vitamin B1, or thiamine, that keeps the mosquitoes away. Without it, it's as if you have a bull's-eye on your skin. I encourage patients who are "bug bait" to take six to nine whole-food B vitamins every day, especially if they have other body signals of B-complex deficiency syndrome.

Some of the body signals I see in individuals who have liver congestion, P-450 dysfunction, or inadequate vitamin B are spider veins in the legs, varicose veins, hemorrhoids, bronzing on the body (especially on the left cheek), gallbladder removal, a slightly swollen or boggy wrist, and crying without reason. B vitamins are needed to break down or process estrogen.

I often see the following history for women who have hormonal issues: They are 35 to 40, have two children, are slightly to moderately overweight, and have a fair complexion. They have uterine fibroids and there is a history of gallbladder removal. The gallbladder, by the way, is not the problem; the real concern is that the liver is so congested that it's causing the bile to be thick and "sludgy."

By far, the most consistent pattern with liver congestion is gallbladder issues. When bile becomes thick and pasty, gallstones appear in the gallbladder. These obstructive lesions can impair the gallbladder's ability to secrete bile. They can literally plug the bile duct, or tube from the liver into the intestines. Your body needs bile as a form of degreaser soap. Fat needs to be metabolized.

Removal of the gallbladder results in some potentially very negative consequences. When you have your gallbladder removed, you impair your body's ability to metabolize fat properly. Historically, issues I see in patients who have had their gallbladder removed are a breakdown in cardiovascular health (leading to heart disease) and cancer. Gallbladder removal is a signal that your body is not functioning properly. It is imperative that you correct the foods you are eating and the chemicals you are putting into your system.

If you have had your gallbladder removed, I would strongly suggest that you eat at least half an apple a day, preferably a sweet apple versus a tart one. This information comes from my study of Indian, or Ayurvedic, medicine. Of course, having your gallbladder, with bile functioning, is better for your digestion. In my practice, I use bovine-sourced bile salts. (See Chapter 17, "Cleansing Protocols.") I have my patients who have had their gallbladder removed take one bile salt tablet a day with their lunch or evening meal and/or when fat is eaten. The next day, I suggest they take two, and on day three, a total of three. On day four, they go back to one. If you continue to take the same amount all the time, your liver will become dependent on the product.

Your liver will continue to produce bile. The gallbladder is a reservoir of bile. When this gland is gone, and you eat foods that need an extra "squirt" of bile, it is not available. You will have incomplete fat metabolism and, as a result, an inadequate amount of oil to serve as a base for hormones. Are you starting to see the picture? Don't give up because you have had an organ removed. Your goal is to eat the right foods, as discussed in Part IV, "You Are What You Eat."

ESTROGEN

I would like to discuss estrogen in more detail in this chapter because I know that if you understand that estrogen needs to be processed properly, you will be able to see the big picture.

Estrogen is one of several female hormones that is a part of the normal female hormone cycle. Estrogen receptors are found throughout the body. You may have heard of a term that I briefly mentioned already: *estrogen dominance* or *saturation*. This occurs when you have more estrogen than your body needs in comparison to progesterone. Estrogen is normally balanced by progesterone. I discuss progesterone in Chapter 3, "Progesterone," and Chapter 8, "Support the Adrenal Glands."

Estrogen is the general term for the several types of estrogen made by the ovaries, adrenal glands, liver, breasts, and to a lesser degree, testicles. Estrogens are steroids. This means they have a particular chemical shape. Steroids, including estrogen and progesterone, can be made from cholesterol. Cholesterol is the building block for other steroid hormones, including cortisone, with its pain-relieving properties. Cholesterol is improperly blamed for so many health issues, but in fact, it is fulfilling its job description. When there is inflammation in the body, LDL (low-density lipoprotein) transports cholesterol to put out the "fire"; thus, LDL cholesterol becomes elevated.

There are three main estrogens that I would like to discuss.

1. **Estrone, or E1. Five to ten percent of estrogen is this type. It is considered a very strong estrogen because of its ability to cause cell proliferation (an increase in the number of cells due to cell growth and division, as in cancer).**

2. **Estradiol, or E2. Five to ten percent of estrogen is this type. It is considered the strongest estrogen, because of its ability to increase cell proliferation more than the other two types, and is the predominant sex hormone present in females.**

3. **Estriol, or E3. Estriol is considered a weak estrogen because it does not cause cell proliferation. However, estriol appears to balance the cell-proliferation effects of estrone and estradiol, conferring protection against their cancer-causing abilities.**

KNOWN FUNCTIONS OF ESTROGEN

1. **Confers female secondary sex characteristics**
2. **Promotes cell proliferation, especially of the uterine lining and breast tissue**
3. **Slows bone loss**

4. Appears to stimulate and protect brain cells

5. Appears to raise HDL levels

6. Increases body fat

7. Creates progesterone receptors

SYMPTOMS OF ESTROGEN DEFICIENCY

1. Hot flashes

2. Night sweats

3. Insomnia

4. Mood swings

5. Mental fogginess, poor memory

6. Vaginal dryness, dry skin and eyes

7. Bladder infections

8. Incontinence, urethral irritations, urinary frequency

9. Headaches, migraines

10. Decreased sexual response

SYMPTOMS OF ESTROGEN EXCESS

1. Heavy bleeding

2. Clotting, cramping

3. Water retention, bloating

4. Breast tenderness, lumpiness, cystic breasts, enlarged breasts

5. Weight gain

6. Postmenstrual headaches and migraines of undetermined origin, one of the most common body signals I see in estrogen-dominant females

7. Depression, irritability, anxiety, anger

8. Decreased sexual response

9. Berry-colored moles

METABOLIC PROBLEMS THAT DEVELOP
WITH ESTROGEN EXCESS

1. Loss of zinc, retention of copper (demonstrated in hair analysis and with the oral zinc sulfate test, available at www.druglessdoctor.com)
2. Cold hands and feet, interference with thyroid hormones
3. Impaired blood sugar control
4. Increased risk of autoimmune disorders over time

A couple of concluding thoughts: Estrogen only functions correctly when it is in the right proportion to progesterone, its primary partner and synergist. In cycling women, these proportions change; in menopausal women, the proportion of progesterone to estradiol falls ideally to around 30:1.

Here is a topic that is not often discussed or understood: We have an overabundance of xenohormones, which are a source of synthetic estrogens. The body is already dealing with estrogen excess or estrogen saturation that is not being balanced by progesterone.

THE PROBLEM WITH XENOHORMONES

Xenohormones are man-made substances that are foreign to the body and have hormone-like properties. Most xenohormones have an estrogen-like effect and so are sometimes called xenoestrogens. The presence of xenohormones, in combination with a sluggish, physically congested liver, is one of the primary reasons women in our society have so many menstrual and fibroid issues. Xenohormones can be absorbed by digestion, inhalation, and direct skin contact.

COMMON SOURCES OF XENOHORMONES

♂ Synthetic estrogens and progestins, as are found in oral contraceptives and conventional hormone replacement therapies

---

♂ All American-grown, non-organic livestock, which are fed estrogenic drugs to fatten them

♂ Petrochemically derived pesticides, herbicides, and fungicides

♂ Solvents and adhesives (as in fingernail polish and polish remover, glue, cleaning supplies, and industrial environments)

♂ Car exhaust

♂ Emulsifiers found in soaps and cosmetics

♂ Almost all plastics, given off especially when plastics are hot or heated (as when a hot wire or rod is applied to cut the plastic film used to wrap meat and vegetables in a grocery store)

♂ Industrial waste, such as polychlorinated biphenyls (PCBs) and dioxins

DISORDERS RELATED TO XENOHORMONE EXPOSURE

♂ Increased reproductive-site cancers in women and men (breast, uterine, ovarian, prostate, and testicular)

♂ Decreased fertility in both sexes

♂ Decreased sperm count in males, both human and animal

♂ Low testosterone levels and abnormally small penis size

♂ Increased incidence of retracted testicles

♂ Increased PMS challenges in women

♂ Estrogen dominance epidemic

STEPS TO AVOID XENOHORMONE EXPOSURE

♂ Avoid all synthetic and horse hormones (oral contraceptives and conventional HRT).

♂ Eat organic meat and dairy. Avoid the fat on non-organic meat and dairy, which is where the xenohormones concentrate.

♂ Decrease or stop using all conventional pesticides, lawn and garden chemicals, etc. Don't contract with conventional lawn services that use sprays that are extremely toxic and full of xenohormones.

♂ Wear protective gloves and clothing when in contact with any glues, solvents, or cleaning solutions that contain xenohormones.

♂ Avoid particle board, synthetic-fiber carpets, and fake woods as much as possible. The chemicals you smell are xenohormones. Think about that when you are around a campfire or use a wood burner at home. I have patients who are sick all winter when they use a wood-burning stove.

♂ Ventilate properly when you come in contact with any of the above-mentioned materials. Think ahead. For example, if you do install synthetic-fiber carpets, do so when the windows can be opened—it takes months to air out the noxious chemicals.

ESTROGEN AND THE LIVER — ACTION STEPS

☐ The most important detail is not to complicate treatment. The answer to your estrogen saturation is to simply change what you are putting in and on your body, so your natural systems can do what they have been designed to do: function at the cellular level and heal themselves.

☐ Do not have any major surgery unless all natural protocols have been attempted and given time to work. If what is occurring in your body is not impairing natural function, such as a fibroid creating a bowel obstruction, be patient. Estrogen dominance takes time to normalize itself.

☐ Adopt a diet that focuses on whole foods versus processed items; see Chapter 20, "The Page Food Plan."

☐ I would suggest that you minimize sugar, conventional processed dairy products, and partially hydrogenated oil (trans fat), which tend to congest the liver.

☐ Refer to Chapter 5 on the lymphatic system, and start bouncing!

☐ Locate a quality source of whole-food B vitamins. Look at the B-complex deficiency chart on page 33. How many symptoms do you have?

☐ Review the labels on products you have around the house, including those you put on your body. How many products do you see that are toxic? Review the list of carcinogens at the American Cancer Society's website.

☐ I would suggest that you eat Dr. Bob's ABCs—apples, beets, and carrots—daily.

☐ Eating cruciferous vegetables like broccoli, cauliflower, cabbage, and Brussels sprouts will assist your body in eliminating estrogen. I encourage our patients to use a couple of products if they do not eat cruciferous veggies: calcium-D glucarate, which assists the liver in the metabolism of estrogen; and diindolylmethane (commonly known as DIM), extracted from cruciferous vegetables and other non-soy plants. Patients who do not like to eat veggies tend to have an acid metabolism; you may want to start by adding veggies that are lightly steamed, sautéed, or stir-fried in olive oil. Veggies promote an alkaline pH, which from my observation, is a healthier state than being acid.

☐ Drink water from a pure source.

☐ Eat organic food; minimize the ingestion of herbicides, pesticides, and artificial chemicals. I want to also point out that many, unknowingly, are exposed to estrogens and other toxic substances when they spend time gardening or golfing or anytime they are in a location where herbicides and pesticides have been applied. It is possible to measure the body's levels of estrogen through urine testing; I would suggest doing this if you have a family history of cancer.

☐ I would avoid soy. Soy has estrogenic properties, and I have found through experience that it can create physiological issues in premenopausal and postmenopausal women.

NOTES _____

_____

_____

_____

_____

_____

_____

_____

_____

FOR FURTHER INFORMATION, see *What Your Doctor May Not Tell You About Premenopause*, by John R. Lee, MD, and Jesse Hanley, MD (Chapter 5). Also cited: Information from the seminar "Balancing Human Hormones," by Dr. Janet Lang, and information from the seminar "The Doctor of the Future," by Dr. Stuart White.

Chapter 3

Progesterone

The hormone puzzle can be complicated. I was a guest at a friend's wedding some time ago and noticed a couple checking into the hotel where the reception was being held. The woman was walking with a cane. She appeared to be too young to have had a hip replacement, so I calculated that she must have been disabled because of multiple sclerosis. As fate would have it, I bumped into her and her husband at the reception. As we were having a conversation about the usual details of life, I just had to come out and ask her why she had the cane—I have an inquisitive spirit. She proceeded to tell me that she had been diagnosed with MS some time ago, and that her history also included leukemia and a few other conditions.

I asked her how long she had suffered, and she said about 15 years. My next question, which was significant, was, "What was going on in your life when all this occurred? Was there a major stress incident?" She confided in me that there had been, and proceeded to share with me that she had had several miscarriages. She also had a hysterectomy and her ovaries removed since then. I bring all this up to you because there are some significant patterns that we need to discuss in this chapter.

One of the main roles of progesterone is to balance estrogen. It is also known that progesterone is produced by tissues other than the ovaries and adrenals, including the brain and peripheral nerves; as time goes on, I am sure other areas will be discovered.

I would venture to say it will be discovered that steroidal hormones are produced in minute amounts by cell membranes. You may be thinking, why, then, do women have estrogen and progesterone deficiencies with menopause? My answer to you is that these cell membranes produce the little extra that is required to help top off what the adrenal glands and ovaries are supposed to produce, but when your adrenal glands are not up to par and your ovaries do not have enough iodine for functioning, even the cell membranes cannot make enough.

Going back to the wedding guest, here are some points I have noticed over time. Women who have a history of miscarriages tend to be low in progesterone, with the associated body signals of low blood pressure, sensitivity to bright light, and salt cravings—typical challenges of stressed adrenal glands. Progesterone keeps the system intact so that the body can carry a fetus to full-term. When there is not enough progesterone, the body innately calculates that there is going to be a deficit. As a result, the fetus is released instead of going full-term. There are several reasons someone might not be able to carry a child to full-term. An autoimmune complex, which creates a poor environment, is often a factor. I have found that women with a history of a miscarriage or two, or even three, also tend to be ones who develop multiple sclerosis, one of many autoimmune conditions.

The woman at the wedding fit this pattern. I want you to understand that this pattern is not going to happen to everyone, but it is more common than you think. She also told me she had cold hands and feet. These are common body signals for low thyroid function. The thyroid needs iodine and other nutrients to make thyroid hormone, just as the ovaries need iodine to assist in making progesterone. She had had her ovaries out with her hysterectomy, probably because she did not have enough nutrients for optimal ovary function. So the puzzle with progesterone is very big. Progesterone is essential in balancing out the effects of estrogen, and in assisting the body to function properly. It is a building block for other steroid hormones.

One last comment about the wedding guest: Her leukemia, which was in remission, could also be a part of the adrenal gland scenario, because when the adrenals are not up to par, the lymphocytes (white blood cells that are the warrior cells in the body) are handcuffed and not able to function optimally. The adrenal glands, as mentioned, are also a part of the system needed to create progesterone. What we are looking at is a mosaic of many tiny tiles that all need to fit together. This fact is often overlooked by conventional medical thinking.

KNOWN FUNCTIONS OF PROGESTERONE

♂ Acts as a natural muscle relaxant

♂ Balances the effects of estrogen

♂ Maintains the lining of the uterus, ripening it for possible pregnancy

♂ Stimulates new bone growth

♂ Helps burn fat for energy

♂ Is a natural antidepressant when balanced with estrogen

♂ May help against autoimmune disease

♂ Functions as a precursor for other steroid hormones

♂ Can increase libido

♂ Increases the sensitivity of estrogen receptors

♂ Is a natural diuretic

♂ Is preventive against breast, uterine, and all other forms of cancer

♂ Facilitates thyroid function

♂ Maintains the developing fetus in pregnancy

♂ Functions all over the nervous system in ways that are not totally known

You can see from the list that progesterone plays a critical role in many functions in the body. Before I list the deficiency symptoms, I would like to share with you that I prefer to help my patients create the environment for their "pharmacist inside" to produce progesterone, rather than apply a progesterone cream. I agree that most women need additional progesterone, and I am aware that there are many very fine healthcare providers who strongly suggest progesterone creams. However, by applying the creams without altering their lifestyle, patients will never get to the real cause of the problem. Certain foods and environmental toxins drain the body's ability to create the substances it was designed to.

I do not recommend progesterone creams unless someone is bleeding very severely and needs progesterone to balance their estrogen. Putting progesterone cream on your stomach, buttocks, and breasts may stop heavy flow but will not get to the cause. I am not saying progesterone creams are wrong, but they do alter normal hormone physiology. What I typically see when I do progesterone and estrogen testing (and this correlates with body signals) is elevated estrogen compared to progesterone from the onset of the cycle. Progesterone typically does not reach a peak like it should at the middle to end of the cycle. Estrogen is typically high from the beginning of the cycle and may dip a bit in the middle. As a pattern, estrogen saturation or dominance creates painful breasts, heavy flow, and headache at the end or beginning of the cycle.

As I have stated before, I have noticed that women with a history of miscarriages tend to have low progesterone levels. Progesterone elevates during pregnancy because of many factors. Again, if it is low, the body will release the fetus because all the factors are not just right for a full-term pregnancy.

Many of my patients tell me they always felt the best when they were pregnant. I believe their progesterone levels were at the high point of their lives, and it just plain old made them feel good. The corpus luteum and placenta take over and make progesterone while you are pregnant. These women probably had an exhausted system normally, and their bodies were not capable of producing enough progesterone. When your progesterone is low, your body will not have enough of this precursor to make the anti-pain, anti-inflammation hormone cortisone. When you are low in cortisone, your hypothalamus, or the CEO of your brain and body, will instruct more cholesterol to be made to create progesterone, which is a precursor for cortisone.

When you have a blood serum assessment for cholesterol, and the number is above normal, it is more than likely because your body needs more progesterone to give you pain relief by fulfilling the need to make more cortisone. Furthermore, sugar creates a demand in the body for more natural cortisone. Are you beginning to see that more is involved in keeping cholesterol down than not eating meat and cheese? In many situations, lowering your cholesterol is harmful to your overall long-term health. It may not appear that way, but if you have pain syndromes, you need cholesterol to make cortisone. I don't want you to go out and begin eating pizza to raise your cholesterol, but I do want you to know that it is inflammation about which you should be concerned. This is a huge puzzle, and you need to look at the consequences of all your choices. View this as a long journey, not a short-term dash.

SYMPTOMS OF PROGESTERONE DEFICIENCY

♂ Premenstrual syndrome

♂ Heavy bleeding

♂ Spotting

♂ Clotting, cramping

♂ Water retention, bloating

♂ Weight gain

♂ Headaches, migraines

♂ Depression

♂ Anxiety, irritability, nervousness

♂ Decreased sexual response

♂ Endometriosis and fibroids

♂ Breast tenderness, lumpiness, cystic breasts

♂ Infrequent menses

SYMPTOMS OF PROGESTERONE EXCESS

♂ Sleepiness

♂ Drowsiness

♂ Bloating, constipation

♂ Depression

I would like to point out that progesterone only functions correctly when it is in the right proportion to estrogen, its primary partner and synergist. In a cycling woman, these proportions change throughout the cycle. In menopausal women, as I have said, the proportion of progesterone to estradiol falls ideally to around 30:1. Remember, estrogen is necessary to create progesterone receptors, and progesterone up-regulates estrogen receptors.

Levels of progesterone and estrogen are best assessed through saliva; the amounts in saliva are going to be the truest. Serum levels are also dependent on other factors, and the hormones are bound with protein. I also evaluate the levels of zinc and copper through hair tissue mineral analysis. I have found that when copper is high, estrogen is high. I generally correlate high copper and estrogen with a female who is fair and has freckles.

The freckles are a result of the elevated copper. I see this occurring in three consistent patterns. When a male or female adolescent is transitioning from a child to an adult, sex hormones start to increase, and the liver is not capable of processing them because of a long history of poor food choices, including pizza and

French fries. This pattern can be accelerated in individuals who are the second child in the birth order. If the mother consumes items such as alcohol, fries, ice cream, and partially hydrogenated oil (trans fat) and is on prescription drugs, the first baby creates an extra burden on her. The liver will not be able to handle all the extra work, and estrogen and copper will go up. Finally, when a woman has her second or third child, she may become a bit overweight and stop exercising, which creates stagnation in the liver once again.

Women like this will often have a history of gallbladder removal because when estrogen is high, the bile gets thick and sluggish. These patients have a history of digestive distress an hour or two after eating because the gallbladder is unable to release the bile (which is thick and pasty) needed to break down fat.

I am sure you have seen by now that the puzzle of balancing human hormones is more than putting a patch on your body, or taking one pill and expecting everything to get better. The success of your long-term health rests on the fact that you will need to make some pretty dramatic changes if you are facing hysterectomy or gallbladder removal.

PROGESTERONE — ACTION STEPS

☐ Have your blood pressure taken while lying down, and then standing; if it drops 10 to 15 points, you will want to refer to Chapter 8, "Support the Adrenal Glands," so you can support your adrenal glands to do their part in creating progesterone.

☐ Take your armpit temperature first thing in the morning for 10 minutes, three days in a row. If the reading is less than 98.7 degrees Fahrenheit, I would suggest you find an experienced healthcare provider who knows how to support thyroid function, and have the TSH, T3, and T4 tests done. You may need extra iodine, which feeds the ovaries, assisting in the production of progesterone. See Chapter 7 for more about the thyroid.

☐ Have you had a miscarriage? If so, you may want to do a saliva test for progesterone and estrogen. If you find that your progesterone is low, that does not mean you need progesterone cream. You want to make sure your adrenals are functioning, your thyroid is up to par, and your liver is doing its job. Study the liver, thyroid, adrenals, and cleansing protocols in Chapters 6, 7, 8, and 17, respectively.

☐ I suggest whole supplementation for the ovaries. [But first, to help you decide which organ(s) you need to support, always have appropriate tests done: saliva for progesterone/estrogen, a thyroid panel, and hair analysis.] Generally, I recommend a few different whole-food products. First, I suggest and find the need for iodine. I use up to 12 milligrams of iodine a day. The iodine will assist the ovaries to make progesterone. Also, I may use either an animal-sourced glandular product or a whole-food supplement combination protocol designed to increase progesterone and not estrogen, depending on the body signals of the patient. If there are symptoms of estrogen dominance, like tender breasts and heavy flow, I use both items just mentioned anywhere from six to nine tablets or capsules a day for several months. This helps support progesterone production.

☐ I do not recommend progesterone cream, unless the patient is at the point of losing her uterus. My experience suggests that when you use progesterone cream, you are literally hampering your body's ability to make its own progesterone. The feedback mechanism used by the brain/tissue loop to assess the amount of progesterone is being altered, even if the progesterone is natural. I always like to get to the cause of the problem. I am not telling you to stop using the cream. I am suggesting that you think about the big picture. Your thyroid, adrenals, and liver may need to be supported. Using the cream may give you temporary relief, but is it helping in the LONG TERM?

☐ I would strongly suggest that you find a skilled, experienced, spinal-adjusting, nutrition-focused chiropractor. This individual could be the answer to nearly all of your issues, as I will discuss in Chapter 10 ("Communication Between the Brain and Tissue Cells"), because your ovaries may not be getting the messages your brain is sending them. The ovaries have a nerve supply. The nervous system controls function. I will discuss elsewhere in the book that I have seen health improve by correcting the spinal area directly associated with innervating, or connecting the brain's instructions to, the ovaries—resulting in improved hormone function. Releasing the subluxation (spinal misalignment and nerve compression) by spinal correction is like turning a tripped breaker back on to an appliance in your home.

☐ Always think about the liver. The liver is critical for proper hormone function. If the liver is not doing its job, estrogen will be up and progesterone will be down. You do not want that, since your body will have a hard enough time trying to balance all the man-made xenohormones, which create the estrogen dominance scenario. Eat Dr. Bob's ABCs every day: half a sweet apple; about one-third to one-half of a cup of organic raw, grated, or baked beets; and several medium carrots.

NOTES _____

_____

_____

_____

_____

_____

_____

_____

_____

_____

PATIENT TESTIMONY:

"Before making Dr. DeMaria's recommended lifestyle changes, I had been dealing with emotions of all sorts during my monthly cycle. Since modifying my sugar consumption and eating healthier, I no longer struggle with these symptoms. I feel better all over. I feel like I can breathe easier, and I also sleep better.

I appreciate Dr. Bob's willingness and his enthusiasm in everything that he does. He is full of Godly wisdom and I am blessed to have him as my doctor."

Jennifer Traxler Miller

Chapter 4

Other Hormones
Affecting the Balance

I would like to discuss several additional hormones that affect the balance of female hormones. Xenohormones, which were discussed in Chapter 2, are by far the most serious of all hormones, and even though they are man-made, they are a part of the whole imbalance.

Hormones that affect hormonal balance include DHEA; testosterone; and the synthetic chemicals that have been developed to replace or support the chemical messengers you already have in your body, i.e., conventional hormone replacement therapy (HRT).

DHEA stands for dehydroepiandrosterone (pronounced dee-hi-dro-epp-e-an-dro-stehr-own). DHEA is a steroid hormone that helps build structure and is classified as an anabolic hormone. It is an androgen steroid produced by the adrenal glands, ovaries, and testes. Men normally have a slightly higher amount than women.

DHEA plays a role in energy, the handling of stress, mood, and immunity. It works inversely with cortisol; when one goes up, the other goes down. DHEA can be used to cushion the ill effects of excess cortisol. It helps decrease insulin resistance.

SYMPTOMS OF DHEA DEFICIENCY

♂ Memory difficulties

♂ Lack of stamina

♂ Lowered mood, depression

♂ Decreased sex drive

♂ Fatigue and exhaustion

♂ Inability to handle stress

♂ Impaired immunity

SYMPTOMS OF EXCESS DHEA IN FEMALES

♂ Irritability, edginess when the dose is too high

♂ Acne, oily skin

♂ Increased facial and body hair

♂ Multiple cysts in the ovaries

I generally do not supplement with DHEA. I have found it is better to support the whole body and adrenal glands and to work on eliminating stress and toxins so that the body can restore its own levels. When DHEA first became popular, I had several patients who required quite a bit of time to stabilize their hormones after saliva testing showed they were overdosing on DHEA supplements taken on the advice of other practitioners. You can create quite a disaster of your own hormones by trying to increase one segment of hormonal supplementation without taking into consideration all of the ramifications.

Testosterone, mostly thought of as a male hormone, is also present to some extent in the female body. Testosterone is a steroid androgen hormone produced in small quantities in the ovaries and adrenal glands. It is made from the precursor progesterone and DHEA in the steroid pathway. Testosterone is an anabolic hormone, which means it helps build body structure. It is not uncommon for me to clinically correlate ovarian cysts with elevated testosterone levels on female hormone panel saliva testing; polycystic ovary syndrome (PCOS) is often associated with low iodine levels.

TESTOSTERONE IN FEMALES

♂ Maintains sex drive

♂ Promotes healthy muscle

♂ Strengthens bone

♂ Helps mood and well-being

♂ Maintains stamina and overall energy

TESTOSTERONE DEFICIENCY BODY SIGNALS

♂ Poor muscle tone

♂ Low or absent libido

♂ Decreased stamina and energy

♂ Decreased armpit and body hair

♂ Weakened bones, osteoporosis

TESTOSTERONE EXCESS BODY SIGNALS

♂ Acne, oily skin

♂ Loss of head hair, male-pattern baldness

♂ Excessive body hair

♂ Aggressive behavior and disposition

♂ Deep voice

Low testosterone can be balanced by focusing on taking stress off the adrenal function and making sure the liver is doing its job clearing synthetic hormones, which create a potential hormonal imbalance.

NOTES _____

_____

_____

_____

_____

_____

_____

_____

_____

_____

Chapter 5

Let's Talk About the Lymphatic System

The lymphatic system is probably one of the most mysterious systems in the body. You really only hear about the lymphatic system from an exercise enthusiast who bounces daily to get his or her clear lymphatic fluid moving—or, unfortunately, from a cancer patient who has been told by his or her physician that the disease has spread to the lymph nodes. The oncologist (cancer physician) would usually say something to the effect of, "It appears that the chemotherapy and radiation only contained the cancer for a while." These are heart-wrenching words to hear echoing through the cortex of your brain.

I would like to introduce you to the mechanics of the lymphatic system. It is literally the sewer system of the body, and it would be in your best interest to take care of it as you would the downspouts on your home, the drain in your bathtub or shower, or the road gutter in front of your house. The lymphatic system is a network of channels that are multitasked in nature. It is one of several lines of defense of your immune system as well as the "freight train" that hauls fuel throughout your body in the form of food particles. It is like the "Patriot missile" line of defense, the infantry and supply chain all in one package.

The lymphatic system carries proteins and fats for digestion and activates lymphocytes (a type of white blood cell warrior). The lymph nodes in a person's neck, including the tonsils, swell and get red when they are DOING THEIR JOB protecting you. Having one's tonsils removed is like disarming a warrior or cutting the wire to the "warning signal" on your car's dashboard. When we are born, there should be little tags on all of our organs that say "DO NOT REMOVE!"

I know we have been told that organs that are commonly removed are not necessary for life. I believe as time goes on we will hear more and more about the negative effects of the surgical removal of lymph tissue. The tonsils are the storage house of sulfur in the body. Sulfur is needed to help maintain cartilage for your structural health. Great natural sources of sulfur include eggs, onion, and garlic. If your lymph nodes are swollen and sore, limit dairy, exercise your muscles, and drink more water. It is very important for you to come to the understanding that when these and other tissues in your body are performing their job descriptions, you DO NOT REMOVE THEM!

Lymph health is promoted by drinking water, increasing activity, and avoiding processed foods and dairy. If your lymph nodes become swollen and sore, usually it is because you are consuming something that is overworking the system. If you continue to do this long enough, you will get some type of chronic condition, possibly even CANCER. Your children are no different. If they continually have swollen glands, DON'T GIVE THEM ANOTHER ANTIBIOTIC and STOP FEEDING THEM SUGAR AND DAIRY. I also encourage lymphatic drainage massage by an experienced massage therapist. It will assist your body's line of defense and create open drainage for toxins that have accumulated in your tissues.

There is a term I think you will find significant and should be a part of your wellness vocabulary: *stagnant* (not flowing or running). Stagnation is something you would like to avoid throughout your organ systems, but most importantly in the lymphatic network. When the lymphatic system is stagnant, you are not going to be working at 100 percent. You really want to keep all the fluids in your body moving at a nice rate, with no congestion or bottlenecks. Some of the primary reasons I see a sluggish or stagnant lymphatic system are overindulging in dairy-sourced products, insufficient water in the diet, and a lack of muscle-moving exercises. Your body needs motion! Motion is life. It is easier to move clear lymphatic fluid than the sludge created when you consume soda (diet soda included), power drinks (loaded with chemicals), alcohol, and/or coffee in place of an adequate amount of water.

The cells in your body are analogous to machines, all working together for the good of the whole. When a machine is operating, there is generally some scrap or waste from the operation. The maintenance crew comes by and picks up this byproduct to take it to the recycle bin. Similarly, your cells have waste, and the lymphatic channels in and around your arms, legs, neck, trunk, and abdomen are a part of the waste disposal system. The waste is eventually going to be processed by the liver, kidneys, and colon for recycling or elimination. Your colon, by the way, has one of the largest concentrations of lymphatic tissue in the body.

The lymphatic system is also the organization that creates the warriors, or lymphocytes, that seek and destroy foreign invaders, or cells that have become abnormal for whatever reason. The lymphatic system sweeps, cleans, and disposes, like the crews in your neighborhood that clean the streets and dispose of the trash, often when you are sleeping in your cozy bed. But the lymphatic system is capable of handling only so much at a time. If the channels used to carry away the debris are congested from overproduction or faulty disposal, the lymphatic system can get backed up.

I see it where I live, when there is an abnormally large amount of rain. The gutters and downspouts on a house can handle only so much rainfall in a certain period. If you have failed to clean out your gutters, or leaves and sludge have accumulated, you can be in trouble. There can be water damage inside the house and an overflow of water into the basement. I also read in the newspaper about how people in our community are displeased with the city for not cleaning out the street sewers that take away water.

Consider another situation: You have two pumps working very diligently during a downpour, and you feel really good about the situation—but all of a sudden, you hear a crack of lightning and the power goes off. If you did not plan ahead with a battery-backup pump or gas-powered generator, you can have a HUGE mess in the basement.

The outcomes of the scenarios I have just described can be controlled. Now, you cannot control the amount of rain, but you have control over the way the water is disposed. Your body is no different. You cannot necessarily control everything that is thrown at your body, but you do have charge over what you do with it. And honestly, you really do have control over the majority of what goes into your body, even the toxins. Let me explain.

First, you want to make sure you are drinking enough water every day. How much is enough? Well, the least amount you should drink is a quart. A general rule of thumb is to drink one ounce of water for every pound of body weight. I personally would not drink over one hundred ounces a day, especially if you start noticing leg cramps at night or when you are walking. You would be getting rid of too many minerals. As I mentioned before, and this is important, avoid using soda, fruit drinks, energy drinks, or coffee as your main beverage. Eat veggies and fruits, as they have high water content. Avoid pastries and goodies that draw water out of the system in order to be processed.

Your colon is a dehydrator. If you continue to eat foods that contain gluten (such as wheat, rye, oats, and barley), you are creating thick and pasty coverings on your intestinal walls. Your body needs water to cleanse the system. The next time you are hungry, instead of grabbing a "little" cracker, cookie, etc., drink a glass of water or have a piece of cucumber, a small tomato, or a piece of celery. You are putting fluid in, which is positive and proactive for your long-term health, instead of creating a negative state.

You want to make sure you are exercising. A rebounder (mini-trampoline) can be used to create a vacuum in the lymphatic channels.

This creates movement of fluid. Again, motion is life. Your lymphatic system does not have the privilege of its own pump, like the cardiovascular system does. Any type of exercise is better than being a couch potato—walking, riding a bike, fast stepping, or dancing.

Several massage therapists assist me at my clinic. They conduct therapeutic massage treatments. One of the recommended techniques, in which they have all specialized, is lymphatic drainage massage. Some of my patients have had the swelling in their body diminish after their lymphatic system was properly stimulated and drained.

I recently presented a workshop on skin health to my patients. I made a comment that the average Western female absorbs, either through friction or natural lip licking, four to seven pounds of lipstick over her lifetime. A massage therapist in attendance said she thought about what I had said and offered an observation: When a female patient came in for lymphatic massage and had lipstick or lip gloss on, normally when the session was complete, the lipstick or lip gloss had been absorbed. She theorized that she was stimulating the flow of lymph fluid in the body. I thought that was a very interesting observation, one that I had not read or heard before. I think that most people who have dry lips don't realize it's an internal problem. Dry lips are a possible signal that you need to increase your water consumption. Most would not think of the lips as a tissue directly linked to the lymphatic channels. If you are a massage therapist and you do lymphatic drainage, let me know if you observe the same phenomenon.

The lymphatic system is not the bad guy. It is critical for your optimal health. Your objective is to keep the lymphatic channels flowing flawlessly. I have observed, as I review the food journals of my patients and case histories, that patients generally have a long history of poor dietary choices. They have focused on foods that do not promote regular, timely, "no assistance needed" bowel movements (that is, without a laxative, herb, etc.). Their diet is concentrated with refined grains and starches. They have toxic-looking skin, which is pale, not pink and vibrant, with many red and brown marks and possibly varicose and spider veins. Little or no exercise is common on the intake history as well. All of these symptoms and conditions result in a stagnant system unable to get rid of the excess scraps from production.

The body is overwhelmed; it does not know what to do with all the excess. At this point, the environment in the body is like a toxic pond or river. Cells begin to break down, and there is cell membrane destruction—oxidation, which is like a massive rusting away. You can slow and stop the oxidation process, which is like the progressive deterioration of steel, by increasing your consumption of veggies during the day. Veggies and fruits are like Rust-Oleum® and combine with the free radicals theorized to be in the process.

The tremendous magnitude of oxidation creates the potential for free-radical or abnormal cell activity. Your hormone levels are not normal. You do not feel good for some time and finally start to have symptoms. A lump appears in your breast, your menses are heavy, and you feel nauseated. Finally, you visit the doctor and many tests are completed on you. Then you are given the bad news at the time of your consultation—you have CANCER.

You make an appointment for further testing with a cancer specialist, who decides to do a biopsy. You wait with baited breath for the results. You are receiving well wishes from friends and family, and e-mails from people with advice on what to do. Finally, you are told the cancer has spread to your lymphatic system. They want to take the nodes out. So now what do you do?

Here is my advice to patients. This is what I say every time, as diplomatically as possible. If you don't change what you are doing, you will DIE! That usually gets their attention and a tear. I am not trying to be abrasive. You are in a battle. You are the "commander in chief" of your army. What you decide to do affects the VICTORY.

You need to take responsibility to fight your own war. What you have done to this point in your life is the reason you are in the situation you are dealing with now.

The big question is, what do you do about chemotherapy and radiation treatment? My suggestion is to consider how bad the current symptoms are and the stage of the cancer. Sometimes, if the cancer is advanced, you may need assistance (chemotherapy or radiation) to get it under control while you are making lifestyle changes. I would locate the book *The Answer to Cancer*, by Dr. Hari Sharma. He details what your steps should be if you are going to have chemotherapy. If your cancer is not advanced, then you have a fighting chance to win the war. I see it all the time in my natural drugless practice. I have had new patients present themselves at my office with tears in their eyes, make the decision to CHANGE, and LIVE. I do not heal them. Their own body does the healing. I coach them. Unfortunately, many come in after the conventional methods have been exhausted and there is nothing else they can do; it is hardly a time to start thinking about making lifestyle changes.

Let me be candidly honest with you, and this is not meant to be unkind to the established way things are done in our society: Chemotherapy and radiation are not the ONLY answers. These forms of treatment do not get to the cause of the problem. They are treating the symptoms. CLEAN MACHINES WORK BETTER. You need to clean your machine. Synthetic HRT treatment for female hormonal issues was standardized by the medical community. Women were dying because of synthetically sourced, horse-urine-based medication. It was extremely significant that the results of a government study were released in 2003, or the drugging of women would have continued. But it was recently reported that HRT is safe and effective for select age groups and stages of hormonal change. Do you understand how IMPORTANT this is? The battle you are in is for your own LIFE.

LET'S TALK ABOUT THE LYMPHATIC SYSTEM — ACTION STEPS

☐ Focus on whole foods that promote bowel movements. Mixed greens and mostly raw (lunch) and steamed (dinner) vegetables should be a regular part of your diet. If you can't handle the taste or texture of raw vegetables, which is common in patients who are very acid in their saliva pH (see Chapter 15), eat steamed vegetables until your body can handle raw ones.

☐ Drink water as your beverage of choice. Avoid processed, pasteurized, homogenized, physically altered dairy, which tends to plug the lymphatic channels. Avoid eating cheese on a regular basis. According to the senior massage therapist on staff at my office, it creates a layer of palpable fat under the skin. She also noted that her clients who are regular cheese consumers have a peculiar odor to their skin, especially their feet.

☐ Exercise your muscles regularly. That means exercise some body part daily. Bounce on a 55cm exercise ball or mini-trampoline.

☐ Stretch your muscles with flexibility exercises using an elastic band.

☐ Tonsils removed? Eat eggs, onion, and garlic, which will provide sulfur. The tonsils are your body's sulfur reservoir. An organic egg a day is safe and good for you. Eat the yolk. You do not need to have toast. Eat poached, hard-boiled, or scrambled eggs with olive oil. Add some spinach, throw in some onions, and what the heck—add a dash of garlic!

☐ I would eat Dr. Bob's ABCs every day: half a sweet apple, several pieces of baked or grated raw beets, and several small organic medium carrots or a large peeled carrot that has been cut up.

☐ Start your day with one-fourth of an organic lemon in pure warm or hot water. This is good for the liver and digestion. I personally would eliminate soda and alcohol, and limit coffee. Soda has man-made chemicals that stress the liver and kidneys. Alcohol, including wine (a media beverage for heart health), even in moderation is still processed, often with sulfates. I know that the literature says it will help your heart; however, eliminating wine and dessert with a meal will promote more life than drinking a glass of wine. This is just a suggestion. Patients who have the discipline to curtail alcohol will lose weight, lower their cholesterol, and get over depression more quickly than the ones who hold on to the "moderation" theory. I see it in my practice routinely.

☐ Seek out a skilled massage therapist who is trained in lymphatic massage.

NOTES _____

_____

_____

_____

_____

_____

_____

_____

_____

_____

PATIENT TESTIMONY:

"When I first came to see Dr. Bob, I had been dealing with a heavier flow, cramps, heart palpitations, psoriasis, mid- and lower back pain, and depression. I had been taking antidepressants, antihistamines, and nasal drops, and using psoriasis creams. Losing my mother was very tough on me physically and mentally, so my daughter suggested that I try Dr. Bob and see what it was like. I am still working on taking sugar out of my diet, and I take 1½ tablespoons of flaxseed oil daily. The most difficult challenge has been to really look at labels and know what to look for, especially hidden sugars.

After receiving my first adjustment and having my "switches turned on," I felt like it woke me up to a new, happier person. I have never looked back. The knowledge and the adjustments have definitely helped me."

S. Dietz

Chapter 6

The Importance of
Optimal Liver Function

Improving health at any level—whether you are an adolescent with an acne issue; a teen with chronic headaches; a depressed 20-year-old; or a woman with a congested gallbladder, heavy menstrual flow, tender breasts, or chronic pain syndromes (and I could go on)—all boils down to this question: Is your machine clean? Let me explain what I mean by a clean machine.

I discussed how significant the lymphatic system is to the body. It is the body's sewer system and cleanup crew. One major reason women have issues with hormone function is that the body is not capable, at our current level of toxic overload, of handling what it is being exposed to.

Estrogen, as you are now aware, is one of the key hormones necessary for the female menstrual cycle. To begin the cycle, estrogen elevates. When its purpose is complete in the cycle, it gradually declines in strength and amount, with progesterone stepping up and taking the dominant position. The lining of the uterus is sloughed off and the whole process starts over; easy, right? Hardly. Estrogen dominance is the key reason most women suffer with so many challenges up to the cessation of menses, and insufficient estrogen produced by the support organs is the reason they have severe problems after menses have subsided.

The liver's purpose as an organ is multifaceted, with hundreds of known functions. It is likely that we will never know everything it does. Our understanding of the liver increases as technology uncovers more possibilities. The Western mind-set is different from that of other cultures when it comes to whole-body function. Healing comes from the inside out, versus the Western premise that disease is something that comes from the outside in. Your body does have to deal with outside toxins, but most of them can be handled if the inside tissue is up to par and not overstressed by toxic choices.

In other parts of the world, the liver metaphorically replaces the heart that we so revere in Western culture. Can you imagine receiving a Valentine's Day card with a liver on the front instead of a heart? In Chinese medicine, another association of the liver is with anger, as described by Jack Tips, PhD, in *The Healing Triad: Your Liver...Your Lifeline.* I often wonder if this is why we have road rage. People are racing around and eating some of their main meals in the car. When I am driving around town and on the highway, I see people with Bluetooth earpieces, a burger in one hand and a soda in the other, scarfing down handfuls of fries. As a society, we are literally trashing our livers with bad eating habits and choices, resulting in a plethora of physical and emotional consequences.

The word *melancholy* can be traced to the term *bad blood*. People with congested, overworked livers tend to be more easily angered— a body signal I notice in many new patients. When I complete an assessment using various diagnostic modalities, liver congestion is generally evident in individuals who have shorter tempers. If you have a history of gallbladder surgery (and there are over 500,000 of them performed a year), it is a sign to me that your liver is not up to par. Taking synthetic, high-potency B vitamins can compound the problem, making the situation worse. I have seen fibromyalgia clear up in women when they get off their high-potency, synthetic Bs.

I was at an event recently when a professional colleague approached me with questions about his wife, who was in her mid-50s. He was beside himself. He was doing everything he could to help his wife's chronic health situation, which included female body signals (tender breasts, heavy menstrual flow, PMS, postmenstrual headache, and spider veins on the legs and thighs) plus constant mid-back pain. His wife then had some discussions with me and decided to come to my office for an assessment. During our conversation, she revealed that she LOVED SUGAR. Sugar is the stealth player in our society that depletes the body of much-needed nutrients for optimal body function. I talked to her just as I am talking to you right now.

I told her, "Sue, you really need to clean up your liver, eat more veggies, and drink more water." Her response was, "Dr. Bob, I do all that. I have taken tons of supplements and done bioidentical hormone replacement, all without any change. So what else can I do?" It is not about what else to take but what to avoid. Your body can work only with what you put into it. Food does more than provide calories; it creates the building blocks for life. Anytime you consume food that has been processed, your body actively needs to do something with it. Sue, like so many women, will not progress past where she is unless she avoids items that stress her detoxification system. I instruct my patients to minimize products that are highly processed or have the potential to be toxic. This includes over-the-counter and prescription medications as well as synthetic vitamins that are stressful to the system.

In the owner's manual for a car, it is suggested that you replace your oil, gas, and air filters on a more frequent schedule when you are in dusty conditions, which create stress on the cleaning mechanism. In such environments, the oil gets dirty and "gunky" quicker. Similarly, there are several protocols that I recommend for liver/gallbladder cleansing. These sensibly affordable procedures have the bonus of being noninvasive and can be done in the privacy of your home. My patients have received outstanding results after following these simple directions and protocols. I will explain the exact details for each procedure in Chapter 17. I have very successfully incorporated these activities to help patients control their own destinies and take charge of their health.

CLEANSING PROTOCOLS

Colonic

A healthy colon is essential to a healthy body. Conventional diets that are comprised of refined, processed food and are high in saturated fats and low in fiber contribute to many problems associated with the large intestine. The elimination of undigested food material and other waste products is as important as the digestion and assimilation of foodstuffs. Waste material that is allowed to remain stagnant in the colon decomposes, increasing bacteria and their toxins.

The colon contains the largest concentration of bacteria in the body. These bacteria provide important functions, such as the synthesis of folic acid, B vitamins, and vitamin K from foods. *Bacillus coli* and acidophilus comprise the majority of the healthy bacteria in the colon, and exist with small numbers of bacteria that can release toxins if not kept in check by the immune system. Waste material permitted to stagnate alters the proportion of healthy bacteria to potentially toxin-producing bacteria, creating the possibility for disease. The latter bacteria decompose proteins and carbohydrates, resulting in the production of toxins. Some of the toxins are thought to be absorbed and become a potential source of disease elsewhere in the body. The purpose of the colon as an eliminative organ is to remove this waste material by mass muscular contraction, called peristalsis. Colon hydrotherapy provides therapeutic improvement of muscular tone, facilitating peristalsis and benefiting the atonic (sluggish) colon. The effects of a stagnant colon can manifest as constipation, halitosis (bad breath), skin blemishes, headaches, low back pain, and lack of energy.

Liver/Gallbladder Flush

For an explanation of the liver/gallbladder flush, please refer to the section "Liver/Gallbladder Flush" in Chapter 17. Reasons to do a liver flush include the following:

- ♂ Blood sugar fluctuations
- ♂ Chemical sensitivities
- ♂ Cholesterol above 225
- ♂ Digestion discomfort
- ♂ Dizziness and/or "the shakes"
- ♂ Dry tongue and mouth
- ♂ Elevated liver enzymes
- ♂ Chronic constipation
- ♂ Extreme fatigue
- ♂ Eye floaters
- ♂ Tender breasts in women and heavy menstrual flow
- ♂ Dry hair and hair loss
- ♂ Headaches
- ♂ Mental problems/depression
- ♂ Muscle and bone pain
- ♂ Nails that peel or break
- ♂ Pain in right side of abdomen
- ♂ Breathing distress
- ♂ Skin eruptions, moles, birthmarks that are growing, acne, psoriasis
- ♂ Susceptibility to infection
- ♂ Unexplained weight gain and/or tendency to gain weight easily

Coffee Enema

Now I am really going to stretch you a bit. My wife, Deb, was diagnosed with cervical dysplasia when she was about 30 years old. This was after our second child was born. One of the points Deb and I learned during this experience was that cells can come and go on a cervical scraping, especially after having a child. We decided that what we were doing up until that point was not promoting optimal liver function in our family. We made a total flip from consuming fried and processed foods, alcohol, and soda to eating living, whole foods that did not burden our bodies with processed or toxic items.

We needed to be committed. There is a point I would like to reiterate by asking you, if Deb would have had the abnormal cells burned or cauterized, would we have been getting to the cause of the problem? No, of course not! To get to the cause, we needed to clean her machine.

After you have a surgical procedure, when your doctor tells you, "We got everything," do not get a false sense of security that you are normal. That statement is speculation that your doctor removed all the abnormal tissue and cells *visible to his or her eyes at the time*. But you need to know that an area in the body, which could be remotely involved, might still be creating the environment that allows abnormal cells to appear.

I cringe when people tell me that an enormous mass of tissue has been removed from their body, and they confidently look at me with the false belief that they are healed. I often learn that these individuals succumb to the same debilitating condition later in life. No one took the time, either out of ignorance or denial of reality, to suggest that these patients modify some aspect of their lifestyle. This is your life! You must take charge of it.

My wife didn't stop at changing her diet. She was told that a coffee enema would benefit her overall health program. Although she really had not done enemas before, let alone coffee enemas, she self-administered coffee enemas regularly for a year. She used a pot of organic coffee, brewed using an organic paper filter. The coffee enema works physiologically because the coffee is very aggravating to the system, and the liver literally goes "berserk" when there is that much insult to it. Now, is the coffee enema something you have to do? Well, let me say this. It is nearly 30 years since my wife started to make lifestyle changes. She has gone in for regular pap smears and other female procedures without ever having an abnormal report. She will do coffee enemas several times a year now, but doing them frequently is no longer important for her because she does not have the ingested toxic overload. We also get colonic irrigation at least twice a year. And we do not willingly put any toxins into our bodies.

Juicing

I am a believer in preventive maintenance. To me that means your life is geared toward promoting life versus treating sickness. It is very apparent to me that most new patients who enter my office have abused their bodies by overeating toxic foods, including pastries, sodas, cookies, donuts, chips, French fries, and the list goes on. They do not exercise, and the thought of drinking anything but coffee, tea, energy drinks, or alcohol is not a part of their daily plan.

If you have been diagnosed with cancer, you will want to heed the following information. I encourage patients who have been diagnosed with cancer to drink at least one quart of fresh vegetable juice daily for a minimum of two months. The juice is to be made in eight-ounce increments and consumed immediately. I suggest the following items in the recipe: carrot, beet, ginger (a small piece), sweet apple, parsley, celery, and cucumber. I recommend one tablespoon of organic green food and one tablespoon of organic flax powder, with five drops of dandelion root/leaf. You can use turmeric instead of ginger in the juice or add it to the mixed green salad that I recommend you eat every day. Turmeric is an anti-tumor food. Please check the ingredients in the green food and avoid any with artificial sweeteners. This combination will assist the body in purifying itself and will also significantly assist in the process of alkalizing the system. Your goal is a saliva pH that is purple on the nitrazine paper, indicating an alkaline pH. Acid promotes cancer, and alkaline promotes life. We live in a society and have diets that are acid in nature.

THE IMPORTANCE OF OPTIMAL LIVER FUNCTION — ACTION STEPS

- ☐ Cleansing is not about taking or doing something; cleansing is about changing the thought pattern that you can eat with reckless abandon and your body will just deal with it. This lifestyle pattern will result in a breakdown in health.

- ☐ Focus on drinking water from a pure source. Minimize the fluids you consume that have preservatives and sweeteners. Your liver has to process any unused chemicals. The more you put in, the harder the organs of detoxification have to work.

- ☐ My primary suggestion is to evaluate what you are putting into your body before you attempt to alter your body's chemistry in order to release existing toxins. Your body physiologically may not be able to release accumulated toxins without distress.

- ☐ Your best mode of detoxification would be to avoid putting sugar, trans fat, and prescription and over-the-counter medications, which are very potent, into your body. These substances are the primary causes of your toxic response.

- ☐ Focus on organic whole foods, especially raw veggies, e.g., broccoli, cabbage, cauliflower, and Brussels sprouts, along with apples, beets, and carrots. See the Page Food Plan in Chapter 20.

NOTES _____

_____

_____

_____

_____

_____

_____

_____

_____

_____

Chapter 7

Fuel the Thyroid to Keep the Body Going

The thyroid is often overlooked in the big picture of female health patterns. I am not sure how many health providers really understand its role in the daily performance of female health. I have many female patients whose entire hormonal puzzle is resolved by adding iodine and tyrosine, which you will learn about later in this chapter.

A challenge you are confronted with as a patient today is that there seems to be a specialist for every system in the body. If the thyroid is not fed the right food, you can suffer from chronic dry skin, morning headaches that wear off as the day goes on, elevated cholesterol, depression, and constipation. So you might visit a dermatologist for your skin, a pain management specialist for your headaches, an internist for your cholesterol, a psychiatrist for your depression, and a gastroenterologist for your colon.

Do you know that it is common for females, both young and old, to visit a healthcare provider for depression? A good percent of the time, such a patient can be at the office with an undetected, subclinical thyroid problem, and still have blood serum testing within normal values. Two significant substances that feed the thyroid to make thyroid hormone are tyrosine (an amino acid, or protein building block) and iodine, which are often deficient in patients who have depression. Tyrosine is known for helping individuals with depression.

Recently, an excessive number of females in their teens and early 20s have come to my office taking not only one antidepressant but oftentimes *two* of these psycho-sensitive medications. What appears to be the indiscriminate distribution of these emotionally addictive drugs is what alarms me. Do you know that the side effects of these prescription medications include a risk of suicide during the first 24 to 36 hours of starting them? Are you aware that suicide is the third leading cause of death in teens?

The pattern for the breakdown of physiology that results in emotional burnout often occurs right from birth. If a child is bottle-fed (versus breast-fed) with soy-based formula from the beginning, he or she is headed for potential challenges down the road. Do you remember having growing pains when you were growing up? Did you experience pain on the front of your knee? Growing pains are a very common body signal for a youngster experiencing low thyroid function. How could that be? The soy found in baby formula is an anti-thyroid food. Children who are not breast-fed are more than likely consuming food that impairs thyroid function from the beginning of life! I have a number of very young patients who have been diagnosed with a subpar-functioning thyroid gland.

I have found that many young women today appear to have an issue with depression because of their food choices. The current generation of young adults was raised by parents who were exposed to convenience foods early in life. Therefore, today's moms ate fries and chicken nuggets, plus an array of convenience foods, during their formative years and have since had children who are now in their late teens and early 20s. Convenience and fast foods are fried in or are overloaded with unhealthy oils that do not make good hormone precursors. The thyroid gland, like other glands in the endocrine system, counts on healthy oil as a basis for making the precious hormones key for the body to function.

"Dr. Bob," you might ask, "why do you think we are having more issues with a low thyroid at such a young age?" There are a couple of logical possibilities, but first I have a question for you: Why are so many kids and adults diagnosed with ADHD, pain syndromes, and heart and hormonal issues? The answer to both of these questions is, primarily, poor fat metabolism. Food today is overprocessed, without enough minerals and vitamins remaining intact. Therefore, you do not take in the ingredients necessary to completely metabolize the food you eat. As I mentioned earlier, soy appears to be in nearly everything, and it depletes one of the key players in metabolism, zinc, along with others.

The biggest issue I see with the thyroid, since it is so significant in the hormonal system, is that not enough iodine is being consumed. Also, many healthcare professionals appear to be recommending the consumption of carbohydrates as opposed to protein. If protein *is* consumed, it is some type of processed "wannabe" meat. Protein from a qualified, natural, whole source is needed for L-tyrosine.

Also, we are living in a culture in which fat phobia is rampant. The public has been so focused on the low-fat diet that getting a drop of good oil to pass the lips of a good percent of the population is tougher than pulling teeth. The media has the general population believing that all oil is bad, so people now primarily eat low-fat, high-carbohydrate foods. Consequently, the thyroid does not have the oil it needs. When the thyroid is unable to function properly, it causes the body to run on low, with no energy; the system is just pulling itself along. You will ultimately gain weight. To correct this pattern, all you need to do is eat whole foods with protein and minerals.

In Chapter 16, "Reversing Unhealthy Patterns," I discuss how significant the thyroid is for preventing destructive patterns that often result in cancer somewhere in the body, especially the breasts. I would like to explain to you in very simple terms how the thyroid operates. Thyroid function is significant for normal bowel movements, and it is an indicator of iodine sufficiency. It seems logical to assume that if the thyroid does not have enough iodine, the ovaries do not have enough either. The ovaries and breasts need iodine for optimal hormone production. Therefore, you could prevent female hormonal issues by considering the function of the thyroid gland.

Your thyroid gland is a small mass of tissue, normally weighing less than one ounce, located in the front of the neck. It is made up of two halves, called lobes, that lie along the windpipe (trachea) and are joined together by a narrow band of thyroid tissue known as the isthmus. (See the drawing in Chapter 1.)

The thyroid is situated just below the Adam's apple, or larynx. During development (inside the womb), the thyroid gland originates in the back of the tongue, but it normally migrates to the front of the neck before birth. Sometimes it fails to migrate properly and is located high in the neck or even in the back of the tongue (lingual thyroid), which is very rare. At other times it may migrate too far and end up in the chest, which is also rare.

The function of the thyroid gland is to take iodine, found in many foods, and convert it into the thyroid hormones thyroxine (T4) and triiodothyronine (T3). Thyroid tissue cells combine iodine and the amino acid tyrosine to make T3 and T4. T3 and T4 are then released into the bloodstream and transported throughout the body, where they control metabolism (the conversion of oxygen and calories to energy). Every cell in the body depends upon thyroid hormones for the regulation of its metabolism. The normal thyroid gland produces about 80 percent T4 and about 20 percent T3; however, T3 possesses about four times the hormone "strength" as T4.

The thyroid gland is under the control of the pituitary gland, a small gland the size of a peanut at the base of the brain. When the level of thyroid hormones drops too low, the pituitary gland produces thyroid-stimulating hormone (TSH), which stimulates the thyroid gland to produce more hormones. Under the influence of TSH, the thyroid will manufacture and secrete T3 and T4, thereby raising their blood levels. The pituitary senses this and responds by decreasing its TSH production. Imagine the thyroid gland as a furnace and the pituitary gland as the thermostat. Thyroid hormones are like heat. When the heat gets back to the thermostat, it turns the thermostat off. As the room cools (the thyroid hormone levels drop), the thermostat turns back on (TSH increases), and the furnace produces more heat (thyroid hormones).

The pituitary gland, as discussed earlier, is regulated by the hypothalamus. The hypothalamus is part of the brain and produces thyrotropin-releasing hormone (TRH), which tells the pituitary gland to release TSH to stimulate the thyroid gland. One might imagine the hypothalamus as the person who regulates the thermostat since it tells the pituitary gland at what level the thyroid should be "set."

When patients come into the office and we do their blood tests, I have noticed that more than half of them have TSH serum levels of less than 2; this is low from my clinical experience. I suspect the reason is that the pituitary, like the rest of the body, needs nutrients to survive. If the pituitary doesn't get enough selenium and manganese, which are depleted by stress, it cannot create the hormones needed by the body. We use whole-food supplements with selenium, manganese, and a pituitary glandular to support TSH production. This phenomenon is also common with patients who have stress on the adrenal glands, which is discussed in Chapter 8. I also consistently see a minimal desire for sexual intimacy in individuals who have a low TSH level; I believe there must be a correlation with the physiological burnout of the system.

There is also an epidemic of "iodine phobia"—physicians have not been encouraging supplementation with an organic source of iodine. Table salt has been used as a tool to deliver iodine to the masses, but it is not really the best-quality source. Commercial-grade sodium chloride (table salt) also contains unhealthy additives, including aluminum and dextrose (sugar), that prevent it from caking.

The public today not only has a fat phobia but a salt phobia. Patients have been told to avoid salt because it raises blood pressure.

I have found that salt may raise blood pressure in about 5 percent of patients (and mind you, that is sodium chloride, the salt the masses consume). I do not consume commercial-grade table salt.

What I really see that raises blood pressure is the huge appetite for sweets. Sugar raises the insulin level in the body and stresses the adrenal glands, raising blood pressure. Your body compensates with increased sodium retention. Increased sodium retention creates more water withholding. When someone does not drink enough water, the blood gets thicker and more concentrated, restricting its flow—probably just the opposite of what you may think (that if you drink a lot of water you will have more fluid and higher blood pressure). Indeed, I see blood pressure elevation in patients who do not drink enough water. Drink *at least* one quart of pure water daily.

I encourage the use of Celtic Sea Salt®, which is harvested from the northern coast of France. Nothing has been added to it. The granules come from the open rock surface, where the salt has evaporated from ocean water. It should be called "sea minerals" instead of "sea salt." Celtic Sea Salt® is an excellent source of minerals, and I encourage our patients to use it liberally.

Nearly every female patient who enters my office today is on thyroid medication of some sort. It might be the standard, Synthroid®, or Armour Thyroid, which has been taken off the market and is produced now by compounding pharmacists. Just as insulin from an outside source does not repair the pancreas, thyroid hormone from a cow or other outside source does not repair the thyroid.

I have observed some interesting issues with thyroid testing. I commonly find a low TSH level in most patients with thyroid symptoms. I recommend animal-sourced glandular extracts to support neurological function and hormone production of the pituitary. These are organ extracts and protomorphogens (materials from the nuclei of cells that contain a blueprint for how the cells function). They feed the organs nutrients and assist in the restoration of cell metabolism.

When doing a serum assessment of their thyroid, I look to see if my patients have the following symptoms. I generally look for at least six symptoms in conjunction with the blood tests that have a predetermined range.

Increased weight	Constipation
Decreased appetite	Mental sluggishness
Easily fatigued	Coarse hair that falls out
Ringing in ears	Reduced initiative
Sleepiness during day	Impaired hearing
Sensitivity to cold	Slow pulse, below 72
Dry or scaly skin	Frequent urination

Other body signals include a morning headache that wears off as the day goes on, thinning of the outer eyebrows and the hair on the sides of the legs, elevated cholesterol, widely spaced teeth, cold hands and feet, dry skin, and growing pains in kids (as previously discussed).

What I have found, as noted above, is that we have three main serum levels to look at. I want to briefly discuss my parameters. If the TSH level is less than 2, I support pituitary gland function. If the TSH level is greater than 2 but less than 10, I support the thyroid gland with a glandular-sourced product. I also make sure the patient is consuming a source of essential fatty acids, including the omega-3 and omega-6 fats. Often I will supplement the patient with a product that supports the RNA and DNA template. It may take six months to two years before changes are seen in the blood serum levels.

I also like to assess the T3 and T4 levels. Generally, I like to see both of these numbers above the midline as I observe the testing reference range from the lab. If the values are at the midpoint or lower, I generally focus on supplementing with an organic source of iodine. I use an iodine product that incorporates both iodine and iodide. Go slow with the iodine; you may notice a skin rash, metallic taste in your mouth, and/or pain over the eyes if you take too much iodine too soon. I also like to supplement with a source of tyrosine and a full-spectrum amino acid. There are many fine companies that make excellent individual sources of tyrosine.

Some individuals have symptoms that appear to indicate they are sensitive to iodine. When you take iodine, it displaces fluorine, chlorine, and bromine; your body reacts to the toxic effects caused by the release of these elements. These symptoms will go away in a few days. Note that fluorine, chlorine, and bromine are located in the same row of the periodic chart as iodine and are actually antagonistic to it. The hostile behavior of these elements to iodine is not usually discussed and is a very common basis for persistent subpar thyroid function.

Taking any supplement, whether it is natural or synthetic, can interfere with some medications. Patients on heart medication may notice heartbeat alterations with iodine. Always talk to a knowledgeable healthcare professional. Do not attempt to take large doses of iodine on your own when you are taking amiodarone, Pacerone®, or Cordarone®.

Japanese women, who have a track record of minimal menopausal symptoms and hot flashes, consume up to 12 milligrams of iodine a day in their food, normally from fish and sea vegetables. I know firsthand, from spending extended time in Japan, that sea vegetables and fresh marine life are a major staple. The Japanese eat as a family and you don't see them eating out at fast-food chains like we do in our Western culture. Their markets are overflowing with fresh fish that is available daily.

The really critical lab value that is a concern is the elevation of T4 in relation to T3. This is a flag to me that the T4 is not converting over to T3. This is usually a sign that the patient may have one of two issues to deal with: stress, with associated high cortisol levels, or high estrogen. Both of these conditions can impair thyroid hormone production. Elevated estrogen interrupts the production of thyroid hormone and creates a loop of negative feedback that results in the thyroid's not functioning. With the bowels and liver not operating at 100 percent, the estrogen builds up, and we have stagnation with estrogen dominance—a tough cycle to break.

I like to see patients' dietary journals to make sure they are eating adequate protein. Oftentimes females do not consume enough protein, i.e., chicken, turkey, and periodic red meat. I suggest that my patients take a full-spectrum protein supplement, containing all the essential amino acid building blocks for protein, to provide the amino acids for liver detoxification.

I have encouraged many women to learn to say "I cannot say yes" to the commitments that put them on overload. This is a polite way of saying "No." Ladies, for you to get to the level of health you desire, you will probably have to assess your commitments, in order to give your body an opportunity to reset itself and to achieve a normal, restful state.

I have patients monitor their armpit temperature while they are following the supplement protocol determined by the blood serum test. Again, an important factor is that they have at least six symptoms from the list of low-thyroid body signals on page 83.

The thyroid can also be monitored by observing the results of hair tissue mineral analysis; you will learn more about this in Chapter 15, on testing. Monitoring includes analyzing the ratios between mineral levels. A common subpar thyroid pattern would include a calcium level that is proportionately higher than the potassium level; the ratio is normally 4:1. There are many tools that can be used to assess the function of your thyroid. Your goal is to wake up without a head-ache and have awesome, smooth skin; regular bowel movements; a vibrant attitude and emotional state; and cholesterol at the 200 level without medication or herbs. That would surely indicate you are going in the right direction, and that you are on the way to optimal, whole-body health—with a finely stoked thyroid gland.

FUEL THE THYROID TO KEEP THE BODY GOING — ACTION STEPS

☐ If you have the body signals described above, take your armpit, or axillary, temperature as discussed in Chapter 3. If you have cold hands and feet, that would be a strong indicator that you may, in fact, have a subpar-functioning thyroid gland.

☐ If your temperature is less than 97.8 degrees Fahrenheit, I would recommend locating a healthcare provider who understands assessing the blood serum thyroid values as discussed above. You would want to consult with that individual and follow the protocol I mentioned for several months, and then be retested. Do not go off your medications without the direct supervision of a qualified professional.

☐ I would not start a supplement protocol until you have had either blood serum analysis and/or hair analysis, preferably both, to establish a baseline for supplementation.

☐ Hair analysis may be of value to determine the state of your tissue levels of calcium and potassium. You would treat according to the lab report results. See Chapter 15, on testing.

☐ Observe how your body signals change over time. That, in conjunction with your other testing, will help plot the course for your female hormone stabilization.

☐ Chlorine is toxic to the thyroid, so I encourage our patients to replace their standard showerhead with one that takes out chlorine. You can smell the difference in the air. I have located a showerhead that has a long life and does not need the filter replaced, because the material is backwashed from the filter.

☐ You may want to consider a urine iodine loading test to assess the amount of iodine in your body. Refer to Chapter 15 or www.druglessdoctor.com for details.

NOTES _____

_____

_____

_____

_____

_____

_____

_____

_____

_____

PATIENT TESTIMONY:

"I had various hormonal issues before making the lifestyle changes recommended by Dr. DeMaria. I had PMS, headaches for several days prior to my cycle, and very tender breasts. I took NSAIDs for cramping and headaches. Following Dr. Bob's suggestions, I eliminated all trans fats, reduced sugar, focused on lean meats and veggies, and cut out most dairy.

Since making these lifestyle modifications, I have virtually no PMS and only minimal cramping. My cycles are very regular!"

Laura Meyer

Note: Portions of this information were referenced from *EndocrineWeb*, http://www.endocrineweb.com/hypo1.html.

Chapter 8

Support the Adrenal Glands

The adrenals are a pair of glands located on top of your kidneys. They are situated right around where your low- and mid-back areas meet. They are by far the most overlooked organs for overall, long-term female health. The adrenal gland is similar to a fuel pump, and your thyroid is like the gas pedal. The two work together in unison with the pancreas, liver, and of course, the rest of the body.

Descriptions of the adrenal glands always seem to use the analogy of responding to a fire. The adrenals are the organs that let you "hightail" it out of a situation when you need to. They create the response in the body that speeds up the heart, gets the muscles the fuel they need, and takes care of all the other details of "getting out of town." Today, in our fast-paced, cell-phone-addicted, Bluetooth-connected, office-in-the-vehicle society, our adrenal glands are exhausted from trying to keep up, constantly putting out all the little-big fires.

What most don't realize is that the adrenal glands are designed as a part of your long-term, backup hormonal replacement system. As time and technology move on, I believe the masses will put as much energy into keeping their adrenals healthy as they do into maintaining their pearly white smiles and keeping their blood vessels clear. The adrenal glands are a part of a sophisticated system of interchangeable, related steroid chemicals necessary for life.

Steroids used in this context are the basic building blocks for the sex hormones in the body.

The chart below has names that I don't expect you to be able to pronounce, but I want you to see the maze of hormones for which cholesterol is a precursor. You will see advertisements telling you that if you take this pill you will lose weight, or if you take that pill your muscles will get big—or, ladies, if you apply this cream, you will have an increased desire to have sex, your bones will get strong, and you won't have heart issues. Adrenal health starts with cholesterol, the designated "bad boy" in health. Cholesterol is not good or bad. It is necessary and does its job.

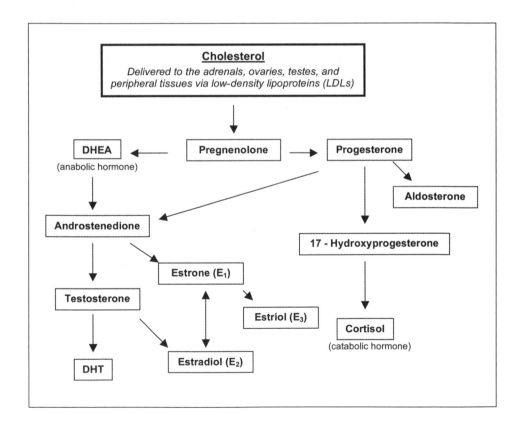

Do you see how adrenal hormone health starts with cholesterol? Cholesterol is the precursor to the important end products of estrogen, progesterone, and cortisol. Vitamin D, an overlooked factor in health, requires cholesterol as a starting component. You read in magazines to take vitamin D so you don't break a bone. I would suggest that you go out in the sun every day. Take extra flax oil and calcium so that the sun has something to work with. The sun converts the cholesterol in your skin to vitamin D. Do you want to help your body lower cholesterol? Then get in the sun. Watch what you are putting on your skin to block out the rays. If you see the ingredient sodium lauryl sulfate, a known potential toxin, on a bottle of sunblock, put it down. Whatever you put on your skin will ultimately enter your body. Lotions and gels are processed by the body and can create cysts! It makes you wonder what is causing cancer anyway—the lotion or the sun! What you put on your skin is absorbed into your body, and your liver has to work on getting it out.

The adrenal gland has two functional portions to it. The inner part is called the medulla, and the outer part is the cortex. I would like to focus on the cortex. Situated along the perimeter of the adrenal gland, the adrenal cortex mediates the stress response through the production of mineralocorticoids (for mineral regulation) and glucocorticoids (for sugar metabolism and cortisone production). It is also a secondary site of androgen (sex hormone) synthesis.

Androgen is the generic term for any natural or synthetic compound, usually a steroid hormone, that stimulates or controls the development and maintenance of masculine characteristics in humans by binding to androgen receptors. This includes the activity of the accessory male sex organs and the development of male secondary sex characteristics. First discovered in 1936, androgens are also called androgenic hormones or testoids. They are the original anabolic steroids. Androgens are also the precursor of all estrogens, the female sex hormones. The primary and most well-known androgen is testosterone—a critical point in our discussion for long-term female health and the reason menopausal women should not have to deal with hormonal issues. (Testosterone maintains libido and structural strength in women.)

The adrenal glands, just like the other glands in your body, need quality food in order to fulfill their job descriptions. It is important to recognize that all hormone-producing glands need oil from a quality source. Therefore, the low-fat diet has been a major obstacle for female well-being. You do not get the right ingredients with a low-fat diet. The focus on calories over quality has created the foundation for poor female health. I personally prefer organic plant oils, especially the omega-3 fats (such as the precursor flax oil), or a "safe" marine-based product. I am currently taking an anchovy- and sardine-based liquid source, available in capsules. I sense over time that the larger fish, like tuna and even salmon, may contain above the "safe" limit of the known toxin mercury. I do not encourage the use of oils sourced from farm-raised fish.

Adrenal fatigue body signals are occurring in epidemic proportions. Most people that I talk with in my practice and throughout America have several common symptoms. I have provided a checklist to help you assess your own potential challenges with adrenal function.

ADRENAL FATIGUE CHECKLIST... HOW MANY SYMPTOMS DO YOU HAVE?

- ☐ Difficulty getting up in the morning
- ☐ Increased PMS
- ☐ Continuing fatigue, not relieved by sleep and rest
- ☐ Worsening of symptoms if meals are skipped or inadequate
- ☐ Lethargy, lack of energy to do normal daily activities
- ☐ Less-focused thoughts, brain fog
- ☐ Sugar cravings
- ☐ Poorer memory
- ☐ Salt cravings
- ☐ Decreased tolerance for stress, noise, disorder
- ☐ Allergies
- ☐ Not really waking up until after 10:00 a.m.

- ☐ Afternoon low between 3:00 and 4:00 p.m.
- ☐ Increased effort needed for everyday tasks
- ☐ Feeling better after supper
- ☐ Decreased interest in sex
- ☐ Getting a "second wind" in the evening and staying up late
- ☐ Decreased ability to handle stress
- ☐ Decreased ability to get things done, less productive
- ☐ Digestion problems
- ☐ Increased time needed to recover from illness, injury, or trauma
- ☐ Having to keep moving ("If I stop, I get tired.")
- ☐ Being lightheaded or dizzy when standing up quickly
- ☐ Feeling overwhelmed by all that needs to be done
- ☐ Low mood
- ☐ Less enjoyment or happiness with life

FACTORS LEADING TO ADRENAL FATIGUE... HOW MANY DO YOU HAVE?

- ☐ Consumption of white sugar and white flour
- ☐ Counterproductive (negative) attitudes, products, and beliefs
- ☐ Lack of relaxation
- ☐ Conventional hormone replacement therapy
- ☐ Smoking
- ☐ Non-prescription drugs
- ☐ Antacids
- ☐ Psychological stress
- ☐ Consumption of devitalized food
- ☐ Persistent fears
- ☐ Unfulfilling employment (dead-end job)
- ☐ Emotional stress
- ☐ Dead-end relationships
- ☐ Lack of sleep
- ☐ Surgery
- ☐ Being in denial about feelings
- ☐ Consumption of junk food
- ☐ Consumption of trans fats/rancid fats
- ☐ Infection, acute or chronic
- ☐ Repeated stresses
- ☐ Financial stress
- ☐ Persistent negative stressors
- ☐ Sedentary lifestyle

- ☐ Deprivation of fun or enjoyment
- ☐ Excessive exercise
- ☐ Allergies
- ☐ Death of a loved one
- ☐ Caffeine
- ☐ Alcoholism
- ☐ Prescription drugs
- ☐ Toxins
- ☐ Marital stress
- ☐ Hormonal imbalances
- ☐ Repeated traumas
- ☐ Oral contraceptives
- ☐ Workaholism
- ☐ Stimulants

I regularly see the following scenario: an infancy on soy-based, high-phytoestrogen baby formula, followed by a childhood focused on snacks and processed and pre-made foods (macaroni and cheese and chicken nuggets). The teen years include soda; relentless cravings for chocolate and peanut butter candies; and fat-sourced, high-trans-fat foods from fast-food venues. Some teens give in to either self-starvation or overeating. Teens become young adults who eat very little fresh veggies and whole foods; the diet is devoid of health-promoting oil and focuses on eating on the run at franchise restaurants. By this time, prescription medications taken incude antidepressants, antihistamines, and/or combinations of pain relievers and antihistamines. Young ladies start to have a heavy menstrual flow, cysts in the breasts, a possible cyst or two in the ovaries, and fibrocystic breast disease. The menstrual cycle is very painful and even debilitating, with a hormone-related headache at the end of the flow. Before she knows it, the young lady sprints into her late 40s. She may be one of the statistics for gallbladder, uterus, and/or ovary removal, and then comes the BIG question: WHAT DO I TAKE?

The adrenal glands are there to rescue you. A part of their job description is to be the backup to provide enough hormones to carry you through all the cycles of your life. A common pattern I see in my practice is the onset of menses before the age of 10, which is often followed by a lifetime of tender breasts and heavy menstrual flow (caused by pre-menopause estrogen saturation) and concludes with challenges in menopause because the adrenal glands now cannot make enough estrogen to support the natural requirements for optimal health.

The adrenal glands are designed to release whatever female hormone you may need. People have an innate passion for sugar; in fact, it is breast milk's sweetness that drives babies to desire to drink it. This passionate craving upsets the very sensitive balance of the production of hormones for sexual function and bone and joint function.

When you consume sugar, your body needs to process it. The adrenal gland must shift the focus of its production to glucocorticoids (mentioned above) in order to process the nutritionally devoid character of sugar. Production of mineralocorticoids and sex hormones suffers. The patient with this history will come in and complain of her back going out easily, a loss of desire for sexual intimacy, and pain syndromes like fibromyalgia.

Let me explain. Your back goes out easily because your adrenals are not making the mineralocorticoids needed to absorb adequate minerals; ligaments require minerals to be strong. As a result, you crave salt. You lose the desire for sex because the sex-hormone portion of the adrenal cortex is focused on processing sugar. Finally, you're in chronic pain because the cortisone used for pain relief is also being used up to process sugar.

You're not going to be a party to be around because you will have a multitude of symptoms related to what you eat. Pain will be with you 24 hours a day, seven days a week. The last thing you want is to have someone wanting to be with you sexually, and you will be craving sugar and salt because you are deficient in minerals. You will more than likely be advised to take an antidepressant because of the stress you are under. The real answer to your misery, however, is to work on breaking the cycle.

If your adrenal glands are exhausted when you are in your 20s and 30s, what is going to happen when you are in your 50s and your body is starving for estrogen? Where is the estrogen going to come from? Your ovaries are shutting down and the rest of your body is totally exhausted. Are you really going to want to take a synthetic hormone based on urine from pregnant mares, trademarked Premarin®?

Gluten, the protein in wheat, oat, and rye products, can create stress on the adrenal glands. I see this consistently when assessing the Adrenal Stress Index™ saliva test. Gluten literally glues the little finger-like projections on the walls of your intestines together so you cannot absorb minerals and nutrients. You can suffer from adrenal exhaustion with pain and hormone syndromes because of oatmeal, cereal, and pastries. I would not eat whole-wheat bread. A food allergy test would be helpful, because when you have food sensitivities, you also may have an essential-fatty-acid deficiency.

I would like to talk to you a bit about a loop I see. I purposely included the chemistry-like chart in this chapter because I needed you to see that cholesterol is a very big player in the scheme of things. Your body will make cholesterol if you don't eat enough of it. Cholesterol is literally in nearly every cell membrane of the body.

Cholesterol is not readily absorbed in water so it needs to be carried by lipoprotein, which I like to call a fire truck. The fire truck that carries the cholesterol to the fire is called LDL; the one that returns it to the firehouse is HDL. If you have recently had a blood test indicating "high cholesterol," and the well-meaning physician suggested a cholesterol-lowering drug, do you know that taking that drug is like shooting yourself in the foot? You're actually shooting the "fireman" and opening yourself up to a list of negative side effects associated with these medications.

Your cholesterol is elevated because your brain has been notified that you need more cholesterol to make the list of hormones in the maze. The questions you need to ask yourself are, why is cholesterol in demand and what is causing the fire? The answers, from my experience and years of looking at diet journals, are complex but correctable: sugar; trans fat, or partially hydrogenated oil; dairy; and the low-fat diet. These items interfere with normal fat metabolism, critical for optimal hormonal health. You will learn more about this in Chapter 22, "Facts About Fat." I have written an entire book on the subject, *Dr. Bob's Trans Fat Survival Guide,* which is available at www.druglessdoctor.com.

Your adrenal glands need cholesterol to do their job. Your consumption of sugar and refined foods creates stress on the adrenal glands to modify production; hence, you will have menstrual issues and eventually menopausal challenges.

SUPPORT THE ADRENAL GLANDS — ACTION STEPS

☐ A real key to long-term adrenal health is coordinating your life so you have time to rest. I know this may not be easy for some, but it will help in your long-term protocol. Sleep eight hours a night, with no lights on. Limit your TV and computer time before bed. Cover the lights on electrical appliances in your bedroom, such as those on alarm clocks, DVD players, VCRs, etc.

☐ Sugar, by far, is one of the most detrimental items for your adrenal health. I would start with three chromium supplements a day to help minimize the cravings for sugar, though I have patients who need up to nine. Gymnema is an excellent herb that reduces the taste of sweet items, one to three supplements daily.

☐ Focus on getting more protein into your diet. Protein helps stabilize the energy burning in your body. You won't have sugar highs and lows. If you consume carbohydrates instead of sufficient protein, your system will burn muscle for energy. Limit protein to three to five ounces per serving so you do not get a compensatory insulin release, starting a cascade of cravings.

- [ ] Avoid sweet fruits, especially bananas, raisins, and grapes. Eat veggies as a snack with some nuts, like almonds, walnuts, and sunflower seeds.

- [ ] If you crave salt, which is a common adrenal fatigue body signal, consume Celtic Sea Salt®.

- [ ] Do not put progesterone cream on your body once your adrenal gland is up to par. Do not take DHEA, as it can throw off your system. Have your saliva assessed for DHEA and cortisol, and support the body with whole-food supplementation, herbal tonics, and adaptogens. You will need a skilled healthcare provider to assist you.

- [ ] You may want to have your blood pressure taken while lying down, and then standing up. Your blood pressure should not drop.

- [ ] Saliva progesterone and estrogen testing helps me develop a proper supplement protocol. I make recommendations based on the results of saliva and other tests, like the sit-to-stand blood pressure test and pupil observation. Normally, a whole-food adrenal product and herb product are suggested, depending on the severity of the gland exhaustion. I also want to say that progesterone production is dependent on enough T4. It is possible to have subpar thyroid gland function with low T4, which sabotages progesterone delivery.

- [ ] I recommend taking whole-food vitamin C up to the point where your stools get loose. Vitamin C is an integral component of adrenal health.

- [ ] I also recommend whole-food vitamin B for patients when their blood pressure is low. You will want to be monitored by an experienced healthcare provider. Synthetic B vitamins may, in fact, aggravate the adrenals.

- [ ] A whole-food pantothenic acid supplement is helpful for optimal adrenal restoration. Pantothenic acid is vitamin B5; it should be balanced with a whole-food B complex, as mentioned above.

☐ You can monitor your progress by assessing your blood pressure.

☐ Hair analysis is also useful to help you monitor your adrenal health. Commonly, I see low sodium and potassium when a patient has stressed adrenal function. Aluminum is often high when the adrenal glands are overworked.

NOTES_____

_____

_____

_____

_____

_____

_____

_____

_____

Chapter 9

Strengthen the Frame and Structure

Osteoporosis is a condition that is very commonly discussed today and is frequently one of the reasons your medical provider will suggest hormone replacement therapy or some other type of prescription. Prescription medicine stops nature from doing its job and, in the long run, will actually *create* osteoporosis. Osteoporosis, simply put, is the loss of the structural density of bone. Think of this process as washing your favorite cotton blouse so often that the brilliant colors slowly begin to fade until, finally, the garment is devoid of color.

It is clear that many physicians do not know the precise cause of osteoporosis, because they treat it with a physiologically incorrect drug—one that stops the body from metabolizing old bone. The public have been positioned as players in the guessing game as to the cause of osteoporosis and have been told that you must take medication to stop it.

There are many reasons that osteoporosis is prevalent. I am sure these possibilities will make sense once I describe them. Not all women in America have osteoporosis. If it was at epidemic levels, one and all would be diagnosed with it. Since all women do not have it, there must be a pattern that creates bone loss for those who do. If I can help you discover your pattern, we can stop it and manage it.

I can tell you that taking one of the new once-a-month, highly promoted, celebrity-endorsed medications only tricks the body and does not get to the cause of the problem. These prescriptions are peddled on a premise of fear—fear that if you do not take them, you will wake up one day and be bent over, staring at your feet.

The medications that women are being told they need to take once every 30 days work by preventing a bone cell called an osteoclast from doing its job. The osteoclast's job is to vacuum up bone cells that need to be recycled. Think of it like the Pac-Man creature going around eating everything in sight. The whole mechanism is very controlled by the innate intelligence that directs how the structural system maintains itself. Your body is in a constant state of transition of breakdown and repair. This occurs at the cellular level. It happens gradually over time.

The real issue with these medications is that they are not getting to the cause of the problem. They are giving the user a false sense of security, just like other medications that treat symptoms versus the cause. Over time, using medications that interfere with the osteoclast's work results in the presence of old, fragile bone where there should be new, strong bone with vitality.

When someone currently on osteoporosis medication has bone density scans performed on various areas, it appears that there is structure, giving the false sense of security I was telling you about; but it is not normal for old bone to be present. Vertebrae can fracture when a person is on osteoporosis medication. I am not suggesting that you stop your meds without making other lifestyle changes. You will want to talk to a healthcare provider who can monitor your progression.

On the x-ray of a new patient with osteoporosis, it looks like the bone has been washed out. The outer margin, or rim, around the bone has what is called a "pencil-thin cortex." This is a characteristic that I evaluate when I am assessing osteoporosis on patient films.

So I want you to think, why do natural-fabric cotton clothes (analogous to bones) fade? Using them causes relentless friction, wear and tear on the small fibers, chemical changes in the dye resulting from sunlight, and the gradual removal of color through washing with detergent. The more you wear and wash an outfit, the quicker you will replace it. But if you take care of the material, and wash it in the appropriate temperature using a mild detergent, it will last longer.

Osteoporosis is something that does not have to happen to a woman when she hits the magic age of 62 or 65. This may be news to you, but osteoporosis actually originates with habits that can start at the very beginning of life; the health of your birth mom is very significant.

I want to reiterate a point. We—and when I say "we," I am including myself in the group—are constantly told by the media (who are fed information by pharmaceutically endorsed studies and freelance writers who get paid to release information) that osteoporosis and other common chronic conditions are controlled by genetics, viruses, and family characteristics. Magazine editors ask experts to write articles that specifically serve the needs of the publication. I know firsthand this is a common practice because I have been solicited to write such articles myself. You should not believe everything you read in a magazine or on the Internet. I would suggest that you look at the bio of the person who contributed a piece of writing. If you see that "so and so is a FREELANCE writer," that is your cue that he or she was paid to find the information required to serve the need of the editor.

I have treated a substantial number of patients who have family members in poor health, yet they (my patients) chose to make lifestyle changes. They started by eliminating the old family recipes, from grandma, and made a new, healthier life for themselves. If someone in your family has an incurable condition, you are not just doomed.

I generally see signs of osteoporosis in new female patients in their late 60s or 70s. I normally do not see osteoporosis in patients in their 40s or 50s unless they have smoked or have a history of obsessive sugar consumption. Smoking is a serious addiction. It depletes the body of minerals and slows the healing of bone structures. Yet not all women I treat have osteoporosis.

I have noted that it is common to see osteoporosis in females who have considerable dental work visible on lateral cervical, or neck, x-rays. This finding, in correlation with my review of blood serum studies and my participation in post-graduate-level training, suggests that there is a common abnormal pattern of having altered serum levels of two minerals. Specifically, I find elevated phosphorus along with low calcium in these individuals. From a functional nutritional perspective, there should generally be ten parts serum calcium to four parts serum phosphorus.

Elevated phosphorus in the body is balanced by calcium. Consuming items with a high phosphorus content, such as grains and soda pop, can create an environment in which the body slowly loses calcium. Phosphorus can also be increased when the body is using muscle for a fuel source because the carbohydrate fuel mechanism is not functioning properly. The altered ratio, heavy on the phosphorus side, can be demonstrated in serum testing and hair tissue mineral analysis. When patients are exposed to this information, they should understand why their faulty eating patterns, based on refined grains and pastries, have been a part of their dilemma. Breads and pastas are regular items in the diet histories of patients with osteoporosis.

There basically appear to be two types of individuals today: those who are very concerned about what they eat, and those who either have no regard for what they eat or feel they are past the point of no return. A patient who changes her lifestyle upon beginning natural healthcare management reduces the potential for developing osteoporosis and other issues commonly accepted as normal in our media-driven society. My patients are reaping the benefits of being countercultural by not following fads, such as the low-fat, high-carbohydrate diet. Just because you read something from a reputable institution does not mean it is accurate.

There have been many reports and headlines in the *Wall Street Journal* suggesting less than honorable things about the results of drug testing. (The WSJ is on a relentless mission to discover nuggets of information from peer-reviewed medical journals.) In other words, the companies reporting information on new prescription medications were lying. I always chuckle when a representative of the pharmaceutical community who does not understand natural care asks me for "documented studies." I often respond, "They can be found in the same study that said XYZ drug you suggested was safe." They know full well that the medication caused harm. Consumers spend billions of dollars a year on osteoporosis medications.

I have post-World-War-II-era patients in my clinical practice who, as adults, started care in 1978. They were in their 40s and 50s and now are in their 80s and are spunky and moving around better than some of the new patients I see who are in their 50s and 60s. They came from a whole different generation of food and activity.

I was raised with food made and eaten at home. We went to a fast-food restaurant only once or twice a year. Today, 30 percent of children between four and nineteen eat at a fast-food establishment every day. You also need to take into consideration that the government feeds 30-million-plus kids every day with food that leaves much to be desired.

I regularly manage patients and their relatives who are interested in making changes for their young families, creating lifestyle patterns that won't lead to osteoporosis. When a female has chronic, challenging menstrual cycles early in life, she will have other hormonal issues when she gets older. It is always best to start a healthy lifestyle pattern right from the beginning.

It normally takes a 40-percent loss of bone structure to show up on an x-ray. The scale used to evaluate an osteoporosis scan is based on findings of women in their 30s; therefore, many women have the potential to manifest osteoporosis in America when they are compared to this scale. I look at several factors when assessing and suggesting a diagnosis of osteoporosis. Calcified rib cartilage is often evident in individuals with a pattern that results in bone loss later found in spinal vertebrae.

It has been suggested that estrogen therapy can slow osteoporosis. But what if we feed the body so it can create estrogen naturally, on its own? From experience, I have seen that improper food choices are one of the major reasons there is an osteoporosis epidemic. Your body has a challenge making hormones when you do not not supply it with the proper ingredients or when you eat nutritionally inadequate foods. Estrogen (in natural or synthetic forms from outside sources) in a compromised but functioning hormonal system is often not properly processed by the liver. The liver is a very significant player in the process of hormone metabolism.

The human body has the potential to make estrogen from several sources. Feeding the body whole foods is one of the better ways to maintain adequate estrogen levels after menopause. In addition, the adrenal glands and ovaries are two of the major secondary postmenopausal sources of estrogen.

When a new patient with osteoporosis comes into the office, she needs to realize that her lifelong eating and exercise patterns have created the state of mineral loss that resulted in her physical condition. In order to see results, you have to come to the understanding that what you have done to your body up to this point in your life is the reason you are the way you are.

To get what you have never had before, you must do something you have never done before. The three Ss—sugar, soda, and stress—are by far the chief factors leading to osteoporosis. Lack of activity is also a very key reason we nearly have an osteoporosis epidemic. Food groups that are acid, like meats, cheeses, and grains, will create an acid environment.

An acid-ash diet promotes osteoporosis. Refer to the chart showing alkaline-ash and acid-ash food groups in the Appendix. Focus on eating enough servings from the alkaline food groups, especially when you eat from the acid-ash food groups.

When sugar, an acid, is consumed, the body's protective physiology forces minerals out of their normal job descriptions to neutralize the effects of the sweet crystals. Guess which area of the body is your mineral reservoir. You guessed it: the bones. Your body will have to take minerals from somewhere—very often it is your skeletal system and your teeth.

Soda has an ingredient in it called phosphoric acid, which creates soda's effervescent bubbles. Phosphoric acid leaches calcium out of the body. I would like you to start observing the teeth of our youth, which are mottled, discolored, or unevenly white. Young people are often heavy soda drinkers or have been overexposed to toxic levels of fluoride. The average American consumes over 50 gallons of soda a year.

I also know that the stress of everyday living can create the redistribution of tissue calcium. I will often complete a mineral tissue analysis of a patient's hair sample from the nape of the neck. In reviewing the analysis, the lab often notes that the patient has plenty of calcium; it is just in the wrong places in the body. Someone under stress can have the adaptive response of having calcium deposit in the hair instead of being what we call "bioavailable," or "for use." The calcium is not ionizable. Stress can also elevate cortisol, a hormone from the adrenal gland. Elevated cortisol, occurring either naturally or from medication, has a calcium-depleting effect. You may want to have a mineral tissue analysis completed to see what your levels are. It is a great noninvasive procedure that can actually give you a road map for your future.

Mineral tissue analysis, unlike serum calcium assessment, gives you a snapshot of your past. It also presents a pattern of what your future may hold. Blood serum calcium can fluctuate quickly because your body is constantly pursuing equilibrium. The process of homeostasis will attempt to balance the minerals in your body by robbing Peter to pay Paul.

One of the visible body signals of stress that I commonly see is cold sores on the lip. I often find that individuals with cold sores are going through personal challenges. Stress creates an acid state, and calcium is required to balance it; cold sores result when a virus takes over due to the lack of calcium. These people nearly always have chronic low-calcium body signals, e.g., leg cramps; menstrual cramps; cold hands and feet; thick, dry, flaky skin; poison ivy, and gray or white hair. The gray or white hair is also a sign of poor metabolism of calcium in the body.

Calcium helps glue cell membranes together. When you run low on calcium, cell membrane defense mechanisms break down, and viruses have the chance to move in through gaps in the cell membranes—producing herpes simplex on the lip. Herpes blisters on the lip are quite common in individuals who have financial, marital, and other personal issues. Also, patients with blood type A seem to have more digestive distress, with poor calcium absorption.

Your body converts the cholesterol in your skin to vitamin D. Vitamin D helps increase the absorption of calcium from the intestines. Think of it this way. Being in the sun will help lower your cholesterol, which is very good. But if you do spend a lot of time in the sun, make sure to eat sufficient calcium-based foods, such as the cruciferous veggies (including broccoli, cabbage, and cauliflower), along with sesame seeds and almonds. A daily dose of sunshine does the body good. It creates calcium movement.

I see this calcium-depleting phenomenon in a lot in "snowbirds" from the North who go to sunny climates during the winter. They will often come home with a cold sore on their lip; further, they will have cold symptoms. I am bringing this up primarily because if you are eating foods with sugar or have a high-protein diet, which is an acid-ash or acid-residue diet, you will have a tendency to get cold sores when you are in the sun or stressed. You are living in a state of calcium depletion. You also have the tendency to be a candidate for osteoporosis. An ounce of prevention is worth a pound of cure.

There is a phenomenon that occurs in the body called the piezo-electric effect. In this response, gravitational pressure placed on supporting bone results in the deposit of calcium at weight-bearing points. If someone does not do weight-bearing or resistance exercise on a daily basis, I can almost guarantee they will have some structural breakdown.

The body's bone structure works just the opposite of a cotton shirt that gets washed out. The more gradual stress you place on bone, the stronger it gets. This is a very significant point for you to grasp.

Have you ever gone snorkeling or seen pictures of underwater vegetation? Think of your spinal structures as sea coral. A coral reef facing the shore has very little resistance splashing on it from the ocean. On the other hand, if the coral is facing the open sea, with strong currents and the resistance of the water forcing itself upon the reef and small structures, it will experience greater growth and branching. In much the same way, calcium is placed on the spinal vertebrae, hips, and other weight-bearing structures for strength and resiliency. Sitting on the couch is very similar to being the coral facing the bay. You would do your body a favor by getting out and moving.

I have noticed, probably like many of you, that typical Western children are rarely outdoors anymore. When my wife and I ride our bikes, we just do not see kids playing outside. I am sure many of you reading this can remember going outside to play first thing in the morning and not coming home till dusk, exhausted from playing with your friends. Considering the shape you are in now (and I am not meddling, just questioning), what will happen to the current generation 30 or 40 years from now? They do not play or run outside, creating a long-term pattern of lack of exercise.

The children in our culture, as one attorney friend of mine said, do not even have to learn the skill of negotiation anymore. All their activities are organized, with referees and coaches telling them what to do. You can find an organized activity for nearly any interest.

Electronic games have replaced TV. Children used to have handheld video game devices that distracted them. Now I see small children playing games on their parents' cell phones—and many have their own cell phones, with all the latest applications.

I suggest that, as a top priority, you become more active. You need to engage in an exercise that gets your heart pumping oxygen, such as riding a bike, jogging, rollerblading, rowing, or jumping on a mini-trampoline—any activity to get the lungs blowing off extra acid. The lungs help stabilize pH, or the acid and alkaline levels. I recommend strength training combined with aerobic activity as a start to improving your overall health.

I am NOT talking about water aerobics, by the way. Water exercise is more appropriate for mobilization than for structural strength. I would take your water exercise one step further, by the way. Chlorine depletes the body of sodium, so I would add a quality mineral supplement to my diet (not the sodium chloride found in commercial table salt). Sodium is needed in the body for many reactions. If you are stiff and sore, you may need sodium, according to Donald Lepore, author of *The Ultimate Healing System*. I encourage my patients to use Celtic Sea Salt® liberally. Swimming or being active in chlorinated water is also antagonistic to iodine and thyroid function.

The thyroid plays a huge role in the osteoporosis puzzle. Having a low-functioning thyroid is a very common condition today. It is estimated that one-third of the world's population has subpar thyroid function. The people in the United States have a very strong tendency not to consume enough iodine. Taking salt with iodine added to it, by the way, does not guarantee you will achieve optimal iodine levels. When you have a low thyroid count in America, you are normally prescribed a thyroid medication by a conventional Western medical practitioner. This medication does not support calcium metabolism, so if you take it during menopause, you can get osteoporosis.

The thyroid gland and its very close neighbors, the parathyroids, are the major players in mobilizing calcium. Between them, the two glands virtually control calcium movement in the body. One of the warnings on thyroid medication is not to take it long-term or bony reabsorption will result, reducing bone mineral density, especially in postmenopausal women. This may cause increased excretion of calcium and phosphorus from the body. I also want you to know that when your level of vitamin D is low, you have the potential for osteoporosis. I would suggest that you get your D level tested. We have kits available on our website; they can be sent anywhere in the world.

Thyroid medication, when taken over time, has the potential to create osteoporosis in menopausal women. As far out as this may sound, it is possible that the thyroid medication you have been taking for years is the primary single cause of your OSTEOPOROSIS. You can check this out yourself by doing a Web search for thyroid medication and osteoporosis. (Synthroid® is a common thyroid medication.) I am not telling you to get off your medication. That process requires assistance from a skilled healthcare provider familiar with natural, drugless therapies.

Hot flashes are one of the significant reasons women are on hormone replacement therapy. I would like you to be aware of the following. Are you ready? One of the primary causes of hot flashes is a low-functioning thyroid gland, with or without medicinal support. So if you are taking thyroid medication, you can lose bone long-term and still have hot flashes. Thyroid medication is really not restoring thyroid function in the first place. Patients who are taking thyroid medication and have hot flashes have presented themselves to my office. When treated appropriately, they are relieved of their hot flashes and are able to discontinue their thyroid medication. It takes time and lifestyle modification. You have to feed the thyroid, which I talk about in detail in Chapter 7.

One of the current medical protocols is to utilize antidepressants as a Band-Aid to relieve the symptoms of hot flashes. It was just recently released that the antidepressants used for hot flashes can have many negative side effects, which include the loss of bone density, or osteoporosis. So we have a Catch-22. My suggestion is to implement the lifestyle changes, mentioned previously, that allow the body to function optimally without symptomatic treatment.

Thyroid issues can actually start very young. I bring this up because, as a natural healthcare provider, I have the opportunity to see patients of all ages. I have seen babies from a few hours old to patients over one hundred years of age. One very common thread I see in youngsters under ten who have the initial body signals of a low-functioning thyroid is a fever of unknown cause.

Do you know what I have found to be one of the leading factors causing a fever? Not enough calcium. This occurs during several important physiological times—when children are teething and when they are ready to have a "growth spurt." At these times, a demand is placed on their calcium reserve.

These same children often also have growing pains. I see growing pains a lot in children who have body signals of a thyroid that is not functioning up to par. Probably the most common symptoms include cold hands and feet. Yes, children can have a low thyroid with an associated low body temperature. I have had children as new patients who have been on thyroid medication from very early in their lives, and some have even had their thyroid surgically removed.

The armpit temperature should be measured in the morning when these children first get up, and used as a gauge to see how they are responding to natural healthcare recommendations. I would also suggest the normal thyroid blood tests, to be evaluated by a healthcare provider who can assess the ranges—even if they are within a laboratory designation of normal. I would not want to see a child put on thyroid medication prior to the completion of a nutritional assessment. Often, stress can cause thyroid problems.

If you remember having the symptoms mentioned above, such as fever, growing pains, and cold hands and feet, chances are your body never got over having a low-functioning thyroid. You may have a calcium metabolism issue that more than likely started when you were very young.

I did when I was a child. I had growing pains and terrible discomfort in various joints in my body, which hurt when I played ball. My parents took me to all types of doctors, who treated the symptoms but not the cause. If you had growing pains as a kid, you will want to work hard to reverse the patterns that deplete your body of calcium. When your calcium reserve is under stress, your thyroid will not function properly.

Let me tie a little of this together for you. If low calcium causes a fever in a child, could it also produce a "fever" or hot flash in an adult? My experience says "yes." For women with osteoporosis and hot flashes, hair analysis reveals that calcium is present in the hair but is not available at the cellular level.

One of the areas most noticeably affected by osteoporosis is the spine, since it has a bearing upon your posture. If your head is in a forward position due to poor posture, it will put additional abnormal stress on your spine. Gravity is either working with you or against you. Your long-term preventive maintenance should include altering your postural mechanics. Seek a skilled chiropractor. Chiropractic adjustments will improve your overall health. See Chapter 10, "Communication Between the Brain and Tissue Cells," regarding subluxation. You will want to do some of the exercises I describe.

Another key to the long-term prevention of osteoporosis is toning the tissues in your body. The patients I attract are tired of being on medications, and they realize that they are the captains of their own ships. I highly recommend that you exercise every day. Let me tell you something: I know your pain. I see it every day. I have patients who are just like you. They are not happy with how they feel and look, but—and this is a big BUT, no pun intended—they make an educated decision to change. Results take TIME. This is not an excuse. You are dealing with physiology.

If you are overweight and unhappy with how you look, the last place you want to go is to an exercise class with women in tights who have been working out for years. I suggest that you find an exercise class for beginners. They are around; you just need to seek one out. Pick a class that best fits your schedule and commit to it. Managing osteoporosis either medically or naturally is a process. It takes determination, discipline, and effort. I see it work all the time for my patients, so it can work for you, too.

Controlling and managing osteoporosis requires a full-spectrum approach. I do not want you to have a false sense of security that taking a once-a-month pill is getting to the cause of the condition. I would encourage you to become proactive in your lifestyle. Do not get discouraged. It has taken time for your body to arrive at the state it is in, and it will take time to restore function. Start today. Look over the following suggestions. These are the same recommendations that I have used for the last 30 years with amazing results!

STRENGTHEN THE FRAME AND STRUCTURE — ACTION STEPS

☐ I would first suggest completing a food journal to assess how much sugar and soda you consume daily. If you are a sugar and soda addict, I would recommend a whole-food source of chromium, which helps minimize those relentless urges to eat sweets. You may need up to nine tablets a day until the craving for sugar subsides. Then I would slowly reduce the chromium to a maintenance level of one or two daily. You want the cravings to stop. I also suggest an herb called gymnema. Take one to three tablets daily. This herb works by reducing the taste of sweets. A mineral tissue analysis of your hair chromium would be a good idea, if you are serious about managing your bone structure.

☐ Focus on eating whole foods that are high in calcium. Now, there may be a lot of controversy over this, but I would personally avoid dairy. (When was the last time you saw a cow eating cottage cheese, milk, or ice cream? They eat hay, grass, and alfalfa.) Instead, every day, make sure you have greens, sesame seeds, and almonds (plant sources of calcium). At least have a place to purchase organic almond butter.

☐ I would suggest a thyroid evaluation (see Chapter 7).

☐ Are you stressed? Most osteoporosis patients are stressed to a point. If you have stress in your mind, your physical body can be impacted. The hypothalamus, which connects our emotional and physical aspects, does not necessarily differentiate between what is real and what is imagined; for example, sad thoughts about a current situation register the same in the body as sad thoughts about a memory. Stress depletes the body of calcium. I caringly tell my patients to learn to say, "I can't say yes," when they are asked to be on another committee or commit to another project. This is a polite way of saying "no."

☐ **What should you supplement with nutritionally?**
My suggestions would be the following:

1. Have a mineral tissue analysis to determine your levels of nutrients.

2. Have your calcium and phosphorus tested, and examine the ratio—which should be ten parts phosphorus to four parts calcium.

3. Have a blood serum test. You want to make sure that your serum globulin level is 2.7. Circulating globulin above 2.7 would suggest that your body is not able to absorb protein and/or you may not have adequate digestive acids to create an environment to absorb calcium.

4. Have a thyroid panel completed, including TSH, T3, and T4 (see Chapter 7).

5. Monitor your armpit temperature as discussed in Chapter 7. You would like to see it at or above 97.8 degrees Fahrenheit.

6. We use a couple of products for long-term maintenance and structural support; the key is optimal wellness supplementation. I have had patients in their 60s reverse their bone destiny readings with supplementation and diet modification. Whole-food manganese is also beneficial and a great source of nutrients for long-term ligament integrity. We use a variety of products for osteoporosis prevention and correction. You want to make sure you have an easily absorbed calcium and protein. There are great plant-based proteins. You would do best to schedule a consultation with me to fashion a strategy for your optimal health.

7. Monitor your bone density. Talk to your healthcare provider and have it done. Now there are tests that measure bone density at the heel. You will want to use the same source or type each time you have an assessment; different procedures have variable reference ranges. It may take up to two years to see a reversal of your levels. Also, if your levels stay the same, that's a success, because you are not getting worse. The restoration of bone density also depends on how depleted you are and on how many children you carried full-term. Do not give up!

Take the results of your tests to an experienced natural health-care provider, one familiar with assessing the findings. Generally, I find that I need to support the thyroid gland, and I commonly recommend a digestive aid. If you are in need of calcium, I recommend an easily absorbed, ionizable calcium lactate.

NOTES _____

_____

_____

_____

_____

_____

_____

_____

_____

_____

PATIENT TESTIMONY:

"I always knew that summer and poison ivy went hand in hand. What I didn't know was that they don't have to! In late May, when my daughter Christa was preparing to leave for her first summer camp counseling position, we stopped at Dr. Bob's to purchase some remedies to have on hand for when she would, inevitably, I thought, get poison ivy. I was surprised when Dr. Bob suggested something so she wouldn't get poison ivy in the first place! I didn't know we had a choice in the matter! We left with a bottle of citrate and L-lysine and I'm happy to report that, after eight weeks on the job, Christa is the only counselor at her camp who has NOT gotten poison ivy! Instead, I got it. Weeding on our church property, I encountered two small "suspicious vines," and not protected by the above-named products, sure enough, I woke up with an eye that drooped like a basset hound's. I was familiar with poison ivy manifesting as a rash, and while there was a little of that, droopy eyes were new to me. I figured the poison ivy would "run its course" in a few days, like a cold. What a mistake! A few days later, I was in the emergency room of the hospital at four in the morning getting an IV with three meds. My ears were like Dumbo's, my head like a basketball, and my big eyes were reduced to tiny slits. I felt like Fiona from Shrek!

Thanks to Dr. Bob, I'll never again believe that poison ivy HAS to be part of my family's summer vacation, but even if it is, I now know a drugless alternative."

Patti Evans

Chapter 10

Communication
Between the Brain
and Tissue Cells

The information I will share with you in this chapter represents the biggest difference between my approach as a natural doctor and that of a Western-trained, allopathic physician. Healing comes from the inside out; cellular restoration does not come from the outside in. Putting pills and potions in or on the body treats only the symptoms. This is a very critical point worth repeating in order for you to understand what it takes for total, long-lasting restoration.

"Successful surgery" is actually an oxymoron. In other words, a successful surgery is one that never needed to occur. By that I mean, the patient should have been instructed early enough in his or her life to engage in activities that *promote* life versus drain it. Empowering patients through education is vital if we want to help the next generations. The term *doctor* actually derives from the Greek word *teacher*.

The natural principle of healing from the inside out is dependent on your brain's being able to communicate to each cell. Interruption of this communication would be very similar to your not receiving e-mails, phone calls, snail mail, or text messages. Could you honestly experience life to the fullest, as you know it now, without this communication? You would do better to incorporate whole-food supplements to restore the nervous system than seek a healthcare provider who promotes medical relief of symptoms while denying that the body functions with a brain-to-tissue-cell connection. I have confronted innumerable healthcare providers who deny that proper nervous system function is necessary for optimal health.

It is a known fact, described in anatomy books, that the nervous system controls the functions of the body. The brain continues on as the spinal cord. Think of the spinal cord as the cable (prior to wireless technology!) that left your personal computer and connected it to your ancillary equipment, such as a printer or a fax machine. The brain, your "personal computer," is so important that it is protected by a bone case called the skull. The nervous system, which is very sensitive, is protected by a bony conduit called the vertebral column; this conduit has 20-plus movable parts.

There are several nervous systems in the body that allow you to function without a conscious effort. Can you imagine if you had to make a thinking effort to breathe, blink, pump your heart, digest your food, and release hormones, all simultaneously? I am not sure you can even blink constantly and count your pulse for 30 seconds. Go ahead and try it.

Visualize your brain as the circuit panel that controls the power in your home. If the switch is off to your refrigerator, how long will it take for the food to spoil, so it cannot be consumed without harming you? Perhaps a day or two?

This actually happened to me a couple of years ago. A squirrel interrupted the flow of electricity from the transformer on the utility pole outside to the electric lines delivering power to the residences in my neighborhood. The power was off for several thousand homes in the area. Fortunately for me, my neighbor is not on the same line, so I was able to connect to his source of power via a large electrical cord and keep the vital appliances functioning. The food did not spoil because I responded very quickly. Your body will survive for only a few milliseconds when the main power is disconnected from your brain to your body.

I have a very significant point I want you to chew on. Do you see, smell, or taste the electrons moving up and down electrical wires? No. But from experience, could you touch the end of an open cord or an electrical outlet without some kind of sensation? Of course not; you would get shocked. Well, here is the point. The brain is sending the same kind of living energy over the wires, or nerves, in your body. You cannot see it, feel it, or touch it. But this power can be measured by sophisticated equipment, just like the power in electrical wiring can be assessed by a trained electrician.

Let's say the same power outage occurred, and instead of connecting to another power source, I called a family member who suggested I go to the gas station and purchase a bag of ice to keep the contents of the refrigerator cold. After several hours, I would need to purchase another bag of ice. This would go on for hours. Well, by now the ice is melting and dripping on the carpet around the refrigerator and making a mess. This would be considered a bad or negative side effect. I may call another friend or relative for further advice. He or she may suggest that I power up a generator or find an alternate source of power. The body is not any different; if you do not have power, you will not work effectively.

"But, Dr. Bob, how does this process happen?" Let me ask you a question. Does gravity ever take a vacation? The answer is NO. Gravity is continuously and relentlessly compressing the very sensitive nerves that are nestled between vertebrae. To compound this, you may have poor sleep and postural habits that cause spinal compromise. You bend and twist at work and play, you have probably been in several traumatic accidents, and you may have started life with a strenuous birth (such as an unnatural surgical cesarean section), all of which can create an environment for breakdown of the spine and the communication network between the brain and tissue cells.

Compression itself can impair the flow of electrical current from the brain to the organ or organs that are waiting for a message. If this happens, over time, the organ or organs will not know exactly what to do; as they become more disconnected from their power source, they start to malfunction. I have seen this phenomenon occur hundreds of thousands of times in my career. You—yes, you—may be suffering needlessly right now because no one ever told you that you should be regularly checked for misalignment in your spine. This misalignment will choke the nerves.

The reason I am very focused on what a person eats is that what you eat affects the integrity of your spinal structure. Water increases the disc height between vertebrae. Smoking and sugar deplete the mineral structure in those same discs, causing them to compress prematurely. As the members of an orchestra need to work together to create harmony, diet and the body must work together to create health.

I need to tell you about a condition occurring in females that is a prime example of what I am talking about and that I have successfully helped resolve on innumerable occasions. By now, you should have learned that the ovaries need to be fueled with minerals, protein, vitamins, oils, and especially iodine to operate at peak performance. You should also realize that the ovaries create hormones, especially progesterone to balance estrogen. I have had patients—and I am sure this has also happened to many of you—who have a postmenstrual headache one month and then do not have a postmenstrual headache the next month. Here is what's going on.

The patient is living with a subluxation in the lower part of the spine and pelvic-sacral area that is interrupting the performance of the ovary by impeding the transfer of information from the brain. If the impairment caused by the subluxation is on only one side of the body, when it's that ovary's turn to work, it is not capable of doing so. How do I know this? Because many women suffer from a German-named condition called mittelschmerz. Mittelschmerz is a medical term used to denote a painful ovary. When the ovary is in pain, do you think it is working at its best? Hardly! By the way, you don't have to feel pain to know if the ovary is or is not functioning properly. Chasing pain by treating symptoms does not answer all the questions, and you really should not cover up pain with a medication.

On many occasions, I have adjusted a patient's lower spine with a specific correction, and after some time has elapsed, she returns and tells me that not only has the ovarian pain stopped, but in that same month, there was no headache—and, in fact, she is headache free. Was it a placebo effect? I know that is what well-meaning allopathic physicians would say, but I can tell you this: I have many very well-educated female patients who would be insulted if you even suggested that it was a placebo effect. Most of these same patients have repeatedly told their physicians about their ovarian pain, and the physicians have glared at them, communicating through body language that they couldn't really help them. I have helped a lot of women labeled "hypochondriacs" who were, in fact, living with subluxation that was interfering with the body's e-mail system. Do you understand what I am saying? This may be YOU! For your WHOLE LIFE!

What happened following the specific spinal adjustment was simple, to say the least. The ovary was finally able to receive the information from which it had been disconnected. I have come to the conclusion, after seeing the effects of subluxation so many times and for so many different conditions, that the organs literally go into a state of self-imposed hibernation and get by with the little information they can get. Over time, if this situation is not corrected or relieved, the body starts to break down, resulting in a state of poor function. I don't mean to scare you, but this can take years. The good news is that, in many cases, if a patient is motivated to make appropriate lifestyle modifications, feed the body correctly, get checked for proper spinal alignment, and reduce subluxation patterns, the body will improve itself to the best it is capable of doing. I have witnessed total and full recovery, using the sequence I just presented, of some of the most intense diagnosed conditions. I am excited to help YOU!

I want to share with you another analogy. I see this occur in nature, and I believe it will help those of you who may not have body signals of poor ovary function. When a tree branch is disconnected from its source through some kind of environmental damage, such as a fungal attack or an attack by insects, the branch begins to decompose and weaken. The tree itself can remain quite healthy for many more years—or the abnormality can create a burden on the tree, causing it to die. In some cases, a storm might be nature's way of getting rid of the unhealthy limb, so that the tree can continue to flourish.

Organs that are not functioning in the body are similar to the branch. When the organ becomes a burden on the body, you will start to experience poor function. The organ is breaking down or decomposing slowly. Sometimes the symptoms you are suffering may not even be related to the organ itself but to a detoxifying organ like the liver, colon, or kidneys trying to process the debris.

You may—and this happens more often than not—see your family healthcare provider, who assesses poor function. You may then be referred to a specialist who isolates the primary organ not operating as efficiently as needed for the body as a whole. It may then be determined that in order for you to survive, this malfunctioning tissue needs to be removed. So you go through with the surgery and feel great for a season. Then what happens when your body has determined that all the parts are not there anymore? You start having other breakdown phenomena, and the cycle continues.

The real challenge is how to assist you if an organ has been removed. First, we need to make sure that all the remaining organs are receiving the vital information from the brain that enables them to contribute most efficiently to support the system. It is not possible to restore the body to its pre-surgical state.

Here is some solid information for getting your spine, nervous system, and posture to operate optimally. Your posture is the window to your spine. If your spine is not in proper alignment—with aligned frontal or front-to-side position—your posture is not optimal. When your posture is compromised, your nervous system is not going to function as well. I have included a set of exercises that you need to complete on a daily basis. Remember, gravity does not take a day off. A healthy spine is a healthy you.

I advise my patients to perform the following maneuvers on a regular basis.

The doorjamb push-up is a simple maneuver designed to pull the shoulders back. A forward head position is not a healthy postural alignment. Stand in a doorjamb (it can be imaginary). Raise your hands to shoulder height or above, place your palms on the doorjamb, and lean into the doorway. Hold this position for five seconds. Do three sets of 15 daily. You may want to find an accountability partner with whom to do these. Your goal is to have your head resting such that your ears are right about at the center of the tips of your shoulders.

To pull your tummy backward, I recommend the cat stretch. Get on all fours, whether in bed or on the floor, and push your back up toward the ceiling. You can complete three to five sets of 25 per day. Regular antigravity exercises will go a long way toward managing your hormonal issues.

You are going to want to have your spinal structure assessed by a passionate, skilled spinal specialist. When I am asked for an out-of-town referral, I encourage individuals to ask around. Go to a health-food store; talk to a personal fitness trainer, yoga instructor, or someone who understands how structure works. I would personally seek the hands of a subluxation-based chiropractor who has studied and is knowledgeable about diet and nutrition.

You need to take some action. Remember, it is okay to go in and interview the doctor. This is your body you are talking about. Another important point for you to remember is that it took time for you to get this way, and it will take time for your body to repair itself. The doctor does not do the healing—your body does. His or her job is to help remove the interference; your job is to do what you can to manage function. Drink water, eat whole foods, exercise, and rest.

DO YOU HAVE ANY OF THESE SYMPTOMS?

☐ Look at yourself in the mirror. Is your posture not perpendicular to the floor?

☐ When you bend over and touch your toes, do you have pain?

☐ Close your eyes and turn your head left and right. Do you hear grinding?

☐ Get two scales. Stand on them both at the same time. Do you weigh more on one side? If your weight is not balanced, you may have a spinal structural weakness.

If you have any of these symptoms, you would do best to locate a skilled chiropractor who works with his or her hands and takes postural spinal films.

NOTES _____

_____

_____

_____

_____

_____

_____

_____

PART II

LEARN HOW TO WAKE UP THE DETECTIVE INSIDE OF YOU

Chapter 11

Common Female Conditions That Are Challenging

You may be plagued by a variety of hormonally based conditions that I have not yet covered. Let me explain to you why I have not discussed all the possibilities. I have come to the conclusion that most of the challenges women suffer from are precipitated by the same factors, i.e., poor dietary choices, toxic buildup, and sabotaged communication between brain cells and tissue cells. I do not want you to think I am not concerned about endometriosis, enlarged uteruses, dysplasia, breast cysts, and ovarian cysts. I am. Truthfully, I would not tell you anything different in the way of cause and treatment. You need to focus on what you are putting in and on your body. You must evaluate what you are doing to yourself.

Let me give you an interesting example of what I am talking about. I have the opportunity to treat several generations of patients in the same family. For one family, I have been privileged to help a woman and her daughter, granddaughter, and great-granddaughter. They are awesome and understand the role of natural choices in overall health. Before I connected with this family, the daughter was in the hospital for several days with idiopathic chest pain (of an unknown cause). She had seen my natural health program on TV and said to herself, "I need to see Dr. Bob." She checked herself out of the hospital and came into the office. I completed my normal intake procedure and determined that through trauma and injury, she had rotated or misaligned a rib. I made a specific corrective maneuver, and her gnawing pain diminished immediately. I further explained to her that the food she was eating (sweet fruits and potatoes) may have created a reflex that threw off the messages from her viscera (organs) to her spine. This is a very common complaint that responds well to natural, drugless treatment. Traditional medicine does not totally understand this cause-and-effect scenario. It thinks "outside in."

She was so excited about what we were able to do for her that she asked me to assess her 16-year-old daughter, who was a model. The very attractive young woman came into my office with very typical issues for a teen: acne, headaches, and menstrual pain. Mom was most concerned that her daughter had been told she had a cyst in her breast and needed to have a biopsy. (A note about terminology: While some say that cysts, tumors, or fibroids are *on* an organ, these abnormalities are actually located *in* the organ's tissues.) The young lady was told to stop consuming items with caffeine, a normal protocol for anyone with breast cysts. I started asking more questions, such as what types of lotions or creams she was putting on her body. She was applying a common "baby oil gel" so her skin would be smooth and vibrant. I have access to a microscope, so we examined the integrity of her blood in a "live state." Much to her surprise, but not uncommon in my experience, she had what appeared to be little "fat globules" in her specimen. I believe that her skin and lymphatic system were absorbing the gel, causing her body to be overwhelmed and unable to process the foreign substance (sodium lauryl sulfate). The body deposited it in the breast tissue, a common reservoir for women in a toxic state (breast cysts). She stopped using the product and has not had a problem since. I strongly advise you to review the American Cancer Society's list of items that are cancerous and to eliminate them from your regimen. Many common ingredients in cosmetics and lotions are actually quite toxic.

Any item that alters the normal physiology of female hormones has the potential to create an abnormal cell response. Birth control pills are dispensed today to teenagers for a variety of body signals, including acne, depression, and irregular and painful menses. I have seen many young teens on birth control pills become chronically ill. They present with various menstrual challenges, including severe menstrual headaches. My experience suggests that women at any age who have been taking any type of synthetic female hormone, for whatever reason, have the potential to develop abnormal side effects. These aberrant effects result from the body's attempt to achieve some type of equilibrium. The medical community's answer to emotional challenges today seems to be an antidepressant or birth control pill. Focusing on putting the right fuel into the system would be a more appropriate answer.

A diet of soda and French fries, with a focus on low-fat, high-carbohydrate convenience and snack foods, is hardly fueling the body correctly. If you are a mom reading this, it is critical for you to relay this information to your daughter. In what seems like a very short period, she could be facing ablation, hysterectomy, biopsies on breast tissue, and removal of ovarian cysts due to the consequences of toxic food choices. Conventional medicine continues to focus on the idea and create the mind-set that nearly all health issues today are the result of some renegade genes from inherited DNA. I treat families in which one family member is attentive to his or her eating and exercise habits and does not have distress. This person asks me how a sibling in another location is facing radical hormonal and/ or surgical intervention. The difference is lifestyle choices.

I have treated all of the previously mentioned conditions the same way. Do assessments on all the glands and functions I have discussed thus far in the book, and treat accordingly. I commonly and consistently find estrogen saturation and toxic buildup. I have had women come into the office with a history of large fibroids in the uterus, combined with elevated estrogen levels. After these women decided to change everything about their lives, the fibroids stopped growing and, in fact, diminished over time.

I have a patient who is an RN and a personal fitness trainer, who once worked for an OB/GYN. She came to my office with multiple cysts in her ovaries that have since been reduced by adding more protein to her diet. This same patient had a fat phobia and never ate egg yolks. She also was literally addicted to soy lattes. Needless to say, she was reading all the latest information in magazines focused on women's health. She was doing everything right. WRONG!

She was headed for disaster. She was addicted to sugar and had chronic left-neck and shoulder-blade pain and a chronic sore throat. She was a mess, like some of you reading this book. I started by suggesting that she take flax oil, one tablespoon per one hundred pounds of body weight; drink water from a pure source; and stop consuming soy lattes! Most soy milks used at coffeehouses have sugar in them. I strongly encouraged her to eat more protein. She listened to everything I said, and guess what happened. All of her body signals improved. It took a little over 12 months, but it happened. She now has a regular menstrual cycle, her throat is better, and her craving for sweets is gone. This same scenario can and does happen to people just like you. I also recommend iodine for patients with ovarian issues, depending on what we find in their assessments.

"Okay, Dr. Bob, I have a mother and aunts who have all suffered from cysts and tumors the size of grapefruits in their uteruses and ovaries, and I do not want cysts and tumors." I understand your concern. You need to change the recipe box. Stop eating and drinking what they eat and drink. Start the proactive recommendations I have suggested. Most of all, stop eating partially hydrogenated fat, or trans fat, or your body will incorporate this fat into cell membranes, resulting in the mutation of cells. This is very serious—I am sure you understand that.

So regardless of the condition you may be suffering from, what you have done to this point in your life must change. If you do not change, whatever the condition is, it will continue to advance and interrupt your life.

Your goal is to clean up your habits, eat whole foods, drink water from a pure source, and not consume any extra toxins. This may mean you will want to stop drinking alcohol. Having two drinks a day can increase your statistical chances of having breast cancer by 25 percent. You must realize that I am describing natural principles; you cannot get a "hall pass" or skip school and get away with it. Your body, when abused and tested long enough, will start to break down.

Let me put it to you this way. Whatever condition you have, whatever name has been placed on it, it will respond if you make the changes I have suggested. Unfortunately, you may appear to be at a point where your body has been beaten up so badly that it cannot turn itself around. Do not give up! I have seen the most serious conditions respond IF you do everything I have mentioned. I have had patients who came into my office with only months to live but have gone on to live for five years or more without medication or chemotherapy. I am currently seeing an elderly woman who came into my office 30 years ago, diagnosed with cancer. She recently told me, and I have heard this more than once, that her biggest challenge is finding new friends, because hers have passed on.

I want you to have an increased quality of life. Your body will do what it needs to do. Follow the steps to optimal health.

COMMON FEMALE CONDITIONS THAT ARE
CHALLENGING — ACTION STEPS

☐ The key, regardless of your diagnosis, is not to get carried away and start taking a lot of different medicines or best-friend-suggested synthetic supplements ("outside in" treatment).

☐ Review Chapters 2, 6, and 17, about estrogen, the liver, and cleansing protocols, respectively. Your goal is to cleanse your system.

☐ You may want to start with a saliva assessment of your estrogen and progesterone levels. If your estrogen is high and your progesterone is low, you need to focus on elevating the progesterone and lowering the estrogen. This is the most common scenario I see with nearly all common female health issues. The liver needs to be supported. You will want to make sure you are taking adequate whole-food B vitamins and consuming NO SUGAR! One other test to consider would be the urine estrogen test, which will provide you with the "good" and "bad" estrogen levels present in your body. Too much bad estrogen may result in breast issues.

☐ It would be wise to have an essential fatty acid and food allergy blood spot assessment to determine your food challenges and levels of healthy fats. We send this kit to clients all over the world. The results can help me help you create an optimal health strategy. We will discuss this more in Chapter 15, on testing.

☐ If you choose to pursue another assessment to locate the cause of your challenge, you may want to consider a thyroid panel. It will give you an idea of your thyroid function and the amount of iodine in your body. If your T3 and T4 are low, you need to make sure you are taking 12 milligrams of iodine a day. I use a whole-food-sourced iodine/iodide combination. Your ovaries need iodine to make progesterone, to counterbalance extra estrogen.

☐ Take your morning armpit temperature when you do the thyroid panel and monitor the degrees as a gauge of your progress. Do the same with your blood pressure, sitting to standing. You can monitor your progress by assessing these simple tests as you follow your protocols.

☐ Start taking one tablespoon per one hundred pounds of body weight of organic flax oil a day. I use the Hi-Lignan Flax Oil® product from Omega Nutrition.

☐ Avoid all processed foods and drinks; drink water from a pure source.

☐ Start exercising regularly. Work something into your daily schedule.

☐ Be assessed for spinal subluxation by a nutritionally based chiropractor. You are going to want to ask around and find an excellent chiropractor in your area or visit my practice.

☐ Take the supplements that are recommended from your testing results. Treat acording to the information in Chapter 18, "What Supplements Do You Need?" You will want to be monitored by your natural healthcare provider.

☐ I would suggest that you eliminate any synthetic, chemical female hormones, including birth control pills. Also, once your adrenal function is up to par, I would eliminate progesterone creams. Your body should be well on its way to making its own. Review the symptoms of hormonal excess and deficiency in Chapters 2 and 3, on estrogen and progesterone, respectively.

NOTES _____

_____

_____

_____

_____

_____

_____

_____

_____

Chapter 12

What Causes
Hot Flashes?

I would like to discuss hot flashes, which are one of the primary reasons women go to their healthcare provider for an opinion. Natural protocols can provide assistance for hot flashes and night sweats. If you suffer from these symptoms, you are not alone. In fact, 85 percent of women in the United States experience some form of hot flashes before or during menopause and in the year or two following menopause. I have new patients in their late 70s who are still having hot flashes—and many who have never had them. When you compare the lifestyles of the individuals with and without hot flashes, you can see how diet and emotional states are a part of the dilemma.

Fifty percent of women will experience hot flashes for years after menopause when they have not received care or are not in optimal health. In our practice, we treat and support their adrenal glands, thyroid, and whole-body function without a patch or cream. We do it internally by restoring their natural body chemistry, all without soy.

Whether you get hot flashes all the time or just once in a while, they can be extremely disruptive to your life. They're not only embarrassing and distracting but can sometimes even be scary. For many, the worst aspect of hot flashes is the sense of powerlessness over your own body.

It's true that during perimenopause and menopause, and while weaning off hormone replacement therapy (HRT), your body is going through a major hormonal transition. The good news is that you can use this time to get in touch with your body and your health; in the process, you can learn to control or eliminate your hot flashes naturally and without drugs. The body's response to stressful situations and environments is a part of the scenario. How you feed your body and the state of your overall health determine the reaction. I have had patients in my office experience a hot flash when confronted with a simple question or statement that was not significant, but to them it was a major obstacle. I am always amazed that so many women are unaware of how their body reacts to certain situations and foods. They haven't been taught to read how their own system works.

Recently, a 39-year-old female MD started care with me. She had been on the "medical merry-go-round" without any success or satisfaction for her trigger finger (a condition in which a small nodule develops in the tendons of your palm and fingers), the bronzing on the sides of her cheeks (indicating liver and adrenal gland stress), hip pain, headaches, and loss of libido. She was at her wits' end when a personal fitness trainer and a massage therapist suggested she receive natural care. I discussed with her exactly what I am telling you in this book, and within two weeks, her hip pain was gone. She had no more wrist and hand pain, her headaches were history, and the breast tenderness she had lived with for years during the latter part of her menstrual cycle was gone. Needless to say, she was very happy. It doesn't make any difference who you are (an MD, DC, DO, ND, PhD, or someone just like you), cell function is cell function.

HOW DO I KNOW IT'S A HOT FLASH?

The symptoms associated with hot flashes vary from woman to woman. Some women feel hot all the time, while others experience "flashes" of being overheated. Here are some physical and psychological symptoms associated with hot flashes and night sweats:

- ☐ An intense feeling of heat in the face and upper body
- ☐ Weakness
- ☐ Feeling suffocated
- ☐ Increased heart rate
- ☐ Anxiety
- ☐ Dizziness
- ☐ Flushed appearance or blotchy skin
- ☐ Nausea
- ☐ Headache
- ☐ Chills as the hot flash subsides
- ☐ Perspiration

WHAT CAUSES HOT FLASHES?

The long-held belief that hot flashes are caused by too little estrogen is not totally agreed upon. There are multiple factors leading to hot flashes, and the truth is that during natural menopause, estrogen levels don't fall until later in the transition. Body signals that include hot flashes are most likely the result of a shift in the balance between estrogen and progesterone; and it is progesterone, not estrogen, that is usually low. You can evaluate your progesterone and estrogen levels by having a saliva assessment. Record your hot-flash activity during the month you measure your levels. I have not seen consistent patterns among women regarding triggers for hot flashes.

You may be surprised that you will have more hot-flash body signals when your adrenal glands are stressed. The adrenal glands and ovaries are your main sources of progesterone. This is one of the reasons I have consistently seen hot flashes in my patients with lumbar subluxation (see Chapter 10). You can understand why many women have relief of their hot flashes with spinal correction (which restores the communication to the ovaries) and dietary changes. Subluxation removal is the secret weapon and reason that so many chiropractors see improvement with this common condition. The ovaries can once again produce the progesterone needed. Actually, the body will create the proper balance of estrogen and progesterone, whichever hormone needs to be innately corrected. Unfortunately, patients are often not properly instructed on nor do they follow through with dietary changes to minimize stress on the endocrine, or hormonal, system. You can take up to 12 milligrams of iodine daily to feed the ovaries. I would avoid soy, since it is an anti-thyroid food, as well as sugar, which is an anti-adrenal food. You want all the organs operating at their best. Feed your body right!

An interesting finding that I see in my female patients with hot flashes is that they have tenderness of the cartilage along the breastbone. I often see this as a body signal in low thyroid function. It is called Tietze syndrome. You would do best to follow the protocol in Chapter 7, "Fuel the Thyroid to Keep the Body Going," to support your thyroid and ovaries.

Whether you are suffering from hot flashes because of the natural fluctuation of hormones during perimenopause and menopause or due to rapidly weaning off HRT, the physiology is very similar. A menopausal hot flash is essentially caused by a mix-up of signals between the brain and the body. As hormones naturally shift during perimenopause and menopause, some women's brains receive confused messages from their bodies, and hot flashes result. The brain, in particular, is affected by fluctuations in estrogen that occur against a backdrop of relatively low levels of progesterone. During moments of extreme estrogen flux, the temperature-regulatory part of the hypothalamus (the CEO of your body; see Chapter 1) misinterprets the message as a signal for elevated core body heat. It responds by sending "release heat" messages to the peripheral body.

To release heat, the body reacts within seconds by increasing heart rate and dilating vessels to circulate more blood, as well as opening sweat glands. Some women have waves of anxiety wash over them, while others might feel heart palpitations. When it's all over, the uncomfortable sensations and panic have passed, but the woman is left in a puddle of sweat.

The sudden impulse to dispel the body of heat is a built-in mechanism to protect us from overheating in intensely warm situations, such as in the throes of exercise, stress, or infection. But when a hot flash overtakes us, we are not truly overheating; the brain just thinks we are. This confusion between body and brain can be mighty uncomfortable and can increase skin temperature by several degrees.

Flushing events and hormonal storms generally subside a couple of years into menopause. Some women, however, will continue to experience them well into their menopausal years. And for women trying to taper off HRT after menopause, hot flashes can return as a result of hormone withdrawal and the subsequent fluctuation of estrogen.

The specific triggers for hot flashes and night sweats are as colorful and varied as women themselves, which is why there is no one-size-fits-all solution.

WHY ONLY SOME WOMEN SUFFER HOT FLASHES

Just as triggers vary, so do hot flashes. In fact, some of our mothers and grandmothers never experienced hot flashes or night sweats at all. Even today, many women in the world make a far calmer and cooler menopausal transition than women in the United States do.

The reasons underlying these cultural differences are severalfold. The absence of hot flashes may result from less erratic hormonal fluctuations, different diets and exercise patterns, or the fact that the brain simply doesn't get its messages mixed up. A transition free of hot flashes may also be the result of better coping mechanisms for stress or having solid support already in place for the elevated demands placed on the body during this time of change.

Although some women have an easier time than others, on the whole it seems that today's menopausal women are suffering from hot flashes more than in the past. This is likely due to our changing world, stressful lifestyles (adrenal gland stress), and how we support our systems nutritionally and emotionally. Women in midlife today are pulled in many directions, between caring for older and younger generations, working full-time jobs, maintaining households, and dealing with marital challenges and financial concerns; their plates are full of responsibilities. I consistently see adrenal stress in individuals with hot flashes. The adrenal glands are your backup source of progesterone, and estrogen needs to be functioning optimally (along with the thyroid) to make it through menopause without hot flashes.

At the same time, the quality of our food supply and our eating patterns are not what they once were. Diets high in refined carbohydrates and processed foods result in less resilience to otherwise normal hormonal changes in the menopausal years. Partially hydrogenated fat, or trans fat, interferes with and sabotages the formation of long-chain fats and fat metabolism, which are needed for hormone function. Trans fat has been commonly added to our foods for the last 30 or 40 years. Amish women do not consume trans fat and do not have the same issues with hot flashes as other American women do.

But the good news is, no matter what your health foundation is or how severe your hot flashes and night sweats are, your body has an amazing ability to heal when you learn to listen to its messages and take steps to support it.

TRIGGERS OF HOT FLASHES AND NIGHT SWEATS

It's helpful to identify the underlying causes, or triggers, of hot flashes. Try tracking your hot flashes in a diary or journal. Are there certain times of day when you are more prone to have them, or do they wake you up at a particular time of night? Are there foods that seem to set you off on a heat wave? Here are some of the common triggers, including foods to avoid:

- ♂ Sugary foods, sweet fruits that act like sugar in the system (bananas, raisins, and grapes), and simple carbohydrates

- ♂ Caffeine, nicotine, and stimulants in general

- ♂ Alcohol (including wine)

- ♂ Spicy foods and hot (in temperature) drinks and foods

- ♂ Hot places, such as saunas, hot tubs, showers, and overly warm bedrooms

- ♂ Anxiety or stressful events or people (adrenal stress)

- ♂ Exercise or any type of activity that heats the body up without allowing adequate cool-down time

While some women see a clear correlation between their hot flashes and triggers, others find it more difficult to make these connections. Once you track your hot flashes for a week or two, you'll very likely spot patterns in how, when, where, and why you get them. From that point, a plan to address the triggers can be developed.

HELP FOR HOT FLASHES

Conventional medicine is turning to antidepressants for relief from hot flashes; this approach is never used in our office. It does not get to the cause of the problem. Often, depression is a result of inadequate nutrients needed for thyroid function; L-tyrosine, an amino acid protein building block, helps to diminish the symptoms of depression.

I have been prescribing natural solutions that effectively address the underlying causes of hot flashes and have achieved results for over 30 years. My approach to resolving hot flashes includes the following:

♂ **Dietary and nutritional support**

♂ **Lifestyle modifications**

♂ **Gentle, natural endocrine support with whole-food supplements**

♂ **Improving spinal function and reducing subluxation**

Time and again we find that women experience rapid and marked reduction in hot flashes and other hormonal symptoms by feeding the body right and cleaning out the liver.

DIET AND NUTRITIONAL SUPPORT

Experience has shown us that women get amazing results by giving their bodies the nutrition they need. Eat a balanced diet of protein; healthy, organic (not synthetic) fats (flax and/or black currant seed oil); complex carbohydrates (especially vegetables); and select fruits (as I mentioned earlier, I do not encourage consuming sweet fruits, such as bananas, raisins, grapes, pineapple, and dried fruit). Vegetables provide your body and brain with the building materials they need in order to function and keep signals from getting crossed. An easy way to add protein to your diet and help hormonal fluctuations is by eating small portions of protein throughout the day. Great choices are almond butter; organic deli meats; hardboiled eggs; and egg white protein with almond, rice, or oat milk. This is important: I do not encourage soy. A source of information on soy and its impact on health is Soy Online Service; in particular, refer to the page on the phytoestrogenic effects of soy and soy's impact on the thyroid, a key player in the endocrine system. Also, the book *Why Am I Always So Tired?*, by Ann Louise Gittleman, PhD, will help you understand the reason soy can be an issue.

There are too many conflicting results using soy. Patients continually obtain great improvement without being on it, and even better when they get off it. Remember, a balanced diet provides building materials that contribute to your hormones and neurotransmitters, both of which affect hot flashes and your overall sense of well-being.

I suggest using a whole-food multiple supplement. I have also seen hot flashes disappear by adding a quality-sourced organic flax oil. I suggest the flax oil with high lignans from Omega Nutrition; use one tablespoon per one hundred pounds. These two items alone will help bridge any gaps in a basic nutrition program and ensure the supply of nutrients your body needs for neurotransmitter and hormonal balance. Your body needs these items when creating long-chain fatty acids in the fat-metabolism pathway.

Stress is finally being recognized by conventional medicine as a significant factor in causing hot flashes. In my evaluation of women with hot flashes, their histories and consultations have revealed a direct correlation between anxiety and the severity and frequency of hot flashes.

Deep, paced breathing and relaxation exercises performed throughout the day significantly decrease the frequency and severity of flushing symptoms, supporting the idea that stress is a major trigger. I have so many female patients who not only have a full-time job creating income for the home but also care for their children, aging parents, and spouses and participate in community activities. These supermoms exist in a world that is pulling at them from all directions. The body can take only so much before it yells for help. Could this be the time hot flashes start?

If you know that relaxation is what you need to calm your hot flashes, you might try a behavioral therapy of taking quiet time and focusing on events and moments that are calming. Many times our health depends heavily on our emotional state. Just as certain foods and drugs can be toxic to your system, stress and negative emotions can be toxic.

Anger is an emotion that mind-body practitioners relate to problems with the liver; in turn, it is often implicated in hot flashes. Learn to identify and navigate negative emotions accordingly, and find ways to give yourself more time for relaxation and re-energizing. There is a great book that goes into detail on how to navigate your emotions: *The Relaxation and Stress Reduction Workbook,* by Martha Davis, PhD; Elizabeth Robbins Eshelman, MSW; and Matthew McKay, PhD. It was a part of my curriculum for my NHD degree.

There is also little doubt that exercise is one of the best things you can do to calm your body and mind. Experience has shown that hot flashes are yet another health concern that exercise can help alleviate, principally by reducing anxiety. Menopausal patients who participated in exercise classes at the office, with my trainer, noticed a reduction in hot flashes. On the contrary, patients with menopausal symptoms who did *not* exercise showed an increase in hot flashes.

When it comes to exercise, I recommend that you time your activity so that it does you the most good. You may want to exercise in the morning or at midday, following natural cortisol levels in the body. If you exercise consistently at night, you are not allowing your adrenal glands to rest like they should. It is also better to avoid dashing off to undertake activities that are stressful or involve a high level of activity directly following your workouts. The stress of fitting exercise into your life can be counterproductive, so make sure it is timed correctly, and you are not overtaxing your schedule or yourself.

Make a commitment to reducing stress, whatever form it takes in your life, even if you have to chip away at it a little at a time. This might mean setting better boundaries at work, at home, or with your community. Learn to value your own well-being enough to say "No."

WHAT CAUSES HOT FLASHES? — ACTION STEPS

☐ I would suggest starting with your axillary (armpit) temperature as discussed in Chapter 7. Use that as a gauge to see how your core temperature is doing. If it is less than 97.8 degrees Fahrenheit, you may want to pursue TSH, T3, and T4 testing. Review Chapter 7 to see how. You may need to supplement with iodine; adding iodine alone often relieves hot-flash challenges.

☐ Is your breastbone tender? It may be Tietze syndome. I commonly see this in my office in women who have hot flashes. Avoid soda; it is throwing off your calcium metabolism, which can create sternum (breastbone) pain.

☐ Have your blood pressure taken while lying down or sitting; then have it taken in a standing position. If it drops, I would suggest you review Chapter 8, on supporting the adrenal glands.

☐ Avoid sugar, pastries, and other refined foods.

☐ Find an exercise that you like; do it at an appropriate time, and be consistent.

☐ Take one tablespoon of flax oil per one hundred pounds of body weight; avoid trans fat and other fake fats.

☐ I would avoid soy products for a month if you have severe hot flashes. Especially avoid coffee with soy milk.

☐ Add deep-breathing exercises to your life.

☐ Find a quiet place and relax regularly.

☐ Organize your day and incorporate your entire family in household chores to reduce your stress levels.

☐ If you are craving salt, use Celtic Sea Salt®. You can use it liberally. Your body is seeking minerals as fast as you are burning them in your stressful life. Minerals are essential to make fat for hormones.

☐ You might consider a mineral tissue analysis to assess your selenium and manganese levels. I historically notice that these two elements are low in women with pituitary stress, which is not uncommon among those "working through" hot-flash challenges. The pituitary gland is working hard to create hormones, and the body is not responding; this may be a "stealth" factor in your unresolved issue with hot flashes.

☐ Follow these steps. You are healing your body from the inside out. Give it time. Please take time to rest.

NOTES _____

_____

_____

_____

_____

_____

_____

_____

_____

PATIENT TESTIMONY:

"The hormonal issues that I had before making lifestyle changes were mainly hot flashes and depression. I was taking three kinds of depression medications over the years. I was also taking ibuprofen and Excedrin® for headaches. Following Dr. Bob's advice, I cut out sugar altogether, and I also cut back on coffee and tea (I'm still working on these). It has been difficult cutting back on coffee, tea, and chocolate. I also have a problem with salt. I am cutting back, but it's really a struggle. I also eat more vegetables.

The only hormonal issue I currently have is a periodic episode of 'night sweats' (if I deviate from my diet). Everything else has gone away. I am completely off the depression medicine, and I hardly have any headaches. If I do, they are minor. I seem to have lots more energy, and I'm not as sick with colds or flu. I always feel good after my adjustments. I feel younger and happier, and I enjoy doing things. My life is definitely better!"

Janet Crumley

Information and documents in part from Marcy Holmes, NP, Certified Menopause Clinician, found at http://www.womentowomen.com/menopause/hotflashesnightsweats.asp.

Chapter 13

Learning from
the Amish

I want to share some insightful information with you. I have a colleague who has been treating Amish families for years. He also treats "the English," the name the Amish affectionately give us typical Americans. He may assess four or five hundred Amish patients every week. I have spent time with him at one of the farms where he treats patients. I have had the opportunity to walk through homes, barns, and outside areas and see how the Amish live day to day and what they eat. What a wonderful experience. It was like going back over a hundred years, before electricity was in even the remote areas of the world. I posed several questions to him about the patients he treated, and I decided to pass on this information to you.

First, I have some questions for you. Have you ever been to an Amish farm? Do you think the Amish have stress? Have you ever seen a buggy traffic jam? Would you get up every day and milk cows? Would you miss an electric dryer? Would you want to eat lima beans, corn, or squash for a week straight?

Now, I am not saying that the Amish do not eat a variety of foods or have time off. I want to make the point that they live today like we did as a society 50 or 60 years ago. Can you imagine not having the modern conveniences that most of us take for granted? Would you want to do your daily activities without electricity?

Being Amish in America, without conveniences, is tougher than you might think. The Amish participate in our lifestyle to a degree, but they do not *own* our conveniences. For instance, they will pay drivers to take them where they need to go.

One critical item that really separates the Amish diet from the American diet is the fact that the Amish do not eat trans fat. They prepare the food they eat themselves. They grow their own produce, which has not been processed and still has the original components in it.

The fact that the Amish eat only food grown on farms in their own area is quite significant. I have read several articles suggesting that you should consume food from within a 350-mile range of where you live. My observation is that Americans today eat food from distant lands and climates. Produce is often picked prior to full ripening and then sprayed with gases to create coloration for "taste appeal." These altered foods are not quite physiologically right and may create distress in the system, especially pain syndromes and digestive troubles.

Let's say you live in a warm southern climate. It is better to focus on foods that are cooling, such as fruits and water-based light vegetables, than on dense, starchy items. Foods that cool should be consumed in the summer, and not in the winter. If you live in a cold region, you want to focus on roots and squashes grown in the north, versus food from a southern climate. I know this may seem new to you. However, I have seen a lot of chronic pain syndromes go away just by having my northern-based, cold-climate patients avoid citrus during the winter. The Amish do not have to be concerned about that because they eat their own food, which is grown locally. Your goal is to create a lifestyle that puts the least amount of stress on your physiological system.

I primarily eat food that is organic, and I can tell you there is a taste difference between conventionally and organically grown items. Organic radishes have a crunch and produce an electrifying zing on your tongue. Organic beans have a unique flavor versus the bland, tasteless beans that have been commercially grown in dead, devitalized soil; sprayed to keep the bugs off; and then canned. Do you know what the Amish use as fertilizer? They use the manure from their animals, not toxic chemicals that have the potential to cause the list of issues I have discussed thus far.

The Amish preserve their food by home canning, and they keep it in cool cellars below or next to their homes. They also dig large pits in the ground to store vegetables through the winter, like the farmers in America did only a generation ago. They live off the land and enjoy the fruits of their labor, knowing exactly what they are eating and where it came from.

Have you ever looked at the ingredients on the label of a food container? Can you pronounce all the names? The best food to eat, according to one of my patients, is food without a label on it. (Yes, you read that correctly!) When was the last time you saw a list of ingredients on cauliflower, broccoli, or cucumbers?

Researchers would have you believe that the stress of modern daily living is the reason you are having hot flashes, and emotional and hormonal distress. The Amish have stress in their everyday lives, too. Their overall health is not what you think it would be. They get sick; they have colds and chronic infections, just like we do. However, they do not appear to have the same hormonal issues that are plaguing Western women: osteoporosis, hot flashes, and hysterectomies.

When you look at the posture of Amish women, you do not see senior Amish women walking around all hunched over. They have a strong structure that serves them well into their senior years. The older Amish folks live with their children and grandchildren, so there is a continuity of family purpose. Today, divorce and the existence of blended families make it challenging for the family network to provide the necessary support. The additional burden created by a challenged family life results in adrenal gland stress and a drain on the hormonal system.

According to my colleague's observations, the Amish do not have osteoporosis to the degree of "the English"; 15 percent of the Amish have bony changes demonstrated on x-ray, compared to 85 percent of the non-Amish in his East Coast practice. I asked him why he thought this was the case. He promptly said, "The Amish work hard every day. They work in the field, in the barn, and in the home. They are used to being labor intensive. They eat whole food that they make themselves from scratch." They are active from the beginning of their lives and continue until they pass on. This is not the way Americans normally live.

Amish children have a lot of responsibility for the survival of the family unit, unlike their non-Amish counterparts. They also enjoy playing outside and having fun in the sun, using their imaginations and creativity.

I would like to present an interesting side note about something I have learned from my patients regarding lack of exercise and activities of the hand. We currently have a generation that was raised on hand-held electronic play toys focusing on thumb movement versus whole-hand dexterity. This trend will continue. Amish children play and work with their hands. They do chores outside. I am not suggesting that we go back to the wilderness; I am suggesting that we would do best to limit children's use of electronic games. Brain development is activated by motion. The whole body is one contiguous unit; motion is life.

Another factor in your long-term health is that you may not be getting enough restful, restorative sleep. Growth hormone is released at night. How hungry are you in the morning when you awake? If you are hungry, it is a good sign that your body is actively creating growth hormone for restoration. If you are not hungry when you wake up, feel worn out, and can only get going with a cup of coffee, you may want to evaluate your sleep habits.

The Amish are able to get more restorative sleep than the non-Amish. They do not look at computer screens or watch TV before they go to bed because they have no electricity. The stimulation you put into your body has a lot to do with your ability to fall asleep and go into a restorative state. The pineal gland, a small mass of tissue in the forebrain, is affected by light. This same gland produces melatonin for sleep. If you are worn out and have the symptoms of adrenal fatigue and burnout discussed in Chapter 8, I would suggest that you limit your exposure to the light from your laptop and other monitors and give your brain a chance to sort out the activities of the day. If you have insomnia issues, do absolutely nothing for at least one hour before bed.

Roughly 30 percent of the patients I treat sleep six hours or less a night; more than 50 percent get less than eight hours nightly. Those on swing shifts or who work nights have some of the greatest challenges with their health because their biological clock never really has time to adjust itself. The Amish go to bed at dusk or a little later and are up at the crack of dawn. They get the restorative benefit of the natural release of growth hormone.

When it comes to aging, the Amish do work very hard, and it does take a toll on their physical body. However, one health factor they do not have to contend with is the damaging consequences of the electromagnetic energy that surrounds us from cell phones, computers, microwaves, and even air travel. We are bombarded daily with invisible electromagnetic particles that we do not think about because we cannot see, feel, taste, or touch them. They harm us by damaging the strands of RNA and DNA in our cells. When the genetic material of our cells is altered, cancer has an opportunity to proliferate. Environmental toxins and electromagnetic contamination will alter your body's ability to operate harmoniously; you will be in a chronic state of disease if you do not address your relentless exposure to these pollutants. We recommend an herb called rhodiola for support if you are one of the Bluetooth, computer, or video game warriors.

The Amish, fortunately, do not need to deal with the negative effects of all of our modern conveniences, and they also do not have to deal with the adrenal burnout that so many people experience.

I have learned many things from observing the Amish. I would recommend that each of us incorporate a bit of "old-fashioned life" into our daily schedule. I would encourage you to go outdoors, take walks, and become active. Think about what you are eating. Focus on foods that satisfy the warming and cooling of your body; don't just ingest calories. I would really try to avoid citrus altogether, especially if you have pain that is relentless and you consume citrus items regularly. Just try it. I consistently get good reports. I know what you are thinking. Where do I get my vitamin C? Try red and yellow peppers, along with other colorful produce, such as asparagus, broccoli, and cauliflower. Oranges are not the only source of vitamin C.

NOTES _____

_____

_____

_____

_____

_____

_____

_____

_____

PART III

JUST TELL ME
WHAT TO DO

Chapter 14

How Do You Exercise?

There are definitely a proactive exercise mind-set and corresponding movement in America today. It also seems that there are two types of individuals: those who are disciplined and stick to it, and those who exercise for a season and then fall off the "weight bench" and go home to sit on the couch.

I know the food industry is bewildering. To whom does it cater? Individuals who watch what they eat *or* those who eat with reckless abandon? Look around you. So many people are overweight and do not even know how to begin to lose weight. Any long-term, successful weight-loss program needs to include daily exercise. Exercising should become as normal as brushing your teeth or taking a shower; it is a significant factor for optimal health. You may want to read *The 7 Principles of Fat Burning*, by Eric Berg, DC. Each individual does best on an exercise regimen tailored to his or her own body and hormonal system.

Motion is life. Activity creates the feel-good hormones in the body. The benefits of exercise also include the following:

♂ **Proper flow of lymph fluid**

♂ **Healthy stress on the heart muscle**

♂ **Piezoelectric effect needed for bone strength**

♂ **Postural and foundational strength**

♂ **More oxygen flow for cellular health**

Exercise helps every structure and organ in your body.

Okay, so where do you start? You are not going to run a marathon or lift your own body weight the first week. You want to go slow and steady, like the tortoise in the fable. The important thing is, you just need to start exercising! You would be wise to have a healthcare provider assess and direct you. You may want to have some blood tests performed, including a basic metabolic panel with your cholesterol, triglycerides, and glucose. You will be surprised how these levels will go to normal with just a bit of movement. You can use your test results as a base to monitor your improvement and be a part of your long-term motivation and evaluation.

You may want to find a handful of exercise partners, not just one or two. You will be amazed at how some people may not be as motivated as you are and will drop out for various "very good" reasons. I recently had this happen with two of my patients. One was having some personal stress and was not able to go to our local college to exercise, so the other thought she would just wait until the first was available. Six months went by and NO exercise was done by either patient. I see this quite often; we wait for others instead of exercise alone.

What kind of exercise should you pursue? Well, there are a lot of options. Some forms of recreation can be considered exercise, since they get your heart rate going. I want you to focus on moving oxygen through activities such as walking, dancing, jogging, and playing tennis or racquetball. It is imperative to engage in movement that gets blood, lymph fluid, and oxygen flowing.

The next type of exercise I would like you to concentrate on is strength training. I encourage both aerobic and muscle-toning activities. I have people in my practice who jog on a treadmill or ride a stationary bike daily but have "loose flesh" around their tummy and arms. Personally, I advocate exercising some part of your body every day. Now, I am not suggesting that you can never take a day off. However, I want you to know that there are so many options available that you can do something different every day of the week without overdoing it on one part. It is your choice.

For strength training, it would be in your best interest to go to a community center, exercise facility, school, church, or someplace where a trained professional can assist you while you are learning a routine for yourself. Now, some routines can become ruts, and ruts are graves without ends, so it is important to vary your workouts. You can go to multiple locations. I have patients who attend three or four different venues in town, and each is either free or has a very minimal charge.

You might use free weights, machines, and/or exercise bands. The possibilities are almost limitless. However, you do not want to overdo it. Your goal should be to slowly put enough resistance against your muscles to create tension, which will increase blood flow and muscle contractions. You will be amazed at how quickly your muscles will respond; they will rejoice with the activity.

I also encourage my patients to use "physio balls." These are the large colorful balls that you see at the gym. They are great for improving your posture and strengthening your core. Core work is also excellent. Pilates and yoga are very good for the soft tissue structures. Other options include tai chi, karate, judo, tumbling, and tae kwon do. I am all for square-dancing, line dancing, belly dancing, aerobic classes, etc. There are books and DVDs available for these activities, so there is no excuse! Just find something you like to do, or several activities that you enjoy, and get involved.

To avoid sore muscles, make sure you are drinking enough water. Sore muscles are often a result of too much acid building up in your body. You want enough water to flush out the acid. Also, make sure you are eating sufficient protein. We encourage egg white protein as a supplement, with rice, almond, or oat milk (not soy or whey protein). You do not have to use a powder; just make sure you are adding some extra protein to your diet, such as almond butter, eggs, nuts, organic deli meats, or beans. I would also suggest that you consume some omega-3 flax oil, for relief of any tendon pain, and Celtic Sea Salt®.

Where do you find the time to exercise, especially if you have little ones at home? You will need to do some co-op work. Get several moms and dads together and work out the details. You may need to actually go to bed earlier and get up a bit earlier. Something may have to go; the best thing to let go of is watching television. Now, if you are an addict and need to be amused, you can schedule your workout around your favorite program or just watch it *while* you exercise. You need to figure out how to make time in your schedule to exercise.

The biggest challenge I see is the patient who is extremely out of shape, overweight, and embarrassed to put on exercise clothes and be seen in public. Well, you are going to need to make some choices. You will need to look around for the right class and organization for you—or start at home. Commit to a regimen, be disciplined, and get to the level you want before making your public debut.

It is not easy, but if you continue to do nothing, in five years, you will be in exactly the same or worse shape as you are now. The average person over 40 loses about 5 percent of his or her muscle mass every decade. When you lose muscle, you lose the ability to burn extra carbohydrates. So the downward spiral will continue if you don't do anything!

HOW DO YOU EXERCISE? — ACTION STEPS

☐ Exercise at least half an hour a day. Do something!

☐ Start with walking; it is by far the easiest and most cost-effective form of exercise.

☐ Drink more water if your muscles are sore.

☐ Eat extra protein, including beans, almonds, nuts, eggs, and organic deli meats.

☐ Vary your routine to include strengthening, oxygen-moving (aerobic), and core-strengthening activities.

☐ ONCE YOU START, DO NOT STOP!

NOTES _____

_____

_____

_____

_____

_____

_____

_____

_____

_____

Chapter 15

What Tests Should You Have Completed?

I would like, once again, to applaud you on your persistence in achieving optimal health. What you have learned and the steps you have followed up to this point have been focused on creating the foundation for long-term health for you and your family.

What we have been discussing up to now may seem countercultural to some of you; most people do not like to change. Given the focus of our society, "Have it your way" and "This one is for you" are about having what *you* want now, without any consequences for *your* behavior. Have you noticed how popular the Food Network is? And have you observed how the hosting chefs tend to be a bit larger every season? There are consequences to what you put in your body.

Deciding which tests to have done can sometimes be overwhelming. There are two main factors to consider at this point: Which tests do I have completed, and what do I do with the results? After answering these questions, you can begin your journey with a baseline.

You can have many different tests completed. Some are often inconclusive, and there is not much you can do with the results. I am also aware that you can learn a lot without being overly invasive. I will describe the common tests I use to direct my treatment of patients. I always take cost into account, since many of these tests are not covered by traditional insurance (which tends to cover symptom-based testing).

Saliva Zinc Test: This very easy, 10-second test requires a bottle of zinc sulfate. We put two full droppers of the solution in a cup. Then we have the patient hold the zinc sulfate in his or her mouth for at least 10 to 15 seconds. We observe the response and the look on his or her face.

Generally, because so many people do not have enough zinc in their system, they do not taste anything; they say the liquid is tasteless. From our assessment, this is an indicator that they may be deficient in zinc. We supplement them with the liquid, at two to three droppers full at least once a day, until they have a bitter taste from the test. A bitter sensation is the sign we are looking for.

The saliva zinc test is very simple and reliable because patients who find the solution tasteless also seem to have other body signals associated with low zinc, including large facial pores, poor memory, cuts that heal slowly, white spots on the fingernails, fatigue, a craving for sweets, and (in men) difficulty emptying the bladder totally at night or during the day because the prostate is swollen. Patients with low zinc often, but not always, have freckles (because high copper is common with low zinc) and eat soy.

A diagnosis of low zinc is confirmed over time with a hair tissue mineral analysis.

Saliva pH Test: We complete this common test on all new patients in our office. The most accurate time to do the saliva pH test is when you wake up in the morning, before you get out of bed. When you open your eyes, slip the test paper into your mouth and then compare it to the color chart. In our office, we do the saliva pH test on all of our patients, regardless of the time of day.

I would encourage you to purchase a roll of nitrazine paper to measure your own pH in the morning. Pre-cut a piece of nitrazine paper and have it ready to be inserted into your mouth before you even sit up in bed. Again, place the strip in your mouth and then observe the color. Generally, I like to see a saliva pH of 6.5. If the pH is low, like 4.5, you will look toxic, because you *are* toxic. You are bathing in the acid excrement from your own cell metabolism. Actually, I have seen a 4.5 pH once, with a gentleman who had pancreatic cancer; he enjoyed an additional five years of life under our care, after he was told he had four months to live.

I am looking for extreme levels of color from this test. If the paper turns yellow, indicating a pH of 4.5 to 5.5, I know the patient is probably acid. We do not want acid. This is a potentially destructive life pattern that, unless addressed, often ends in cancer. Patients with this pH are eating acid-producing foods. (See the pH chart, "Alkaline-ash and Acid-ash Food Groups," in the Appendix.) Sugar creates an acid pH. These patients **must** change their eating and drinking patterns if they want to live a long and healthy life. Normally, they do not drink adequate water but enjoy soda, coffee, tea and alcohol.

On the other hand, if the color of the paper is purple, indicating a pH of 7.5 to 14.0, the result is alkaline. Patients with an alkaline pH will more than likely not die of cancer, but they may have digestive distress and/or pain syndromes because they are too alkaline. This state often occurs when people eat TOO MANY FRUITS. They are addicted to juices, especially citrus. They will often have pain in the middle of the muscle in their upper arm. It is common to find that women, especially over 40, who have deltoid bursitis (pain in the upper arm/shoulder region) are too alkaline. Cut back on the citrus and try adding a good organic apple cider vinegar. We use an apple cider vinegar product from Omega Nutrition.

Changing your diet for three months is not necessarily going to alter your pH immediately. It may take anywhere from six months to two years to do that. One other point about pH: The lungs are your best tool for balancing an acid pH, by blowing off acid during breathing—so good posture is needed. Human cell physiology ends with an acid waste product. Drinking water will give relief to those who suffer from arm and leg pain caused by nerves inflamed by pyruvic acidosis (due to carbohydrate metabolism).

After you have a handle on your pH level, and you have adapted your lifestyle accordingly, you need to check you pH only periodically. I would suggest once a month or so. Do it more often if you are under active treatment for some type of destructive health process.

Saliva Test: In my experience, individuals with parasites also have yeast infestation. This may be a reason that pizza and bread are "craved"! A simple test called the saliva test can be completed as a screen. Generally, if the result is positive, you more than likely have parasites and yeast.

First thing in the morning before brushing your teeth or eating or drinking anything, spit into a glass of cold water. If the saliva goes to the bottom of the glass, whether in a long string or strings, or bunched up in a ball, yeast may be present in your system. If the saliva stays afloat on top of the water, this suggests to me that there is not enough yeast present to create challenges.

Saliva Hormone Test: Saliva testing is a very logical and useful tool. There are hormones and constituents in body fluids that can be evaluated. You need to be careful, just as with a blood test, to look at the whole picture; especially note the body signals you are having when the tests are being completed. I generally do not do serum hormone analysis because the hormones are bound to protein; in saliva, on the other hand, hormones are in a free state and give a better picture of hormone levels.

I generally test for two hormones with saliva. I like to evaluate progesterone and estrogen. I know there are other hormones that can be evaluated, such as DHEA, testosterone, and cortisol. This testing can be very useful but, as a rule, I do not recommend a lot of "outside in" hormone-type supplements. My focus has been on feeding the body and letting the body heal itself by making the hormones it was designed to make. I have used a lot of the popular "media nutrients" but have found that I get long-lasting results by coaching a patient on how to eat right and let the body do its own thing.

I would recommend a saliva test to establish a baseline for your progesterone and estrogen levels. You can then plan a lifestyle that will improve your hormonal health. For an accurate assessment, you should discontinue the use of progesterone creams for about three months before you take samples from your saliva.

Blood Spot Tests: Technology helps me assess many conditions now that I was not capable of assessing years ago. Laboratory evaluation of a blood sample taken from your finger with a lancet in the comfort of your own home or our office (if you live nearby or plan on visiting us) gives me the information I need to create a strategy to help your hormonal system return to normal. We have the ability to assess your essential fatty acids; protein levels; food sensitivities; vitamin D; and TSH, T3, and T4 levels. Nearly all the tests you may have previously completed at a local lab can now be done from anywhere in the world using a blood spot test.

Urine Iodine and Estrogen Testing: It is now possible for me to use your urine to determine two very important levels in your body. Optimal health requires appropriate levels of iodine. Iodine is required by every cell in the body. In my experience, patients with a chronic health challenge commonly have subpar iodine levels. If you have cold hands and feet, feel tired, have constipation and depression, and wake up in the morning with headaches, you might consider the urine iodine loading test.

The other urine test I strongly encourage all women with a family history of cancer to take is the urine estrogen test. Two types of urine levels are assessed; without going into all the scientific terminology, one is considered "good" (2-hydroxy urine) and the other is considered "bad" (16-hydroxy urine). I encourage patients with elevated 16 levels to eat more cruciferous veggies and focus on creating a "healthy liver" strategy. This very important test helps me gauge the current estrogen levels in the body. I have discovered that controlling and managing estrogen saturation is the key to providing quality preventive care for men and women. I would encourage you to consider this test in your long-term strategy for maintaining proper hormone levels.

Armpit Temperature: Taking your armpit temperature is a simple procedure that will give you some insight into your core function. It is not specific for any condition; it is a guide and tool that I use in my practice. I suggest using a shakedown thermometer. Prepare it by shaking it down the night before and putting it on the nightstand by your bed. When you wake up in the morning, before you get out of bed, place the thermometer in your armpit. Hold it there for 10 minutes. Do not move. Look at the reading. It should be 97.8 degrees Fahrenheit or higher. If it is lower than that, I generally suggest a TSH, T3, and T4 blood serum test for thyroid function (see Chapter 7 for more information). If you use a battery-operated thermometer, hold it in your armpit for five minutes before you turn it on.

Blood Pressure: We take our patients' blood pressure in three positions. First we take it while they are sitting on the exam table; then we take it while they are lying down; and then we immediately have them stand, and take it again. Our main focus is what happens to the person's blood pressure when he or she goes from lying down to standing. I have observed that women, especially, tend to have low blood pressure when they have hormonal issues.

This test provides a snapshot of how the adrenal glands are responding. The adrenal glands are your backup source of female hormones, especially the much-needed progesterone; this is very critical for you to understand. The adrenal glands, as discussed in Chapter 8, are significant in making all your hormones once you approach menopause. You do not need a compounding pharmacist or soy-based bioidentical source of "outside in" hormones. You need to support the adrenals, and this is a simple test to evaluate their function.

Generally, the blood pressure of females with hormonal issues is 100 systolic over 60 diastolic. This is low. I know you may have well-meaning physicians who will tell you that this low reading is great. It is not. When you have low blood pressure and/or it drops from a sit-to-stand position, you would do best to eliminate fruits and sugar from your life. These items are creating unnecessary stress on the adrenal glands. There is a great book for you to get, *Adrenal Fatigue*, by James Wilson, PhD, ND. It will help you with your adrenal gland restoration program.

Leg Blood Pressure: I have another noninvasive test for you to do if you are in a quandary with different metabolic issues. One such common problem I see is leg cramps at night or cramps that wake someone up from sleeping. This is often a body signal of poor calcium metabolism—not calcium deficiency, as one would think. When I do hair tissue mineral analysis in the office, patients generally have enough calcium in their body. The real issue is that the calcium is not available for cell metabolism. Most patients scurry around attempting to get the mega calcium pill that will make their bones strong. The real answer is to get the calcium into bioavailable solution so it can be useful. By the way, I do not suggest calcium carbonate, coral calcium, or calcium sourced from over-the-counter digestive aids.

I also utilize the leg blood pressure test if someone has leg cramps that are consistent, which may indicate a need for potassium. Drinking distilled water and, in some cases, reverse-osmosis water can result in mineral challenges. It is imperative that you consume organic vegetables and select fruits, such as pears, plums, and apples.

Here is the procedure we use. You can take this information to your doctor for him or her to follow. We put the blood pressure cuff on the patient's calf. We pump it up to at least 200 mmHg. If the patient is in relentless pain before it gets to 200, we back off.

Now, here is an interesting tip for you. I am sure you are aware that a nitroglycerin pill, once inserted into the mouth of someone with chest pain, will work quickly. It takes only seconds for the vessel spasm around the heart to relax. This response occurs quickly because you are activating the oral-lingual neural (brain) route. The chest pain will be relieved within seconds because the flow of blood has been restored due to the nearly immediate communication from the brain cell to the tissue cell.

Well, the same physiology occurs when you put an organic iodine tablet into a patient's mouth and retake the leg blood pressure. If the patient is in need of iodine to help move calcium, making it bioavailable, you will see the blood pressure reading burst through 200 without a grimace on the patient's face. Iodine is very commonly deficient in patients and consistently creates this response. We have successfully used this procedure with a variety of products and conditions. I see the same response with a dry source of omega-3 fat. In conducting the test, we use a source of flax and various glandular tissues, including ovary and thyroid extracts. (See Chapter 18 on supplements.) There are many causes of leg cramps, such as a potassium deficiency and reduced blood flow from poor circulation, which is why you want to be assessed by a skilled, experienced healthcare provider. **Do not do this on your own.**

Twin Scales: In our office, we weigh patients on two scales simultaneously so the patients can see how they are balanced. The reason we do this is because people often carry weight more on one side than the other. A postural imbalance can often result in wear and tear on the knees, hips, and ankles. I see curved spines, along with bladder, uterine, and vaginal challenges, as a result of weight-bearing imbalance. If the pelvis is in a forward position, there can be a pulling on those structures. The goal of this assessment is weight balanced on both scales, and an aligned posture, perpendicular to the floor.

Clinical Testing: It is possible to have your urine and blood evaluated further for body function. You may want to discuss available testing with your healthcare provider. Toxic overload, how your body is responding to nutritional protocols, and your levels of fatty acids can be determined with today's technology. We have been using blood spot testing to assess essential fatty acids and food allergies. You can order a test kit and complete it at home, anywhere in the world. Go to www.druglessdoctor.com for details on how we may assist you in having testing done to create a logical program for your health restoration.

Palpation: Palpation is touch with purpose by your healthcare provider. I "see" with my fingertips. An experienced massage therapist assesses by touching a client, and palpation assessment helps me create protocols for my patients. I evaluate the integrity of soft and hard structures along the spine and skeletal system. You would do best to locate a healthcare provider who uses his or her mind *and* hands as a part of the intake process. Healthcare providers tend to get detached from the reality of letting the patient's body tell them what may be the root cause of the problem. Don't get caught on the merry-go-round of endless laboratory testing. I am not suggesting that you refuse testing; however, attempt to locate someone who can make evaluations with his or her hands. Following are some interesting areas you may want to have palpated.

♂ **I generally palpate an area of tenderness on the left sacroiliac joint (found on the lower left pelvic area, mid-joint line) with patients who have uterine congestion with their menstrual cycle. Stimulating the area with a forceful, light touch and/or percussion creates relief.**

♂ I will often palpate the outside of the right knee in patients with chronic gallbladder issues. A tender right knee is a consistent body signal with these patients. If they have had their gallbladder removed, they need to think back: Did they have pain in the right outside knee? They need Dr. Bob's ABCs (apples, beets, and carrots) along with bile salt. (See Chapter 18 on supplements.)

♂ Feel your wrist with a light touch. Does it feel boggy with fluid accumulation? If yes, it is a sign to me that your body is retaining water and you would be a candidate for more flax oil or precursor omega-3 foods such as walnuts, greens, and cold-water ocean fish.

♂ Have an experienced chiropractor or massage therapist palpate your left neck, left shoulder, and mid-back area. These are the most common areas where I see relentless, gnawing pain that does not abate with analgesics. The pain is referred from internal organs, especially the pancreas and liver, and increases with foods that create inflammation and alter fat metabolism. These are not necessarily bad foods, just ones that commonly cause pain, such as dairy, sugar, and sweet fruits (bananas, grapes, pineapple, raisins, and any dried fruit). The nightshades can create pain in the same area; they include tomatoes, potatoes, green peppers, and eggplant. Once again, these are not necessarily bad foods. They contain solanine, which is an alkaloid substance that can create discomfort when your liver is congested.

♂ An experienced healthcare provider can tell you a lot by touching the area of your chief complaint.

Here's an observation: It is quite interesting when you have someone look at you with a trained eye and/or ask observational questions (questions based on looking at you). Let me give you some examples of what I observe in my patients or ask them about. This list could go on for pages.

♂ I always shake a patient's hand. The texture and temperature of the skin tells me about his or her thyroid and even fat metabolism. Cold hands suggest low thyroid function. Dry skin can occur when not enough oil is being consumed.

♂ White spots on the fingernails might suggest a zinc deficiency. Fungus under the nails may be a severe yeast or fungal challenge that is systemic (throughout the body). I see severe fungal issues in patients with chronically compromised adrenal function.

♂ Bronzing of the left cheek is a common body signal of an overworked liver, along with a lack of whole-food vitamin E. Dark circle under the eyes are apparent in dairy consumers. Freckles suggest high copper.

♂ Old acne scars on the face suggest liver congestion as a teen; if it was not corrected, it can still be an issue.

♂ Large facial pores are commonly seen on patients who do not taste the zinc in the saliva zinc test.

♂ Skin tabs around the neck area, as well as bronzing patches on the neck and face, are usually more common in patients (even teens and adolescents) who have a toxic diet.

♂ Cold sores or fever blisters on the lip or lips, especially chronic or multiple, frequent ones, suggest to me poor calcium utilization and stress. This is often seen in patients with poor digestion.

♂ Widely spaced teeth, thinning hair, and bulging eyes may suggest a thyroid that is not functioning at one hundred percent.

♂ Spider veins on the legs and thighs, varicose veins, and hemorrhoids suggest estrogen saturation and a congested liver.

♂ I commonly see an elevated left shoulder on posture assessments of patients who have a passion for sugar. A pancreas that is overworked and stressed from handling sugar appears to weaken the shoulder support structure, resulting in the elevated position of the left shoulder. This is the norm today. Test me on this. Look at your shoulders. If they are level, eat a candy bar or piece of cake and see what happens. I am telling you, it is a consistent pattern.

♂ I have also observed that a patient with a dropped lip on the right may need potassium, and a patient with a dropped lip on the left may need sodium. Potassium is easily sourced from cucumbers, while sodium can be safely found in celery.

♂ Patients with bowed legs may need more minerals, which can be depleted by stress, an acid pH, or even parasites. Ground-down teeth or complaints of jaw pain and grinding of teeth at night may also signal parasite challenges. This can often be assessed with a nutritional microscopy evaluation. Also, there tends to be an elevated white blood count in patients who have quite a parasite challenge. These individuals also tend to eat pork and sushi, have cats, and generally have many health challenges that are difficult to correct.

♂ I also observe patients' pupils. Those who have larger than normal pupils tend to burn more carbohydrates. I see this frequently in my female patients who are stressed; do not eat protein; and are on a low-fat, high-carbohydrate diet.

♂ Smelly feet are an indication of congested detoxifying organs. The feet assume the role of "backup kidneys." Toxins need to be released. The kidneys are overworking (causing high blood pressure) because the liver is compromised. The liver is compensating because the colon is sluggish and not releasing fecal material. The colon is sluggish because you're not drinking adequate water and not consuming vegetable fiber. And if your thyroid is not getting enough iodine and protein, it is creating a stagnant bowel. So, your smelly feet may be caused by poor choices on your part. You don't need foot powder. Change your habits.

Acoustic Cardiogram: An acoustic cardiogram (ACG) provides a snapshot of the nutritional status of the heart. Acoustic cardiography is generally utilized by healthcare providers who use whole-food supplements. Heart tissue is very sensitive. The sounds created by the valves snapping shut are translated into a mechanical graph on paper. I use the ACG as a tool to provide insight into a patient's need for whole-food B vitamins, liver function, mineral requirements, adrenal health, cardiac strength, and endocrine function. The heart muscle's reaction to what you eat is almost immediate. It is amazingly accurate. Here is an example of what I see: The heart graph reveals sharp projections on normal closure sounds. But when someone has congested liver tissue, the "soggy" liver cells impede blood flow, creating roundness to the valve closure—which is demonstrated on the graph. I use the ACG in conjunction with other assessments. This tool gives me considerable insight into a person's condition. You can go to www.ifnh.org to locate a healthcare provider in your area who has one of these awesome tools that can be of assistance in your health restoration.

Mineral Tissue Analysis: I learn so much from mineral tissue analysis. A lot of companies do this procedure and attempt to sell you their product line. I am not saying you should or should not partake in that. I use mineral tissue analysis or hair analysis to evaluate many functions of the body. The lab does make recommendations; I generally review them and make my own decisions based on the need of the patient and other findings mentioned here. Briefly, the facility I use provides ratios of various levels of minerals that work together synergistically or antagonistically.

For example, if a patient has low sodium and potassium, I assume he or she may have sluggish adrenal function. This is confirmed clinically with body signals of sluggish adrenal function and the fall of blood pressure from sitting to standing. If there is an imbalance in the calcium and potassium ratio, I look for low thyroid function. An imbalance in the calcium and magnesium ratio suggests blood sugar stress. Elevated sodium levels suggest inflammation. Elevated potassium may indicate blood sugar stress and the associated inflammation. You can see that there are patterns you can look for that would assist you in your long-term plan. I have determined, through clinically based experience, that patients who have elevated and even toxic aluminum levels generally have poor adrenal function.

I have consistently observed elevated mercury and liver spots with low selenium, and a craving for sugar with low chromium. I see high manganese in those who drink well water, and elevated phosphorus in patients who have poor carbohydrate metabolism. Elevated phosphorus is a result of consuming muscle for energy. The average American loses about 5 percent of his or her muscle mass every decade after 40. You know those areas of floppy flesh under your arms? We call those "happy Helens." They are commonly seen in patients with poor carbohydrate metabolism. I also notice elevated copper and low zinc with low insulin, as I mentioned previously. Cigarette smokers commonly have elevated cadmium. The mineral tissue analysis, when used with other procedures, truly can give you a road map for improved health.

I have given you only a very small snapshot of what you can learn from mineral tissue analysis. You will always want to correlate all your test results to formulate a plan of action. Restoring your health is not about taking something; it is about change! I do not agree with providers who do one test and make many suggestions without looking at the whole picture.

X-ray Assessment: I routinely complete postural or standing films on my new patients. Gravity alters mechanics and creates the misalignment or subluxation that may be creating your challenges. Subluxations are real; I have managed them for thousands of patients, with spectacular results. I discuss this in great detail in Chapter 10. Here are some thoughts you will want to pass on to your healthcare provider:

♂ **I notice rotation or twisting subluxation in the lumbar (low back) area with women who have ovary symptoms, including estrogen saturation. The ovaries are necessary to create progesterone to balance estrogen.**

♂ I commonly find rotation subluxation at the first and second lumbar areas in patients who have a history of gallbladder removal. The titanium clips used to secure arteries are adjacent to the rotation subluxation. This is the case over 90 percent of the time. I also reveal this to my patients who have characteristics of potential gallbladder problems (they are fat, fair, female, and 40) and especially if they have freckles and at least two children.

♂ I have noticed a common condition in the upper-mid-back area of patients with improper dietary choices: a mechanical malposition called a patho-biomechanical subluxation. Recognizing this condition is significant, because it is commonly overlooked. The structural change is evident when we look at the spinous process, the bony projection from the center of the arch of a vertebra. In the malposition I observe, the spinous processes are not found in the center. A true mechanical lesion, or subluxation, results in the spinous processes shifting as a unit in one direction. This is an important finding that you may need to show an experienced chiropractor. The misalignment, when corrected, can open up a whole new level of improved health.

♂ A lateral x-ray of the neck, or cervical, area should reveal a C-shaped curve. This normal arc, or curve, is 45 degrees. When I observe a lateral or side cervical film showing less than that amount, I encourage treatment to normalize the position. Patients have a greater chance of compression fractures and osteoporosis when their cervical curves are decayed and less than 25 degrees.

WHAT TESTS SHOULD YOU HAVE COMPLETED? — ACTION STEPS

Tests can be quite frustrating. You would do best to have the ones completed that do not require invasion of your body, as a blood draw or biopsy does. There may be a point at which these tests are necessary, but I would not suggest that you start there. Focus on correcting your findings to be near normal and then continue. See how you are doing. Give yourself time! Too many patients and book readers want everything done yesterday.

☐ Take your armpit temperature. Also, take your blood pressure, from a sitting/lying down position to standing. If your blood pressure drops 10 to 15 points, you need to support your adrenal glands (see Chapter 8). If your armpit temperature is low, refer to the information on the thyroid in Chapter 7.

☐ The thyroid panel, in the hands of a knowledgeable healthcare provider, can save you a lot of anguish. Go to Chapter 7 to learn more. If your thyroid is not up to par, the nutrients needed to get it going can reverse depression, constipation, and poor ovary function—the three major players in hormonal health.

☐ Mineral tissue analysis is a noninvasive procedure that tells you much about what is going on in your body. I personally have used it to help many patients make a plan to restore their health.

☐ Be sensitive to how your body is functioning. Many female patients have had excessive scraping done on their cervix and uterus, which aggravated a condition. I would suggest that you get opinions from physicians from different groups. There are some who may be a bit more aggressive than others. If you do have cells that are abnormal on a Pap smear, I would wait a month or two and make changes in your daily habits. Oftentimes, I see reversals in smears. You might think about using a different form of contraception. You might be pressured not to wait to have a procedure performed, because the cancer could spread. I would suggest that you seek other professional advice.

- [ ] You may want to investigate breast thermography versus x-ray mammography. This tool does not use radiation.

- [ ] Have your areas of main complaint palpated and assessed by an experienced practitioner.

- [ ] How do you look? Is your body aligned and perpendicular to the floor? Your posture, or alignment, can be compared to observation assessments and correlated with postural x-ray films.

- [ ] It would be reasonable to complete a postural x-ray, especially in the lumbar area, if you have pelvic-area issues. I normally complete anteroposterior and lateral films of the spine in a standing position. I also use the films to assess levels of decay, osteoporosis, and mechanical aberrations.

It is imperative that you have someone who is experienced look over your tests in order for you to get to the cause of your challenges.

NOTES _____

_____

_____

_____

_____

_____

_____

_____

_____

_____

Chapter 16

Reversing Unhealthy Patterns

I would like to begin this chapter with the acknowledgment that there are many dedicated individuals who have devoted their lives to treating patients and assisting them with their health. I am not suggesting that you discontinue their services. But I would like you to comprehend that YOU are the captain of your own ship, and it is OKAY to seek options when it comes to your personal health. I know from experience that NOT everything proclaimed by well-meaning individuals is necessarily right. If you are repeatedly contacted by a healthcare provider to schedule an "elective surgery," I would get a second opinion from someone in another group or hospital network.

The area I am most passionate about is partially hydrogenated fat, or trans fat. The healthful claims made regarding this man-made substance were incorrect from the very beginning. This one item has created ENORMOUS financial opportunities—and losses—for entrepreneurs. At one point, eight billion pounds of trans fat were manufactured in one year. I would like you to chew on that for a minute or two.

I have had the opportunity to collect many articles and journals over the years I have been in practice. The insights I have gained from pioneers in the health field are presented in this book. One individual from whom I have gleaned so much is David Frähm, ND.

I have learned from Dr. David that there are restorative and destructive health patterns. If you can discover a negative pattern, modify it, and even reverse it, there is a very good possibility of restoring normal function. Sound easy? Well, it is and it can be. Unfortunately, it appears to me that destructive patterns become physiologically addictive. Just eat one chip! Only one donut! The comment I hear most (and this may be you) from patients about their food addictions and lack of discipline is, "But, Dr. Bob, I only had a small piece of my favorite apple pie." As they say this, they make a small triangle with their hand.

I have consistently seen, and helped reverse, destructive patterns in patients who had some dreadful conditions. The toughest cases, such as occurred with one woman who was in my care, are those in which the patients have tears in their eyes. This woman has been an awesome patient of mine for more than 10 years. I know what you may be thinking: "If she was your patient, why did she get sick?" There is an old cliché, "You can lead a horse to water but cannot make it drink." Just because someone is a patient and shows up does not mean he or she will follow everything I recommend. In this case, the woman refused to drink water, and she loved to eat sweets.

She came into the office with tears in her eyes, looking at me apologetically, as if she had let me down. "Dr. Bob," she said, "I have cancer in my body, and they want to do surgery and chemotherapy. I don't know what to do, and I do not want to have surgery." I hear that a lot from new patients. Human nature is very predictable. She, like so many others, had been addicted to destructive habits and extreme work stress; when the "C" word finally registered in the cortex of her brain, she raised the white flag and gave in to constructive, life-promoting habits.

Although she did have surgery, and her uterus was removed, she opted not to do chemotherapy and radiation. Instead, she made a total about-face in her health patterns. She eliminated cooked and processed foods, she juiced (with carrots, beets, celery, cucumbers, apples, parsley, and turmeric), she had colonic irrigation therapy, and she drank a measured amount of water throughout the day. She also applied a castor-oil pack to the liver area and received additional corrective spinal adjustments to restore nervous system function. She has had several blood tests over the last three years. All the scans and tests are now negative for any destructive growth in her body.

A coworker of hers had also been diagnosed with cancer at the same time. Her coworker opted to go the traditional route, with surgery, chemotherapy, and radiation. Her friend, unfortunately, passed on in less than six months. I don't know what type of cancer her friend had, and I don't want to speculate. But I know you have heard this scenario many times; someone does everything he or she is told to do and still dies.

Your socioeconomic status truly does not make a difference: Rich and poor alike can be stricken with cancer. Yes, I know early detection and treatment are preached to everyone. Cancer results in premature death more often than most would like to accept, and I wonder if the "seek and destroy" treatment does more harm than good. I cringe when I hear infomercial-sounding advertisements on the radio from respected hospitals that have a military-like approach to "destroying" cancer cells (as if they have discovered a new secret weapon). Long-lasting success requires changing what you are doing.

Recently, I was a guest on a radio program. The host was a fine, well-educated, financially established individual who asked me some questions about cancer. He went on to say that his wife had had cancer, and he surmised on the air that she had succumbed due to an overdose of chemotherapy.

Over the years, individuals have come into the office diagnosed by various world-renowned health institutions. I have noticed that a variety of people have the same medical diagnoses (e.g., fibromyalgia, depression, idiopathic pain syndromes, chronic fatigue syndrome, acid reflux/GERD, etc.), and they share a common pattern of nutritional deficiencies and toxic overloads.

We who study these conditions are like detectives, looking for causal patterns in each case. Nutritional starvation at the cellular level and toxic overexposure result in very poor health. Can you tolerate being in a smoke-filled room? Would you want to swim in a Porta-Potty tank? Addressing underlying deficiencies and overloads is foundational to any health restoration plan.

In my years of working with patients who have developed cancer, I have seen that this same truth applies. Individuals with a history of cancer appear to share common underlying patterns of nutritional deficiencies and toxic overloads. Addressing these patterns has proven fundamental to restoring long-term health to the body.

When someone comes into the clinic with destructive health issues, I am not treating his or her cancer. I am assisting the body to reposition itself to normal function. To treat cancer means to attack symptoms...the cells and tumors. I do not do that.

Attacking the cancer medically can be a potentially helpful strategy to slow the progress of the illness while the patient's healing immune system is resetting itself to optimal function. That is why I suggest patients maintain their relationship with their medical physician. If the situation does not progress with conservative natural care, the condition may warrant surgery, radiation, and/or chemotherapy.

Very often, people come in at the end of the destructive process of treating their cancer, reaching for a long-shot miracle. In his book *The Answer to Cancer,* Dr. Hari Sharma, MD, suggests that some conditions may need chemotherapy and other medical treatments before they can successfully be treated naturally, because the body may not be capable of reversing the attack of cancer on its own.

The underlying pattern of nutritional deficiencies and toxic overloads that allowed destructive conditions like cancer to develop in the first place must be addressed. So, then, what is the pattern of underlying deficiencies and overloads that always shows itself in breast cancer?

- ♂ **Low thyroid function (not enough iodine in the diet to feed the thyroid), which leads to...**
- ♂ **Stagnant colon function, which results in...**
- ♂ **Sluggish liver function, which leads to...**
- ♂ **Unbalanced estrogen recycling (compounded by not enough progesterone production by the ovaries), which leads to...**
- ♂ **Zinc depletion, which leads to...**
- ♂ **Essential fatty acid depletion**

These six issues appear to be common among the women I consult with, either before or after they have been treated with a medically diagnosed condition of breast cancer.

Here is how the interplay between these areas transpires. When the liver and colon have become sluggish due to low thyroid function (lack of iodine), the body cannot break down excess estrogen and remove it adequately from the system.

A thyroid functioning at subpar levels is the leading cause of constipation; the primary cause of constipation is lack of fiber and water. The body also needs a steady supply of magnesium for bowel function. Magnesium can be sourced daily from a mixed green salad that you incorporate into your lunch routine.

The excess unbalanced estrogen gets stored in the fat cells of breast tissue when it is not properly eliminated. This is a key source of estrogen saturation and the cause of breast cancer, from my observation. The second source of estrogen saturation is undernourished ovaries, which result in inadequate production of progesterone. The body requires 10 times the amount of progesterone as estrogen. The ovaries are one of three organs that need iodine to function optimally; the other two are the thyroid and breasts.

When estrogen is in a state of saturation, the body's zinc stores are depleted. Not only is zinc essential for proper immune system response to fight off cancer cells, but without it, essential fatty acids cannot be processed and absorbed. EFAs are necessary for the production of healthy new cells. (Check out Chapter 22, "Facts About Fat.")

This is one of the many reasons the low-fat diet has been so detrimental to the female population of the Western world. Unfortunately, many women have been on the low-fat/no-fat diet for years. A 32-year-old mother of three came into my office recently. When she was 26, she underwent a hysterectomy due to a fibroid tumor. She was now overweight, and when I said the word *fat* (referring to flax oil), you would have thought I said the word *POISON*. I want to point out that she also fit the potential breast-cancer pattern of being overweight, fair, female, and freckled. "Freckles?" you are thinking. I have seen that individuals who have low zinc (which we assess with the zinc sulfate test) will also show high amounts of copper in their mineral tissue analyses. Patients with high copper tend to have freckles; the copper overload appears on the skin. Freckles are common in patients who have fair skin; low zinc; and a racing mind when they go to bed at night, even though their bodies are exhausted.

Another finding is white spots on the nails. A young man said to me that he thought the white spots on his nails were calcium spots. Indeed they were not; rather, they were a sign of zinc deficiency. There are over a hundred known enzymatic functions of zinc, which include improved memory, healing, and sugar stress control. That is why I test every new patient for zinc deficiency. You should get a bottle of zinc sulfate and do the test yourself. Continue zinc supplementation until you taste the zinc sulfate. (See Chapter 15.)

I also see females with low zinc and high copper, which can be tested with hair tissue mineral analysis. They also may have a history of having their gallbladder removed. High estrogen tends to thicken bile. Gallbladder removal, revealed on a medical history form or during a conversation with the patient, is an area that needs to be addressed.

You can see that zinc is a huge part of the pattern. When your zinc is low, you will have a tendency to lose your sense of taste and smell. You may always be tired because your body needs zinc to make insulin. Insulin is necessary for the movement of glucose, or blood sugar, into cells. Without enough zinc, you will experience the result of poor glucose movement—no fuel to burn. You will be tired. Ann Louise Gittleman, a very knowledgeable healthcare provider and researcher, and author of the book *Why Am I Always So Tired?*, does an excellent job describing in detail the reason zinc is critical for the energy cycle. I would encourage you to look up her books.

Do you notice that you scar easily? If you do, this is also a body signal to me that you may be low in zinc and high in copper. There is a condition called keloid formation, which is overgrowth of new skin. I have confirmed through mineral tissue analysis that keloid formation and a lot of scars occur with high copper levels. Women who suffer from postsurgical adhesions, which may be more challenging than the problem for which surgery was performed, may need to supplement with zinc to stop the adhesions from advancing.

Zinc is also discussed in Chapter 22, about fat metabolism. It is a critical ingredient in the formation of long-chain fats. Incorporated into cell membranes, fat is used by the body to make hormones. Zinc's role is to be a part of the metabolic pathway. When you are zinc deficient, your body will not have all the ingredients required to do its job effectively.

Recently, a patient shared a new term with me: *bed picnic*. I know what you may be thinking, but it's not about SEX! She had suffered silently for two years with a condition that no one seemed to be able to figure out. She was depressed and overweight, had shoulder and hip pain, was unable to breathe through her nose, and had lost her senses of smell and taste. That didn't sound like a picnic to me.

She ate for comfort, partly because her husband was often away due to his work schedule. She created a ritual that she called a bed picnic. When it was picnic day, she would plan what she was going to watch in her bedroom. She would start the festivities with either a purchased DVD or video, or a TV program. Then she would call the pizza place and have food delivered at a specific time. Her pillows were fluffed, and soda, chocolate, and chips were nearby on the nightstand. I could not believe all the planning that went into the event.

The woman had consulted with many doctors without success. Her uterus, cervix, and ovaries had been removed years earlier. She was frustrated because she had missed the last two years of playing with her grandchild and was so depressed that she had created the picnic routine as a means of escape. I know someone reading this knows what I am talking about and can relate to this.

"So, Dr. Bob, what did you do?" you ask. Well, I know you read Chapter 10 on communication and subluxation. This patient not only had a pitiful diet, she had an upper cervical or neck vertebra that was totally out of normal position. After studying the assessment, including radiographic films and infrared thermography, I gently and specifically made my first correction. I routinely call patients to see how they respond after their first correction. She related to me that nothing miraculous had occurred that evening. It always amazes me that everyone wants a miracle pill or potion—or, in the case of spinal corrective care, a miracle adjustment. However, the next morning when she woke up, much to her amazement, she was breathing through her nose and her sense of smell had returned. She was in shock and, of course, incredibly excited.

When she got into her car, she noticed something: It smelled like stale perfume. She realized that she had been literally bathing herself in her fragrances. Since she could not smell, she had sprayed and sprayed until her smell threshold was reached. Needless to say, she has made a total about-face in her habits. She is following a simple plan that I have made available for you in Chapter 20, "The Page Food Plan." Do you put on more than two bursts of fragrance? Do you eat and eat to satisfy your suffering? If you do, it is time to have a zinc assessment. Then you should start following the Page Food Plan. Also, do you walk by or know people who smell like they're wearing a bottle of perfume? If you do, politely tell them what you just read. Do you know why? Because I am teaching you to be a detective, and putting on too much perfume could be a sign of a destructive pattern that may end up as something very serious, resulting in needless suffering and premature death.

You should have learned that all the parts of the body are interdependent. Please go to Chapter 6 and read about the liver's role in this interdependence. Also refer to Chapter 22, on fat metabolism. The thyroid and ovaries are discussed in detail in their own sections (Chapter 7). We are not talking about one symptom but a whole group of symptoms. Remember, you are the captain of your own ship, and you get to determine your diet and activities for the day.

I advise my patients to limit their soy consumption. I actually would prefer that women age 25 to postmenopausal not consume it. Now, I know this may be the opposite of what you read in magazines, but what I see (not what I read in magazines) is that soy and wheat tend to deplete the body of zinc.

Bioidentical hormones are sourced from soy, which is one of the reasons I discourage "outside in" hormones. I would rather have my patients support their body and have its organs make the needed hormones. You have the best pharmacist right inside of you, making exactly what you need...provided you feed it the right nutrients.

I tend to see high aluminum levels in the mineral tissue analyses of individuals who eat soy. Become a label reader. You should not drink soy milk. Instead, I would recommend rice, almond, or oat milk. I am not sure why so many people feel they need to consume some type of milk, for example, with their cereal. I don't encourage typical cereals, made with sugar and wheat. I would prefer that you start your day with half an apple with nut butter on it rather than with a breakfast cereal.

I have described some destructive patterns along with strategies for reversing them. You do not have to be diagnosed with cancer to require a correction in what you are doing. You might start with a condition like endometriosis, an abnormal growth of cells that occurs because the body is being fed the wrong foods, and the detoxification system is on overload. You may be experiencing digestive distress that is aggravated by eating fatty foods. Is it your gallbladder? If onions, radishes, cucumbers, and green peppers cause you indigestion, it could be. In my observation, these foods commonly create digestive gallbladder distress.

So many of the conditions you are experiencing are a part of a bigger picture. Your whole body, not just one system, is impacted by what you do. You now know that there are several systems in your body, and they are significantly interconnected; breast and uterine tissues are seriously impacted by excess estrogen, which is not cleared, in part, due to liver congestion. Cysts and cancer tend to develop in breast tissue, which, again, is very sensitive and impacted by estrogen overload. I want to remind you that you do not have to live in fear that you are going to get a condition because someone in your family, at work, or at church has it. What you choose to do affects every aspect of your body. You don't have to live in fear, but you would do best to live in reality—recognizing that many of your health challenges have been with you since the beginning of your life.

REVERSING UNHEALTHY PATTERNS —
ACTION STEPS

☐ Start with tests you can perform yourself. Look at yourself in the mirror. Examine your posture, skin, eyes, teeth, and hair. What do you see?

☐ Have serum TSH, T3, and T4 testing. Then have the results assessed.

☐ You may want to have your saliva tested for progesterone and estrogen, and treat accordingly.

☐ A properly interpreted hair analysis can potentially forecast health challenges years down the road. It will take time to correct the current conditions that could possibly result in future illnesses.

☐ Have an experienced chiropractor (who understands the role of diet and nutrition) and a hands-on healthcare provider assess your spine and test results. It is okay to work with your natural doctor, a medical doctor, and other healthcare providers. Wisdom is with many counselors.

NOTES _____

_____

_____

_____

_____

_____

_____

_____

_____

_____

PATIENT TESTIMONY:

"When I first came to see Dr. DeMaria, I had various hormonal issues. I had anxiety, depression, unpredictable periods, unexpected periods, late periods, and overall a very irregular menstrual cycle. I had previously been taking Ortho Evra (birth control patch) and Zoloft®.

Following Dr. Bob's advice, I eliminated sugar and dairy and considerably reduced my consumption of soy and wheat products. However, it was difficult for me to give up hot chocolate, and the sugar was the hardest to eliminate. Also, I take the whole-food supplements he suggested—they made a remarkable difference.

The most obvious improvements that I have gained are that I no longer experience depression or anxiety, and my cycle is more regular. My face has cleared up, also. I am not experiencing menopause yet. However, being under Dr. Bob's care has changed my body and issues that I always related to hormones."

Stephanie Morales

Chapter 17

Cleansing
Protocols

Cleansing your system can be accomplished several different ways. My patients always seem to want to do a cleanse. I have told them repeatedly that the best way to cleanse their bodies is to stop dumping toxic foods and beverages into them. I do have to congratulate them, however, because we see awesome results in our practice after patients have completed one or several of the following protocols. They know that if destructive habits are not corrected, the consequences might be surgery or even death.

I have included details of what we suggest our patients do. These procedures may not be for you, and that's okay. You may have some other type of remedy, and if it works and has helped in the past, then by all means go for it. Most of the items discussed can be purchased at a health-food store or from a natural healthcare provider. You can always go to our website (www.druglessdoctor. com) for product information. Study all the information and do not try to do everything at once.

The upcoming instructions for applying a castor-oil pack are easy to follow. If you have any type of skin issue, tender breasts, or a heavy menstrual flow, doing this procedure at least once a week for a year would be excellent. I have seen very severe skin issues, cervical dysplasia, and a feeling of general malaise improve because of the castor-oil pack.

CASTOR OIL

Let's talk about castor oil. Using castor oil may seem like an "exotic" approach to increase immune system efficiency, but in reality, it is a simple treatment to improve function without negative side effects. I have used castor oil in my practice since the late 1970s, and the only side effect I have ever noticed is that the patient may end up with oily clothes. Therefore, I suggest you have a "castor oil" outfit: shorts and a T-shirt.

In many ways, castor oil is a very unique substance. While most of us are familiar with its uses as a remedy for constipation, folk healers in this country and around the world have used castor oil to treat a wide variety of conditions. Its effectiveness is probably due in part to its peculiar chemical composition.

Castor oil is a triglyceride fatty acid. Almost 90 percent of its fatty acid content is ricinoleic acid. Ricinoleic acid is not found in any substance other than castor oil. Such a high concentration of this unusual unsaturated fatty acid is thought to be responsible for castor oil's remarkable healing abilities.

Ricinoleic acid has been shown to be effective in preventing the growth of numerous species of viruses, bacteria, yeast, and mold. This would explain the high degree of success in the topical use of the oil for treating ailments such as ringworm, keratoses (non-cancerous, wart-like skin growths), skin inflammation, abrasions, fungus-infected fingernails and toenails, acne, and chronic pruritus (itching). Generally, for these conditions, the area involved is simply wrapped in cloth soaked with castor oil each night. Or if the area is small enough, a castor-oil-soaked Band-Aid® can be used.

Castor oil's antimicrobial properties, while very impressive, comprise only a small part of the story concerning this mysterious oil. The topical, antimicrobial uses of castor oil described in the previous paragraph are very interesting, but the most exciting use of castor oil is in packs and poultices for deeper applications (such as those affecting lymph and glands).

Much of the current use of castor-oil packs in the United States can be attributed to pioneers in natural healing. Time after time, they recommend the use of castor-oil packs based on reports given over the years by many natural healers. The technique is still practically unknown or shunned by most healthcare professions today. This is probably due to two reasons: First, it's just too simple. It's hard for most people to imagine that something as simple as castor-oil packs could have a profound effect on any health problem. Second, in our present healthcare system, positive results alone are not the critical factor in determining whether a treatment will be accepted by the medical establishment.

Everybody, except probably the poor patient, now seems to be more concerned about how something is *supposed* to work than whether it actually *does* work. Castor-oil packs improve the function of the thymus gland and other areas of the immune system. Patients using abdominal castor-oil packs have had significant increases in the production of lymphocytes.

When castor oil is absorbed through the skin, several extraordinary events take place. The lymphocyte count in the blood increases. This is a result of the oil's positive influence on the thymus gland and/or lymphatic tissue. The flow of lymph increases throughout the body, as discussed in Chapter 5, speeding up the removal of toxins surrounding the cells and reducing the size of swollen lymph nodes. The end result is a general overall improvement in organ function with a lessening of fatigue and depression.

Rubbed or Massaged Directly Into the Skin

Castor oil can be used as a massage oil and seems to be especially effective when applied along the spinal column. If the oil is massaged into the body, the direction of the massage should always follow the same path as the underlying lymphatic drainage system.

Conditions Responding to Simple Topical Application

Often, there is no need for castor-oil packs; amazing results can be obtained by simply applying castor oil directly to the skin. Following is a short list of some of the more common ailments that simple topical application can remedy:

- ♂ Skin dryness and flaking
- ♂ Wounds
- ♂ Skin cysts just below the surface
- ♂ Muscle strains
- ♂ Ringworm
- ♂ Bursitis
- ♂ Warts
- ♂ Itching
- ♂ Fungal and bacterial infections
- ♂ Abdominal stretch marks
- ♂ Liver or "age" spots
- ♂ Ligament sprains

CASTOR-OIL PACK

I suggest that you speak to your healthcare provider about castor-oil packs. You may think that a treatment like the castor-oil pack is low-tech, but I have seen mononucleosis respond quickly, dysplasia of the cervix return to normal, and long-standing digestive distress normalize using this procedure. It works, but I would not use it without having a discussion with your healthcare provider. You are promoting liver function, and it may be something to postpone until you modify your diet.

Castor-oil packs have been employed for health benefits since antiquity. Reportedly, they were used in ancient India, China,

Persia, Egypt, Africa, Greece, Rome, North America, and South America. Common usage had been for improving elimination capacities; stimulating the liver and gallbladder; healing lesions and adhesions; relieving pain; reducing inflammation; and increasing lymphatic circulation, which draws acids and poisons out of body tissues. More modern applications of castor-oil packs include as a treatment for gastrointestinal problems, lacerations, and skin disorders such as psoriasis; as a way to evacuate the bowels; and as a vehicle for introducing medications into the body. Generally speaking, you may wish to employ castor-oil packs to assist your body in its healing efforts in any of these areas.

Necessary Articles (available at www.druglessdoctor.com)
- ✓ Castor oil (100 percent pure, cold-pressed)
- ✓ Wool flannel (cotton flannel should not be used)
- ✓ Heating pad

Procedure

1. Fold the wool flannel so that it is three or four layers thick.

2. Saturate the wool flannel with castor oil.

3. Place the saturated wool flannel in a baking dish and heat it slowly in the oven so that the pad becomes hot but not too hot to place over your skin. With your oven on low, watch the pad carefully so as not to burn it.

4. Rub some oil into the skin on your abdomen.

5. Lay the warm—not too hot—wool flannel over your abdomen.

6. Cover with plastic wrap.

7. Cover with a heating pad for one hour. It is important to keep the area as hot as possible. This is why a heating pad is recommended instead of a hot water bottle. A hot water bottle cools too quickly and does not maintain a consistent, very hot temperature.

8. Remove the flannel and wash your skin.

9. When finished, store the flannel in the baking dish, covered with pastic wrap, or in a Ziploc® bag. It does not have to be refrigerated. Castor oil is very stable and does not go rancid like other oils do.

10. If the flannel becomes discolored, showing other than the normal color of the oil on it, this will probably be due to the drawing of toxins out of the body. I have had patients who brought me their cloths stained with vibrant red, yellow, green, and even purple. When this occurs, wash or discard the flannel.

The flannel can be left on for longer periods if desired. A typical use cycle would be three consecutive days per week for as long as needed. It can be done more often if desired.

Castor-Oil Pack Benefits

Obviously, conditions known to be related to poor drainage of the lymphatic system will tend to benefit from this type of therapy. These would include complaints such as the following:

- ♂ Chronic fluid retention accompanied by swollen joints and pain
- ♂ Arthritis
- ♂ Upper respiratory infections involving the sinuses, tonsils, and inner ear
- ♂ Colon problems like Crohn's disease and colitis
- ♂ Gallbladder disease
- ♂ Boils
- ♂ Liver cirrhosis, hepatitis, enlargement, or congestion
- ♂ Menstrual-related congestion
- ♂ Appendicitis
- ♂ Hyperactivity
- ♂ Constipation, bowel impaction, or adhesions
- ♂ Swollen lymph nodes
- ♂ Bladder and vaginal infections

I really encourage my patients of both sexes to use the castor-oil pack as a regular part of their preventive-maintenance program. It is a low-budget, low-tech but highly effective system.

COLONIC IRRIGATION

Colonic irrigation is best completed by an experienced technician. A small speculum is inserted into the rectum. Water is released into the colon and expelled simultaneously through the speculum. The colonic-irrigation water reaches deeper into the large colon than an enema. The whole procedure lasts about 45 minutes, with 15 minutes for you to sit on a toilet to expel the remaining water. It really is an invigorating experience, and I believe it should be a part of one's long-term health plan. It literally cleanses the side walls of the colon (often lined with debris) in individuals who do not drink enough water or do not eat vegetables and are heavy on grains. This procedure also will help men prevent prostate cancer.

LIVER/GALLBLADDER FLUSH

The next (at home) procedure that can be used is the liver/gallbladder flush. This protocol can be quite controversial; I get e-mails about it from all over the world. I am aware that the information here can create a mix of opinions. However, I have seen this procedure work for many without any adverse effects. Let me tell you that you are going to be further ahead by working on cleaning out your system with this protocol than by dealing with the bad effects of ablation, hysterectomy, or even cancer.

The naysayers of cleansing are not of the opinion that toxins and certain foods are detrimental to your health. Many of the medications that they suggest are actually the *cause* of various modern health problems. I continue to have patients who follow the protocol for the liver/gallbladder flush and have what I call "sightings," or body excretions, in the toilet. These "sightings" would be any material released from your digestive system and bowels the morning after you follow the protocol. The liver/gallbladder flush stimulates the digestive system, including the liver and gallbladder. I know from my own experience that there are times, after eating particular foods (especially certain oily foods), when there is what feels like a huge gallbladder release. It seems like only seconds and my digestive system is rumbling; a bowel movement follows almost immediately, usually with a loose stool.

I have patients who tell me that when they follow the protocol, they find what looks like sludge, mucous, or green balls in the toilet. I am interested that the patients have had a release, and that the system has had some type of discharge of fluid. I also have patients with minimal or no response. These patients appear to have livers that are as hard as a rock when they are touched or palpated, with very little activity. The liver can sometimes be felt under the right rib cage. The lower portion can also be observed on an x-ray. I bring this up because women with spider veins, hemorrhoids, and varicose veins can improve their overall health by first applying the castor-oil pack once a week, for two to three months, followed by a colon irrigation and a liver flush. One of the positive side effects of cleansing is that the skin starts to clear up. This is a good sign of detoxification of the system and indicates that you're getting a grip on estrogen dominance.

Procedure

1. Drink high-quality, organic apple juice for three days, at least one full quart each day; eat as normal. The malic acid and pectin in the apple juice help soften residual material in the gallbladder and liver tissue. I would eat at least one sweet apple every day, half in the morning and half in the evening. Eating an apple a day for a month prior to the flush is a very good idea; by now you should be thinking about eating an apple a day for life.

2. Take phosphorus liquid twice a day for three days. The phosphoric acid will soften residue in the gallbladder. Add 45 drops of liquid phosphorus to the apple juice you are

drinking. In other words, you are taking 90 drops of liquid phosphorus every day. It is easy to divide the quart of apple juice into two pints, using 45 drops per pint.

If you cannot tolerate that much fruit juice, or are diabetic, use distilled water instead of apple juice, or try unsweetened cranberry juice. If you use water, you must increase the amount of liquid phosphorus. Take 45 drops three times a day with the water. That is 135 drops a day.

Add five drops of peppermint oil each time you put the liquid phosphorus into apple juice, unsweetened cranberry juice, or distilled water. This will assist the gallbladder-release mechanism.

WARNING: You must follow this step. If you won't take the liquid phosphorus, don't go on the program. One woman followed only Step 3 of the program, involving olive oil and lemon juice. But she omitted the liquid phosphorus. She passed material but was advised not to do that again, because if the accumulated material is not softened by the liquid phosphorus before it comes out, it will remain hard and can irritate the bile tubes or ducts on the way out. You don't want this to happen. It is recommended that you follow the entire program and discuss it with an experienced professional who has helped others follow a cleansing protocol like this.

3. On the third day, after the last meal of the day (before bed), mix the following together: a cup of high-quality olive oil and a cup of pineapple juice, grapefruit juice, or natural spritzer. Add the juice of one whole lemon (organic is best). Stir. The juice or spritzer serves the purpose of helping to get the olive oil down. You hardly taste the olive oil. (This program originally included Epsom salt, but it was too harsh on most people.)

4. Immediately after you drink the olive oil, go to bed for the night. Pull your knees up to your chest. Lie on your right side for half an hour. The oil will stimulate the gallbladder and liver. These organs will not know what to do with all the oil, so they will overcompensate and throw off whatever may be stagnant in the gallbladder. It is best for you to lie on your right side as long as you can while falling asleep. A

lot of reactions occur because of the gallbladder's response to flush the residue stones out of the colon.

5. <u>Have a colonic</u>. We have seen better results when patients have colonic irrigation prior to the flush. This clears the pathway for residual elimination. We also encourage, after your flush, that you have another colonic. If you have regular yearly colonics, I would recommend doing the colonic *after* the flush.

6. <u>All females</u> who pass any residue, including green "fatty capsules," and are estrogen dominant (determined by saliva testing) should take a beet-based supplement, three daily, until their estrogen levels become normal. Estrogen saturation is complicated by a slow-moving flow of bile and congested liver function.

7. <u>Regarding frequency</u>, if you are really sick (such as you have cancer), consider doing the flush once every few weeks for a few months. Everyone is different. There are no absolute rules. For prevention, do it at least once a year. Others do it more frequently. You will notice that the material passed is often green and floats.

Protocol Options

Our experience with patients who have completed the flush has allowed us to fine-tune the procedure for better results. It appears that there is no guarantee that you will pass anything. We have reports of individuals passing a small amount of material, while other patients pass a huge amount. Read the following data to improve your chance of substance elimination.

♂ Fair females with freckles who have had one or more children will have better results taking one beet product, several flax capsules, and one bile salt tablet or capsule three times daily for three months prior to the three-day program. These supplements aid the liver in "softening" and releasing material. I would minimize cooked food and eat more whole, fresh, raw fruits and vegetables (see the special note below) during this time.

♂ Females on HRT products, birth control pills, and recent long- or short-term medication should follow the protocol mentioned above.

♂ Females with a history of hysterectomy would get a better response with a combined beet and bile supplement.

♂ Anyone with a history of gallbladder surgery would also get better results by adding a beet and bile supplement. The best way to incorporate a bile product is to take one the first day, two the next day, three the third day, and back to one on day four. This protocol will not create confusion in your natural bile production.

Special Note: Material that accumulates in the gallbladder is often the result of eating a high-acid diet; foods burn to either acid ash or alkaline ash after digestion. All meat and dairy products, as well as nearly all cooked produce, burn to acid. The body needs to stay slightly alkaline to remain in good health. It makes acid ash as a by-product of metabolism but does not create alkaline ash. This must come from the diet. If the diet consists primarily of animal foods and/or cooked produce, the body must rob the bones of calcium (an alkalinizing mineral) to keep the bloodstream from becoming acid. But before going to the bones, the body raids the gallbladder. From the bile stored there, it removes the organic sodium (another alkalinizing mineral). What is left behind is cholesterol, which hardens. To protect against gallstone formation, change your diet. (This special note was taken partially from Dr. Frähm's *Health*Quarters *Monthly,* June 2002.) *Always consult your healthcare provider with any questions on the procedure.*

COFFEE-ENEMA PROTOCOL

First, check with your natural physician before beginning this protocol. I would suggest doing a coffee enema daily or at least four times a week for the first four months of your program. Thereafter, do it as needed—that is, if and when you feel toxic or experience problems with elimination.

The coffee enema is believed to be useful in aiding the liver in its detoxification processes, as well as aiding the colon in its activities of elimination. The efficient removal of metabolic waste and toxins through the colon is vital to the maintenance of health and the prevention of illness.

The coffee enema may be performed at any time that is convenient for you. It usually takes from 30 to 60 minutes, depending on the person. It is best to choose a time when you will feel unrushed and will generally be undisturbed.

Most people prefer to complete the enema in the morning, because doing it in the evening tends to keep them awake or disrupts their sleep. Others find that their sleep is not at all bothered and prefer to do it in the evening.

Some find it preferable to perform the enema before a meal, while others prefer to do it after a meal or between meals. There is really no best time to do the enema; it is a matter of individual preference.

Necessary Ingredients

COFFEE—It must be organically grown. Commercial/conventional coffees are loaded with herbicides and pesticides. Organic coffee is available through health-food stores and select coffee outlets. Never use instant or decaffeinated coffee.

ENEMA BAG—Any bag designed for enema usage is acceptable. Most patients have found the type designed as a combination enema/douche bag to be preferable to the combination enema/douche/hot water bottle. The former conveniently has a permanently open, wide mouth at one end, allowing the easy addition of liquid, whereas those of the hot-water-bottle variety require constant sealing and unsealing.

COLON TUBE—A 30-inch colon tube is required. The two-inch enema nozzle that usually comes with the enema bag is insufficient for the high enema. Colon tubes are generally available from a hospital supply or drug store.

LUBRICANT—A lubricant is required for insertion of the colon tube. Any natural lubricant is acceptable; avoid any commercial, chemical lubricants. Natural herbal ointments are available from health-food stores. Chickweed herbal ointment can be used. Natural oils or butter can also be used.

Preparation

Coffee may be prepared using glass, stainless steel, or enamel cookware. Never use aluminum or Teflon®.

Un-boiled coffee prepared using the drip or Toddy® method is preferable. However, the use of an electric percolator is acceptable. You can also just use a saucepan: Fill the pan with a quart of pure water. Bring the water to a boil and immediately turn off the burner. Add the desired amount of ground coffee and steep until cooled to the desired temperature; strain and use.

Distilled water or water purified through reverse osmosis is the water of choice. Tap water is generally unsuitable for drinking or for enemas in a health-building program.

Use anywhere from one teaspoon to four tablespoons of coffee grounds to a quart of water. Your coffee enema solution should be at room temperature or only slightly warmer at the time of usage. Coffee that is too hot or too cool may cause your colon to contract, resulting in difficulty performing the enema.

Procedure

If you are having regular bowel movements, the enema is preferably performed *following* a bowel movement rather than preceding one. When you do coffee enemas on a daily basis, you may not accumulate enough bulk to continue to have regular movements. If this is the case, you should not strain to have a natural bowel movement before the enema, as this may result in hemorrhoids. When your program of daily enemas is discontinued, your normal daily bowel movements will resume. The enemas will sufficiently serve to evacuate the bowel if you do not have a natural movement.

1. **Arrange an area on the bathroom floor to infuse the coffee solution.**

   Most people lie on an old towel atop a throw rug or folded blanket situated on the bathroom floor. The coffee is infused when in a prone position, so most people make the floor as comfortable as possible. Prop some pillows against the wall and use the time for reading or making phone calls in comfort.

2. **Find a place from which to hang the enema bag.**

   It should not be higher than about two feet off the floor (assuming you will be lying on the floor). If the bag is too high, the solution will flow with too much force, causing discomfort.

3. **Hang the enema bag from the place you have chosen.**

4. **Connect the colon tube to the plastic nozzle on the end of the tube that comes with the enema bag.**

5. **Close off the hose leading to the colon tube with the attachment provided, to prevent the escape of any fluid.**

6. **Add the coffee solution to the enema bag.**

7. **Open the flow control and allow a little coffee to flow to the end of the tube and out into the sink, toilet, or bathtub, just enough to eliminate any air in the tube.**

8. **Lubricate the first several inches of the colon tube.**

   Additional lubrication may be applied to the rectum to aid in the insertion of the colon tube.

9. **Insert the colon tube into the rectum.**

   Most people prefer to accomplish this while lying on their left side. Ideally, the tube should be fully inserted. How this is best accomplished soon becomes a matter of individually learning through trial and error. Everyone has a different colon in terms of twists and turns, as well as degrees of contraction and relaxation. For some, it is a simple matter to fully insert the tube. For others, it requires patient, gentle effort. It is often helpful to allow the slow inflow of solution while inserting the tube. Also, many find that twisting and turning the tube while gently pushing facilitates its progress. Others suggest that momentarily withdrawing the tube slightly and then proceeding with its insertion can help get around "tough corners" (the various bends and turns in the colon). Under no circumstances should any force be used. The whole procedure should be very easy and gentle. Many people are simply unable to fully insert the tube. That is all right. You should just insert the tube as far as your colon will easily allow. It usually takes experiencing several enemas before you become comfortable with the procedure and adopt your own individual means for doing it.

10. **Allow the coffee solution (one quart) to flow into the colon.**

    The rate of flow can be regulated with the control apparatus. When the flow is completed, you may remove the tube or leave it inserted during the course of the enema. Many people prefer to leave the tube inserted with the valve left open, as it will allow any gas present in the colon to escape.

11. **Lie on your left side for five minutes, on your back for five minutes, and on your right side for five minutes.**

12. After the 15 minutes, you may expel the enema.

You should not strain to hold the enema. If you feel the need to expel it before the 15 minutes have passed, you should do so. *No straining of any kind should be done at any time.* The whole process should be very effortless.

Exactly how many coffee enemas you use on a regular basis will depend on your individual metabolism. You should expect to feel a sense of ease and well-being on the completion of the enema. If you experience jitteriness, shakiness, lightheadedness, nervousness, weakness, etc., you will need to decrease the strength of the coffee solution.

The coffee enema can definitely be an adjunct to your overall cleansing program. How often you decide to do it is determined by how willing you are to make other changes. I personally would not do it more than once per week. I prefer doing it first thing in the morning, but you can choose a time that works for you. Caffeine is entering your body, so if you do the procedure at night, it may keep you awake, especially if you have a compromised liver. I know some may think that the caffeine is harmful. Let me respond with this thought: The huge long-term benefit of introducing several cups of organic coffee into your body far outweigh the negative effects of medication and the disfigurement of a "successful surgery," with loss of organ function.

CLEANSING PROTOCOLS — ACTION STEPS

☐ I recommend that you perform the castor-oil pack first and then the colonic, followed by the liver/gallbladder flush. The coffee enema can be performed at the end of this sequence, or at any time following the colonic; the coffee enema enhances the long-term deep-cleansing effects of the colonic.

I have provided you with several internal cleansing options. The sequence I have laid out for you is the one I advise for my patients. The castor-oil pack is a noninvasive treatment designed to help liver/gallbladder function. The liver flush and coffee enema protocols put something into the body and may cause some nausea and discomfort. I also encourage colonic irrigation as a regular, twice-a-year event.

Speak to your healthcare provider before completing a liver/gallbladder flush. You may want to have your liver enzymes checked, including SGOT, SGPT, and GGTP. These levels show how your body is responding to your current therapeutic approach and will provide a baseline for how your body responds to the protocol to be employed. Many of the medications prescribed today require testing of blood levels on a regular basis for your own safety, to monitor whether the medications are creating a toxic state in the body.

You have an awesome base now. Do not try to do everything in one month. This is a two-year project. Give it time. Listen to your body. If you notice nausea and cramping, slow down. Always go SLOW!

NOTES _____

_____

_____

_____

_____

_____

_____

_____

_____

Chapter 18

What Supplements Do You Need?

I am contacted nearly every day by clients and e-mail subscribers from around the world who want to know what supplements to take for particular conditions. I generally suggest that they improve their food choices first. One challenge I continually see is that individuals are consuming media-driven nutrients that create dysfunction—even though these items are said to be good for them. One example is yogurt, which is touted as a great source of calcium. I have found that yogurt also creates chronic left-neck and mid-back pain, chronic sinusitis, asthma, liver congestion, bowel dysfunction, and allergies. Yogurt has more sugar per serving than ice cream. Sugar creates a condition in the skin called glycation, in which protein and sugar combine to create wrinkles. I know what you are thinking: "Dr. Bob, where do I get my calcium?" My standard response is, "The same place cows do: plants!" Also, soy depletes the body of zinc and can actually increase the symptoms of estrogen dominance. I discourage the consumption of both yogurt (made from cow's milk, including Greek yogurt) and soy. I am making this recommendation because when patients follow it, they respond over time.

The latest fad is the unnatural addition of extraordinary amounts of omega-3 fats to many foods, creating the false sense of security that you will be healthy by eating these foods. I suggest eating foods that are *naturally* high in omega-3 fats, such as plant-sourced flax oil, mixed greens, walnuts, and green beans. Eat a variety of organic whole foods. Do you honestly think it is logical to add omega-3 fats to foods that do not normally have them in their structure?

I do not advise taking synthetic, petrochemical-based vitamin E capsules or high-dosage vitamin C. I encourage my patients to eat a variety of vegetables every day, along with apples, pears, and plums. I have found that most patients cannot tolerate eating sweet fruits without getting pain and inflammation along their left neck and shoulder area. I encourage non-gluten grains and sprouted bread. I would avoid "white whole-wheat bread." It is sourced from hybrid modified seeds.

Your goal should be to eat a mixture of raw and steamed vegetables and to avoid canned and frozen foods. There are many national food-store chains that offer a wide variety of organic vegetables. Any time food is prepared commercially, high temperatures are used to process the veggies, which have often been picked prematurely. I am not trying to make this hard but to be helpful. Plan ahead so you don't just revert to eating what you are accustomed to.

I encourage the following items, which I use in my practice. (I am not going to give you daily quantities because those should be determined by an experienced natural health doctor after an assessment of your health.) There are many excellent companies that manufacture supplements. I do not have experience with them all; go to www.druglessdoctor.com to see the items we use for our protocols.

- ♂ **A multiple supplement**—I use a whole-food multiple-vitamin product available to healthcare providers. (See the Appendix for the products I suggest.)

- ♂ **Calcium lactate or calcium citrate**—These are ionizable products, which means they are easily bioavailable to the system. They are acid forms of calcium, unlike calcium carbonate, which is alkaline and hard to digest. Often, patients come into the office with a bag of calcium that is sourced from calcium carbonate, which is more challenging to get into the system. We use the leg blood pressure test to assess the amount of calcium lactate to be used. Hair analysis can help determine the amount of calcium needed. Eat sesame seeds, almonds, and mixed greens for calcium.

♂ **Protein**—Protein is necessary for every aspect of normal function. I have observed that women who exercise on a regular basis have cysts appear in their ovaries because they lack protein. Dr. Donald Lepore, in his book *The Ultimate Healing System,* discusses the lack of threonine as a precipitating factor for ovarian cysts. We use a variety of plant- and animal-based protein products that are whole-food sourced. I do not suggest whey. I like egg white, rice, and pumpkin proteins; iodine also prevents ovarian cysts.

♂ **Minerals**—Minerals are the spark plugs to the body. You can have an awesome-looking vehicle and use the best fuel, but if you lack spark plugs, you will have a misfiring engine. Also, you'll lack energy and experience exhaustion. Zinc deficiencies are a common source of low energy, according to Ann Louise Gittleman in her book *Why Am I Always So Tired?* I strongly encourage the use of Celtic Sea Salt®, from the Grain & Salt Society; it is available on our website. It is even being added to conventional canned soups. Also, you will want to make sure you are incorporating this source of minerals into your diet if you are drinking reverse-osmosis water. The process of water purification removes minerals, and you do not want to create a mineral-deficient state. Refer to the information in Chapter 15 on hair analysis and the leg blood pressure test.

♂ **Organ support tissue**—In my practice, I recommend a supplement protocol determined by the organ I have found to be a major source of the patient's issues. Conventional medical practitioners focus on symptomatic pharmaceutical care and are more than likely not aware of the information I am about to share. I support the function of the liver, adrenals, thyroid, ovaries, and brain with a variety of whole-food supplements. You will want to be assessed by your healthcare provider before you embark on your own regimen. I focus on pure, whole-food neonatal/adult glandular tissues that are available to licensed healthcare providers. I would *not* just walk into a health-food store and take products off the shelf that sound good.

♂ **Iodine**—This element is a critical component in your hormone restoration program. I would suggest that you have your thyroid profile completed as discussed in Chapter 7. A skilled natural doctor will be able to assist you by evaluating your T3 and T4 levels. I have found that most people can use up to 12 milligrams of iodine a day. I use organic-based iodine/iodide combination products.

♂ **Herbs**—Herbs are an asset to your program. A huge variety of herbs can be used to assist you on your restoration journey. Your goal is to support adrenal, liver, thyroid, and ovary function. A common herb I use is chaste tree, which stimulates ovary function and supports the adrenals with licorice root. Milk thistle helps restore liver function. I do not normally recommend herbs specific for female hormones. We do suggest combinations, depending on saliva, mineral tissue, urine, and serum assessments. I have found that when restoration of the organs is supported, the body will make its own bio-necessary hormones. I know that many people get symptomatic relief using media-established herbs; I personally prefer to re-establish normal function through appropriate lifestyle modifications.

♂ **Soy and bioidentical supplementation**—If you are currently using this approach and feel confident with how your body is responding, I would continue with it. However, patients I treat every day, around the world, tell me about their issues with soy-based products. I consistently hear from people who take soy and bioidentical products who are not achieving the positive results portrayed in the media; they are depending on an "outside in" product that is really not promoting functional restoration. You will need to discuss your options with your natural drugless doctor.

The Center for Science in the Public Interest (CSPI), a well-respected watchdog organization, stated in the September 2005 issue of its *Nutrition Action Healthletter*, "Researchers don't know whether soy can lower the risk of breast cancer." I have read the findings of many authorities. I have not consistently read research agreeing that soy was a positive factor for women. If I were you, I would not consume soy. There is no guarantee that it will give you the effect you may be seeking.

There are many more items that can be used; these are the more common ones, with which I get consistent results. Your goal with any supplementation program is to take in food that does not promote physiological stress. The endocrine organs, being supplemented, can once again function by themselves. Sugar, hydrogenated and partially hydrogenated oils, and dairy will defeat your goal of optimal endocrine health.

Note: A source of information on soy and its impact on health is Soy Online Service—in particular its page on the phytoestrogenic effects of soy and soy's impact on the thyroid.

NOTES _____

_____

_____

_____

_____

_____

_____

_____

_____

Chapter 19

How to Get Off Your Medication

L et me give you the real facts, which I see in my natural healthcare practice. Every day, new patients come into the office very frustrated; they don't feel well, and no one seems to understand why. They want to get off their medications and do not even know why they were put on them in the first place. I will be focusing on the medications I commonly see in my practice: antidepressants, thyroid medications, proton-pump inhibitors, and pain medications.

Do not go off your medication without first speaking to your healthcare provider; work together, because this is a team effort. I have found that most practitioners today know that their patients are proactive and have access to information about natural remedies. Enlightened healthcare providers, the ones "in the know," are now accepting Hippocrates's statement from centuries ago, "Let food be thy medicine and medicine be thy food." This simple and profound principle is rapidly gaining acceptance.

I just finished interviewing a patient who, when she was in her early 20s, was put on Paxil®. She told me that within three days, the side effects of the medication put her on the couch for a week. She did not want to go into the kitchen because she was afraid to pick up a knife; she was not sure what she would do with it. She had anxiety, depression, and fear. She did not want to be in social settings. Can you imagine that? Well, it is true. There are millions of

Americans, including many of you reading this, who are depressed and do not know what to do about it.

Let me continue with her story. Her physician had switched her from Paxil® to Zoloft® before she entered my office. She also had psoriasis when she came in to see me. She had not experienced natural spinal corrective care before. Within three months, she was off her medication. The regimen I prescribed for her included taking one tablespoon of organic omega-3 flax oil every day and receiving spinal adjustments.

When my treatments were nearly completed, she mentioned that she could not believe she was better and that otherwise she would probably never have been able to get out of the cycle created by antidepressants. She did not know why she had become depressed and had anxiety. This scenario is very common. Young females often enter my office taking Paxil®, Prozac®, Zoloft®, Wellbutrin, or Abilify®—or either Paxil® or Prozac® combined with either Wellbutrin or Abilify®. What a combination!

If you are depressed, how should you handle it? If you are currently on medication, I am first going to suggest that you have a conversation with the physician who prescribed it. He or she may not understand what you want to do and may not know much about supplementation. My long-term experience suggests that if you do what my patient did, you will be heading in the right direction. She started with one tablespoon of organic omega-3 fat for every one hundred pounds of body weight. She eliminated trans fat, or partially hydrogenated fat, from her life. Sugar was now excluded from her diet. She came into the office and had her spine checked for subluxation. She followed the recommended protocol, and within three months, she was asymptomatic. To get results, you must make some changes. This same patient was, and is, very active. She exercised regularly. Losing weight was not a part of the problem. She needed to get OIL into her body. Your body will use the oil to create the right fat for your brain.

I have patients who come into the office suffering from cold hands and feet. They wake up with morning headaches; are tired, fatigued, and overweight; have high cholesterol; and are constipated. Sound like you? It is the most common set of body signals I see. These patients are normally on some type of thyroid medication with no plan to restore thyroid function.

I generally have them get the lab tests discussed in Chapter 7; then I treat them accordingly. When I see a woman with these body signals, I make sure she is taking enough iodine. I usually recommend at least 12 milligrams a day. This is the amount that females in Japan typically consume in their daily diet of sea vegetables and marine seafood.

Japanese women have fewer menopausal symptoms and other common Western body signals (such as hot flashes) than Western women do. If you are on thyroid medication, you will want to monitor your thyroid lab values with the assistance of your healthcare provider. We support the thyroid with neonatal, animal-sourced nucleoproteins that promote proper function; you can obtain these products from a trained natural healthcare provider. I also focus on reducing estrogen and cortisol levels by encouraging the reduction of sugar and cleaning up the liver. High estrogen and cortisol levels impair the conversion of T4 to T3.

I have also seen, by observing thyroid-stimulating hormone from the pituitary gland (TSH levels), that up to 50 percent of patients with impaired function of the thyroid appear to have low TSH. In addition, I have noticed low selenium and/or manganese levels in hair analyses.

To feed the pituitary, I recommend a brain glandular supplement and a whole-food vitamin E. I may also recommend a whole-food chlorophyll product. These items contribute nutrients for pituitary integrity. Patients with brown "liver spots" commonly need a whole-food source of vitamin E. I generally have patients take the products mentioned above for three months and then reassess. I also encourage them to take flax, whole-food iodine/iodide, and minerals. In addition, I like my patients to take a quality whole-food multiple supplement. The supplements mentioned in this section are sourced from whole foods.

You should not go off any medication without being monitored by your healthcare provider or someone skilled in low-dosage supplementation. One needs to understand the role of TSH, T3, and T4.

Another product I see nearly as much as thyroid medication and antidepressants is digestive aids. Patients often take Nexium®, Prilosec®, or Tagamet®; you may have been told to take an over-the-counter remedy, such as one of the many calcium-enriched products.

If your digestive system is not working at 100 percent, your body will not be up to par. You need to absorb nutrients. If you do not have enough acid or enzymes, your body will not get the resources it needs. Many articles and advertisements promote the fact that you have too much acid. This is only half right. You have too much *inorganic* acid produced by fermentation of carbohydrates and/or putrefaction of protein in your stomach because there is not enough *organic* acid to process food properly. Your stomach becomes a compost pile. We can assess enzymes from the pancreas utilizing saliva and stool samples.

I had a guest on a recent TV program who was in her mid-70s. She told me that she had been healthy her whole life. She went on to say that she had been having GERD (gastroesophageal reflux disease) symptoms for 15 years that she had learned to live with. After coming into my office for treatment, much to her surprise, within three months, her GERD was gone. We encouraged her to stop eating sugar, which depletes the B vitamins necessary to make the badly needed digestive acids. I also completed spinal correction to her mid-back, or thoracic, region.

It is estimated that up to 46 percent of people with digestive distress also have mid-back strain. I encourage using Swiss or physio balls, as explained in Chapter 14, to strengthen the mid-back area.

HOW TO GET OFF YOUR MEDICATION — ACTION STEPS

☐ If you are considering discontinuing your medications, you should always talk to the prescribing physician. You should not even think about going without your prescriptions unless you plan on changing your lifestyle, including your diet and activities.

☐ Work with a natural doctor who is experienced with helping the condition you have, without medication. Do not attempt to self-prescribe.

☐ Follow what you have learned so far. Eat whole foods and avoid processed, liver-plugging, thyroid-draining items.

☐ Soda, sugar, trans fat, and dairy are leading items that may be a part of your challenge.

☐ If you take birth control pills, you might think about seeking another option. Birth control pills create a very serious hormonal imbalance in the body and can be a cause of liver distress and estrogen dominance, creating an environment for dysplasia.

NOTES _____

_____

_____

_____

_____

_____

_____

_____

PATIENT TESTIMONY:

"Before making Dr. DeMaria's recommended lifestyle changes, I had been dealing with hot flashes and sweats. I also had been taking various medications: water pill, Coumadin®, heart pill, Xanax®, Lipitor®, and Requip®. Following Dr. Bob's advice, I stopped eating sugar, which was very difficult. I was a junk-food eater!

The information and care provided by Dr. Bob have improved my life 80 percent. I feel much healthier. Dr. DeMaria and his office staff are the greatest. They are always there for their patients!"

Alda Wohliber

PART IV

YOU ARE
WHAT YOU EAT

Chapter 20

The Page
Food Plan

Patients always ask me what they should eat. I get this question on a regular basis. One of my post-graduate training classes was a part of the curriculum of the International Foundation for Nutrition and Health (www.ifnh.org), which utilizes the Page Food Plan protocol in its training. I have adapted the plan in my office and have found it to be very logical—and effective. We focus on eight or ten different foods, and that is the extent of it. Today, most kids eat only about three foods, i.e., pizza, macaroni and cheese, and chicken nuggets. Of course, we cannot forget America's favorite vegetable—the French fry. Adult eating patterns are really not that different. Few people want to explore food choices beyond what they are used to.

While teaching one of my workshops ("The Drugless Approach to HRT") in my office, I noticed a very conservatively dressed woman, whom I did not know, staring at me the whole time I was speaking. I was beginning to think she was from an espionage group. I came to find out that she had started looking at me with bewilderment after I mentioned that beets can lower your cholesterol 40 percent and can help clean up the liver. She—as God is my witness—did not know what a beet was or what it looked like. WOW! I know there are going to be foods and items discussed in this book that will be foreign to you. Do not get discouraged! I do not expect you to make immediate changes. Just try something new and be adventurous.

This food plan is designed to help you create and maintain "balanced body chemistry." Dr. Melvin Page's plan, which falls into two phases (Phase I and Phase 2), is not only extremely helpful but in many cases essential to control blood sugar imbalances as well as all other types of imbalances in body chemistry. Dr. Page based his food plan on the research of nutrition pioneers Dr. Weston Price and Dr. Francis Pottenger, who showed the relationship of diet to both physical and emotional health. At Page's famous clinic, blood chemistry panels were done every three to four days on all patients. The food plan was validated when the blood chemistry panels of thousands of Page's patients normalized without any other intervention.

Many of today's popular diets are based on Dr. Page's work. He emphasized removing refined carbohydrates (such as sugar and processed flour) and pasteurized or processed cow's milk from the diet. In the upcoming food list, notice that the percentage of carbohydrates is indicated. Dr. Page felt that it was not only important to eat quality proteins and fats but quality carbohydrates as well.

The longer you are on this food plan and the more closely you follow it, the easier it will be to stick to. This will result in your feeling and looking much better than you did with your past eating habits. As you become healthier, your cravings for foods that aren't the best choices for you will actually diminish. Old habits are hard to break; take your time changing your diet so you won't slip back into your old way of eating. If this happens, however, tell your healthcare provider as soon as possible. You may need nutritional supplements to help you get back on track, by reducing cravings, etc.

FOODS TO EAT AND NOT EAT—
THE PAGE FOOD PLAN

Proteins: Eat small amounts of protein frequently. It is best if you have some protein at each meal. It need not be a large amount at any one time; in fact, it is best to stick to smaller amounts (two to four ounces of meat, fish, foul, or eggs). Both animal and vegetarian sources of protein are beneficial. Choose a variety of meat products and try to find the healthiest options available, i.e., free-range, antibiotic-free, organic. For most people, eggs are an excellent source of protein. Eat the whole egg; the lecithin in the yolk is essential to lowering blood fat and improving liver and brain function.

With any protein, the way in which you prepare it is critical. The closer a protein is to raw or rare, the better it is for you. Remember, any time meats and vegetables are heated to over 110 degrees Fahrenheit, crucial enzymes are damaged and lost. Avoid frying. Grilled, boiled, steamed, soft-boiled, and poached proteins are best.

Vegetables: Eat more, more, more! This is the one area where almost everyone can improve his or her diet, and it is an especially important area for you. Always look for a variety of veggies, although make the green, leafy type your preference. This type includes spinach, chard, beet greens, kale, broccoli, mustard greens, etc.

As stated above for proteins, the quality of your produce (fresh and organic preferred) and the method of preparation are critical. Raw vegetables are the best, with lightly steamed or sautéed your second choice. Use only butter or olive oil to sauté. When eating salads, try not to eat iceberg lettuce; rather, consume lettuce with a rich green color, sprouts, and raw nuts. Do not make salads your only choice for veggies.

Fruits: Most people wrongly try to drink their fruits. Fruit juice is loaded with the simple sugar fructose, which is shunted into forming triglycerides and, ultimately, is stored as fat. Without the fiber in the fruit, juice sends a rapid burst of fructose into the bloodstream. When you do eat fruit, keep three things in mind. First, eat only one type of fruit at a time, on an empty stomach. Second, avoid the sweetest fruits and tropical fruits—except papaya, which is very rich in digestive enzymes. (Fruits from colder climates are preferred.) Third, eat only the highest-quality, fresh, organic fruits when possible.

Carbohydrates: This is a very tricky area. There are three clas-sifications of carbohydrates: complex, simple, and processed. Unfortunately, for most patients suffering from imbalance prob-lems, almost any carbohydrate is a no-no. It is a physiological fact that the more carbohydrates you eat, the more you will want. Craving carbohydrates is a symptom of an imbalance; you can use this craving to monitor your progress. Overall, eat vegetables as your carbohydrate of choice and limit grains; even whole grains can be troublesome. When you do eat whole grains, have them only in moderation, and only at dinner. If you start the day with carbo-hydrates, you will most likely crave them throughout the day; then you will eat more, and it's downhill from there. Absolutely stay away from white breads, muffins, cookies, candies, crackers, pastas, white rice, and most baked goods.

There is another dark side to processed carbohydrates that is not talked about much—the connection to weight gain, elevated cholesterol and triglycerides, heart disease, and cancer. You do not even need to know the details to grasp how much trouble carbohy-drates can be.

Wheat and Grains: There has been a tremendous amount of debate regarding grains. Whole, unprocessed grains can be rich sources of vitamins and minerals; however, with soil depletion and the special strains of grains that modern agriculture has developed, it is not clear what nutrients remain. The two predominantly used grains in this country are genetically engineered and have five times the gluten content and only one-third the protein content of the wheat from which they were derived. This high gluten content is to blame for many patients' allergic reactions. I have discovered a lack of omega-3 oils in patients with gluten sensitivity.

When scholars studied disease patterns and the decline of various civilizations, they found that many degenerative diseases developed when cultivated grains became a major part of the diet.

Chemicals naturally found in certain grains lack the appropriate enzymes, and the carbohydrate content of grains makes them a source of trouble for many individuals. Our opinion at this time is to minimize grains such as wheat and barley. Unprocessed rye, rolled oats, and brown rice can be considered on occasion to give you more variety. Some of the Danish and German brown breads, like pumpernickel, seem to be nutritious.

Sweeteners: Use only a *small* amount of raw tupelo honey or stevia as a sweetener. Use absolutely NO NutraSweet®, Splenda®, corn syrup, or table sugar. Although Dr. Page did not allow raw sugar cane, it does provide the nutrients to aid in its metabolism. If you cheat, be smart and use only small amounts of it with a meal.

Fats: The bad news is that you probably do not get enough of the right fats in your diet. Please use olive oil (cold-pressed, extra virgin), walnut oil, flax seed oil, and grapeseed oil. (Do not heat flax oil.) These oils are actually beneficial, as long as they are cold-pressed. When cooking, use only raw butter and olive oil. These are the only two oils with which it is safe to cook. Avoid all hydrogenated and partially hydrogenated fats! **They are poisons to your system!** Never eat margarine again! Also avoid peanut butter. Eat all the avocados and raw nuts you desire.

If you think eating fat will make you fat, think again. When you eat fat, a chemical signal is sent to your brain to slow down the movement of food out of your stomach. As a result, you feel full. It is not surprising that recent research is showing that those who eat "fat-free" products actually tend to consume more calories than those who eat foods that have not had their fat content reduced. ("Low-fat" usually means high sugar and high calories.) In addition, fats are used not only for energy but for building the membrane around every single cell in your body. Fats also play a role in the formation of hormones, which make you feel well and function well. It is far worse to be hormone depleted from a low-fat diet than it is to overeat fat.

The sickest patients we see are the ones who have been on a fat-free diet for a long period. Choose your fats, like your carbohydrates, wisely—this program is *not* suggesting fried or processed foods.

Milk Products: Forget *pasteurized* cow milk products (milk, certain cheeses, half and half, ice cream, cottage cheese, and yogurt). If you only knew all the potential problems caused by pasteurized milk, you would swear off it forever. Dr. Page discovered that milk was actually more detrimental than sugar for many people. (Man is the only mammal that continues to drink milk after weaning.) Avoiding dairy will make it much easier for you to attain your optimal level of health and hormonal balance. *Raw* butter and kefir (liquid yogurt), however, are excellent sources of essential nutrients and vitamins. Goat and sheep raw cheeses and milk products are great alternatives because their genetic code and fat content are apparently more similar to those of human milk. However, we should still be cautious using these products.

There has been a lot of hype about replacing dairy with soy milk and rice milk. While these sound like healthy alternatives, they are really highly processed foods that are primarily simple carbohydrates. You are better off doing without these as well. Of course, Vitamite®, Mocha Mix®, and other dairy substitutes are highly processed, nutrient-depleted products that honestly should not be considered food.

Liquids: Water is best to consume, and then herbal tea. You should drink a minimum of one quart of water a day. Avoid all soda. I would limit coffee. Fruit juices are forbidden because of their high fructose content and dumping of sugar into the bloodstream. An occasional glass of vegetable juice with a meal is probably okay, but water really is best.

If you enjoy wine or beer and still insist on drinking it, there are some guidelines. First, drink only with meals. Red wine has less sugar and more beneficial polyphenols than white wine. Most of the good foreign beer is actually brewed and contains far more nutrients than the pasteurized chemicals called beer made by the large commercial breweries in the United States. Less is better. Drink these beverages occasionally rather than regularly. Because coffee and alcohol force you to lose water, you will have to drink more water to compensate. Personally, I would eliminate alcohol.

The most important life-giving substance in the body is water. The body's routine depends on a turnover of about 40,000 glasses of water per day. In the process, your body loses a minimum of 6 glasses, even if you do nothing. With movement, exercise, and sugar intake (that's right), etc., you can require up to 15 glasses of water per day. Consider this—the concentration of water in your brain has been estimated to be 85 percent, and the water content of your tissues, such as your liver, kidney, muscle, heart, intestines, etc., is 75 percent. The concentration of water outside your body's cells is about 94 percent. The more concentrated water outside the cells wants to move into the cells to create balance. The urge water has to move is called hydroelectric power. It is the same power generated by hydroelectric dams (like Hoover Dam). The energy made in your body is in part hydroelectric. None of us would mind a little boost of energy!

EAT SMALLER AMOUNTS MORE FREQUENTLY

Eating a smaller amount reduces the stress of digestion on your energy supply; eating small meals conserves energy. Give your energy generator a chance to keep up with digestion by not overwhelming it with a large meal. The average length of a meal in the United States is 15 minutes. In Europe, the average meal takes one to one-and-a-half hours. Little wonder Americans suffer such high rates of digestive disorders! When digestion is impaired, yeast overgrowth, gas, inflammation, food reactions, etc., result.

Another reason for eating smaller meals is to prevent ups and downs in your blood-sugar level, so you end up craving less sugar. As mentioned earlier, you can overwhelm your digestive capacity. You can also overwhelm your body's ability to handle sugar in the blood. Since the body will not (or should not) allow the blood-sugar level to get too high, insulin and other hormones are secreted to lower the blood sugar. Oftentimes, the insulin response is too strong and, within a short period of time, insulin has driven the blood-sugar level down. As a result of low blood sugar, you get a powerful craving for sugar or other carbohydrates. You then usually overeat, and a cycle of up-and-down, yo-yo blood-sugar levels results. Depression and lack of energy are a part of this cycle. Eating smaller meals, again, will virtually stop this cycle.

Eating smaller meals also has advantages for your immune response to ingested food. It turns out that a small amount of food enters the blood without first going through the normal digestive pathway by way of your liver. As a result, this food is seen by the body not as nourishment but as a threat that will stimulate an immune reaction. Normally, a small immune reaction is not even noticed; but if a large amount of food is eaten (or if a food is eaten over and over again), the immune reaction can cause symptoms. Over time, disease will develop.

By eating smaller amounts, the size of the reaction that occurs is small and inconsequential. A large meal, and thus a large assault on the immune system, might cause many symptoms of an activated immune system, including fatigue, joint aches, flu-like symptoms, headaches, etc. This reaction was called metabolic rejectivity syndrome by the late nutritional pioneer Arthur L. Kaslow, MD. Through thousands of his patients' food diaries, he compiled a list of high-risk foods that is much the same as Dr. Page's.

Important Note: When in doubt about a food, don't eat it. If it isn't on the list, wait and ask your doctor or nutritionist about it on your next visit. The Page Food Plan is designed to help you reach optimal health as it has for tens of thousands of Dr. Page's patients. Many are in their later years without signs of degenerative diseases, such as heart disease, arthritis, cancer, and osteoporosis. This plan is not intended to make you suffer or sacrifice. Quite the opposite is true, as you will be delighted with the physical and emotional improvements you will experience from the food your body was designed to run on optimally. And what you eat and drink at the occasional party or evening out is not going to be significantly harmful to your nutritional balance in the long run. So go ahead and enjoy—but very moderately.

Lastly, as with all things that are beneficial to your health, it is hard to start, but the longer you use this food plan, the greater the benefits you will realize from it. Relax and enjoy the benefits!

Each of your meals must include some protein. The easiest sources are meat, fish, poultry, and eggs. (Count two eggs as three ounces.) Vegetarians must combine proteins carefully and consistently using a different calculation. An easy way to calculate the ounces of protein to be consumed in a day is to divide your ideal body weight by 15. This is not a "high-protein diet." Like many people, you already eat this much protein during a day, but you eat it mostly in one or two meals instead of spreading it out evenly over three to five meals. If you are more physically active, eat more protein.

90 lb. IBW = 6 oz. per day or 1¾–2 oz. of protein per serving
105 lb. IBW = 7 oz. per day or 1¾–2⅓ oz. of protein per serving
120 lb. IBW = 8 oz. per day or 2–2¾ oz. of protein per serving
135 lb. IBW = 9 oz. per day or 2½–3 oz. of protein per serving
150 lb. IBW = 10 oz. per day or 3–3⅓ oz. of protein per serving
165 lb. IBW = 11 oz. per day or 3⅓–3¾ oz. of protein per serving

---

I would like to explain how to use the following food guides. They are based on the glycemic index, which will be discussed in Chapter 23, "Sweet Alternatives and the Glycemic Index." The glycemic index measures how fast glucose travels in the system, affecting blood-sugar levels. Phase I of the Page Food Plan focuses on items that are lower on the glycemic index. They will affect your blood sugar more slowly, creating a steady flow of blood sugar rather than spikes that produce an insulin rush. The vegetables listed are loaded with minerals, especially if you focus on organic-sourced products. These particular foods will assist your body in utilizing the protein you are consuming.

After two weeks or so have passed, you can add the foods from Phase II, which has veggies that are higher on the glycemic index— meaning they will stimulate a bit more insulin and get blood glucose into the cells quicker. Personally, I avoid the 12-to-21-percent carbs group in Phase II. I would strongly encourage you to eat only the fruits on the list. I have found that people in our culture have major health challenges because they consume too many sweet fruits.

PHASE I FOOD PLAN
FOR BALANCING BODY CHEMISTRY

PROTEINS: MEAT — FISH — FOWL — EGGS
(SEE PROTEIN CHART FOR INDIVIDUAL PORTION SIZE, PAGE 239)

VEGETABLES: No Limit on Serving Size

VEGETABLES 3% or less carbs	VEGETABLES 6% or less carbs	VEGETABLES 7–9% carbs	OTHER FOODS In Limited Amounts
Asparagus	Bell Peppers	Acorn Squash	Butter, Raw
Bamboo Shoots	Bok Choy Stems	Artichokes	Caviar
Bean Sprouts	Chives	Avocado	Cottage Cheese, Raw
Beet Greens	Eggplant	Beets	Dressing: Oil/Cider Vinegar Only
Bok Choy	Green Beans	Brussels Sprouts	Jerky
Greens	Green Onions	Butternut Squash	Kefir, Raw (liquid yogurt)
Broccoli	Okra	Carrots	Milk, Raw
Cabbages	Olives	Jicama	Nuts, Raw (except Peanuts)
Cauliflower	Pickles	Leeks	Oils: Vegetable, Olive (no Canola),
Celery	Pimento	Onion	preferably cold-pressed
Chards	Rhubarb	Pumpkin	**BEVERAGES**
Chicory	Sweet Potatoes	Rutabagas	
Collard Greens	Tomatoes	Turnips	Beef Tea
Cucumber	Water Chestnuts	Winter Squashes	Bouillon: Beef, Chicken
Endive	Yams		Herbal (Decaffeinated) Teas
Escarole			Filtered or Spring Water
Garlic			
Kale			
Kohlrabi			
Lettuces			
Mushrooms			
Mustard Greens			
Parsley			
Radishes			
Raw Cob Corn			
Salad Greens			
Sauerkraut			
Spinach			
String Beans			
Summer Squashes			
Turnip Greens			
Watercress			
Yellow Squash			
Zucchini Squash			

☺ FOODS EATEN CLOSEST TO THEIR RAW STATE HAVE THE BEST DIGESTIVE ENZYME ABILITY.
☺ TAKE FLUIDS MORE THAN ONE HOUR BEFORE OR MORE THAN TWO HOURS AFTER MEALS.
☺ LIMIT FLUID INTAKE WITH MEALS TO NO MORE THAN 4 OZ.
☻ NO PROCESSED GRAINS, WHITE FLOUR, SUGAR, SUGAR SUBSTITUTES.

PHASE II FOOD PLAN
FOR BALANCING BODY CHEMISTRY
PROTEINS: MEAT — FISH — FOWL — EGGS
(SEE PROTEIN CHART FOR INDIVIDUAL PORTION SIZE, PAGE 239)

VEGETABLES: No Limit on Serving Size

VEGETABLES 3% or less carbs	VEGETABLES 6% or less carbs	VEGETABLES 12–21% carbs	OTHER FOODS In Limited Amounts
Asparagus	Bell Peppers	On Limited Basis	Butter, Raw
Bamboo Shoots	Bok Choy Stems	(Only 2–3X/Week)	Caviar
Bean Sprouts	Chives	Artichokes	Cottage Cheese, Raw
Beet Greens	Eggplant	Celeriac	Dressing: Oil/Cider Vinegar Only
Bok Choy	Green Beans	Chickpeas	Jerky
Greens	Green Onions	Cooked Corn	Kefir, Raw (liquid yogurt)
Broccoli	Okra	Grains, Sprouted	Milk, Raw
Cabbages	Olives	Horseradish	Nuts, Raw (except Peanuts)
Cauliflower	Pickles	Kidney Beans	Oils: Vegetable, Olive (no Canola),
Celery	Pimento	Lima Beans	preferably cold-pressed
Chards	Rhubarb	Lentils	
Chicory	Sweet Potatoes	Parsnips	
Collard Greens	Tomatoes	Peas	
Cucumber	Water Chestnuts	Potatoes	
Endive	Yams	Seeds, Sprouted	
Escarole		Soybeans	
Garlic		Sunflower Seeds	
Kale			

VEGETABLES 7–9% carbs	FRUITS	BEVERAGES
Kohlrabi		
Lettuces		
Mushrooms — Acorn Squash	Limited Quantity	Beef Tea
Mustard Greens — Artichokes	On Limited Basis	Bouillon: Beef, Chicken
Parsley — Avocado	(Snacks Only)	Herbal (Decaffeinated) Teas
Radishes — Beets	Apples	Filtered or Spring Water
Raw Cob Corn — Brussels Sprouts	Berries	Red Wine Only (3 glasses max)
Salad Greens — Butternut Squash	Grapes, Papaya,	
Sauerkraut — Carrots	Pears, Prunes	DESSERT
Spinach — Jicama	(Fresh)	Plain Gelatin Only
String Beans — Leeks		
Summer Squashes — Onion		
Turnip Greens — Pumpkin		
Watercress — Rutabagas		
Yellow Squash — Turnips		
Zucchini Squash — Winter Squashes		

☺ FOODS EATEN CLOSEST TO THEIR RAW STATE HAVE THE BEST DIGESTIVE ENZYME ABILITY.
☺ TAKE FLUIDS MORE THAN ONE HOUR BEFORE OR MORE THAN TWO HOURS AFTER MEALS.
☺ LIMIT FLUID INTAKE WITH MEALS TO NO MORE THAN 4 OZ.
☹ NO PROCESSED GRAINS, WHITE FLOUR, SUGAR, SUGAR SUBSTITUTES.

THE PAGE FOOD PLAN — ACTION STEPS

☐ I would suggest that you read the Page Food Plan slowly and analyze what you are eating. You will achieve the progress you desire and expect only by making changes and following the guidelines.

☐ If sweets are your challenge, I would suggest that you focus on eating more complex carbohydrates sourced from veggies. These items will stabilize your cravings for sweets. You may need to seek a source of chromium and Celtic Sea Salt®, which will also help reduce sugar cravings.

NOTES _____

_____

_____

_____

_____

_____

_____

_____

_____

_____

Chapter 21

Food Transition Guide: Shifting Your Diet

Ihave several food charts for you to use as guides in your transition to optimal hormonal health. These guides cover four basic food areas: proteins, carbohydrates, lipids, and other foods. Regardless of the articles you may have read about magic herbs that will control your symptoms, surgeries that will give you relief, or other "outside in" modalities, you will not get the permanent, consistent results that you want and deserve unless you change what you have done up to this point.

I often hear from patients, "Just tell me what to do." Often, they do not actually want to hear what to do because that means change. I am sure you have figured out already that this is serious. Unless you do something different, you may be facing surgery and possibly even chemotherapy and radiation.

Use the four transition guides to help you shift your diet as part of your new lifestyle and to support you as you follow Phase I and Phase II of the Page Food Plan. You can utilize the Page Food Plan in your transition to optimal hormonal health. Modify the way you cook, if necessary. Keep it simple. You want quality, organic food in your system. Keep in mind that wheat, oats, and rye may aggravate a gluten issue.

TRANSITION CHART I

Foods to Avoid PROTEINS	Foods to Enjoy PROTEINS	
Eliminate Immediately	**Acceptable** *Experiment with These*	**Vital** *Primarily Use These*
Meats with additives, such as luncheon meats packed with nitrites (bologna, salami, etc.) Meat with hormones, etc. Processed cheese Processed eggs Processed chicken raised in small coops, injected with antibiotics, etc. Pork Pasteurized, homogenized cow's milk Yogurt with sugar and toxic additives	Meat without additives, hormones, antibiotics, etc., raised free-range on organic feed Deep-ocean and pure-lake fish Milk, cheese, and yogurt derived from nuts and grains Goat's milk, chèvre, and feta cheeses (Goat's milk is very close to human milk constituents.)	Sprouts Fresh, raw nuts and seeds: flax, chia, pumpkin, sunflower, sesame, almond, pecan, Brazil, walnut, filbert, etc. Nut butters Nut milks Organic eggs

TRANSITION CHART II

Foods to Avoid CARBOHYDRATES	Foods to Enjoy CARBOHYDRATES	
Eliminate Immediately	**Acceptable** *Experiment with These*	**Vital** *Primarily Use These*
Sugar: white, brown, turbinado, sucrose, glucose, corn syrup, fructose, etc. Chocolate Processed carbohydrates such as white flour and white-flour products White rice Anything packaged or canned with sugar, salt, or toxic additives Processed pasta Ice cream with sugar and toxic additives	Raw honey, blackstrap molasses, barley malt syrup, pure maple syrup Whole-grain bread Whole-grain pasta Grain/nut ice cream without toxic additives or sugar	Vegetables: squash, carrots, celery, tomatoes, beets, cabbage, broccoli, cauliflower, leeks, turnips, radishes, lettuce, etc. Fruit: apples, pears, plums, etc. Sea vegetables Whole grains: brown rice, millet, rye, barley, etc.

TRANSITION CHART III

Foods to Avoid LIPIDS	Foods to Enjoy LIPIDS	
Eliminate Immediately	**Acceptable** *Experiment with These*	**Vital** *Primarily Use These*
Oils that are rancid or overheated Rancid animal fats, such as lard, bacon drippings, etc. Anything deep-fat fried Artificially hardened fats, such as margarine and shortenings	High-oleic safflower and sunflower oils Butter	Raw, cold-processed oils: olive, coconut, sesame, flax, almond, walnut, avocado Raw, unsalted butter Avocado Fresh, raw nuts and seeds

TRANSITION CHART IV

Foods to Avoid OTHER	Foods to Enjoy OTHER	
Eliminate Immediately	**Acceptable** *Experiment with These*	**Vital** *Primarily Use These*
Coffee, tannic-acid teas, excess alcohol Common table salt (sodium chloride) Any commercial condiments with sugar, salt, or toxic additives Commercial soft drinks made with toxic additives and sugar	Pure grain coffee substitutes Not more than one glass a day of non-chemicalized wine or beer Aluminum-free baking powder Soft drinks made without chemicals, sugar, or toxic additives Celtic Sea Salt® Vegetable salt and kelp	Herbal teas and seasonings Organic apple cider vinegar Homemade condiments without salt or sugar Freshly juiced vegetables and fruits Reverse-osmosis water

Chapter 22

Facts
About Fat

Food is essential for life. Man cannot survive without it. Americans love food. Look around: People in social and business gatherings often consume snacks and overprocessed and wheat-based foods. We are not lacking in food sources. We have megastores with endless rows of tasty morsels, which is part of the dilemma: There's just too much food, and not enough time committed to burning off the excess weight we gain.

I can't go on without mentioning consumption of the wrong fats and its role in balancing female hormones! The creation of man-made fats, the industrial alteration of fats, and misinformation from the media about fats have created an enormous negative impact on society's current level of health. I am not totally convinced there is an easy answer for the dilemma we are facing. People are dying, disabled, chemically dependent, surgically altered, and living in pain due to misunderstanding fat. Many a gallbladder has been removed because of the congestion effect of fat on an already overworked liver. Our current medical system is fueled socially and economically by a misinterpretation of the nature of cholesterol and fats. Pharmaceutical companies and the conventional medical establishment generate billions, not millions, of dollars lowering cholesterol to prevent heart attacks. Yet research suggests it is inflammation of the vessels, not elevated cholesterol, that creates heart attacks.

Whom do you believe? When did this all start? Why did this happen? What is the problem with trans fat anyway?

Here we go! Fat can be a challenging and hotly debated subject. I plan on keeping this discussion logical and simple. Poor fat function can be the primary reason you are having so many challenges with your hormone levels. You body needs fat for optimal hormone function.

You should know the names of fats and understand their activities so you can make logical decisions about what to eat. Like them or not, fats are incorporated into your body for fuel and to build cells, tissues, organs, and hormones. Cell membranes are made of fat; the quality of your cells is dependent on the fat you eat or don't eat!

Saturated fats are solid at room temperature. They can be from plant or animal sources, although most are from animal sources. It has been suggested that fat from animal sources is the major cause of heart disease. Whether from plant or animal sources, saturated fat was branded "bad" fat. Some scientists correlated saturated fat with high cholesterol and heart disease. What is not commonly known is that saturated animal fat ALSO contains "healthy" monounsaturated fats and is in itself not bad, but only a part of a larger cause.

Monounsaturated fats are liquid at room temperature and thicken in the refrigerator. An example of a monounsaturated fat is olive oil. It can be heated to moderate temperatures and is what I use to sauté food. It also tastes great (depending on the source) on a huge variety of foods on which you would normally put butter. There is a classification of monounsaturated fats called oleic acid. Oleic acid is found in olive, almond, pistachio, pecan, avocado, hazelnut, cashew, and macadamia oils, as well as in the membranes of plant and animal cell structures. Oleic acid keeps arteries supple. It melts at 55 degrees Fahrenheit. I wanted to bring this up because you may see this classification on food labels.

Polyunsaturated fat molecules are **liquid.** They do not get hard at room temperature, and they remain liquid in cool environments.

I have evidence based on observation that I want to share so you can get the **BIG PICTURE**. Fats and oils found in nature, in their raw, uncooked state, are neither bad nor good. Heat modifies fat molecules in monounsaturated and polyunsaturated fats. Imbalanced fat eating (with a heavy focus on saturated and heated vegetable oils) is what creates a scenario for unhealthy bodies. Researchers have only recently discovered and announced that inflammation is a possible cause of heart and vascular disease. After studying fats for over 35 years, I do believe that red meat obviously is a factor in heart disease. But I do not feel that cholesterol is the main reason for inflammation; it is a part of the body's process to protect itself. Personally, I believe the leading cause of inflammation is sugar.

CHOLESTEROL AND YOUR HEALTH

Udo Erasmus, an expert in the area of fat metabolism, said in his book *Fats That Heal, Fats That Kill*, "There is no other substance as widely publicized by the medical profession—and no bigger health scandal. Cholesterol can strike terror into the minds of misinformed people. The cholesterol scare is BIG business for doctors, laboratories, and drug companies." I just thought I would start this off with a BANG for all of you who are new to understanding how the body works. People do have heart attacks with normal cholesterol while they are on drugs that trick the body into having low cholesterol. This is a very serious issue, and I thought it was time for you to know the truth.

Cholesterol is a hard, waxy substance that melts around 300 degrees Fahrenheit. It is essential for our health, but we do not need to obtain it from food. The body can manufacture cholesterol from simple substances derived from the breakdown of sugars, fats, and proteins. This occurs especially when our total intake of these foods supplies us with calories in excess of our body's requirements.

The more calories (especially sugar), red meat, and other nonessential fatty acids (soy, canola, partially hydrogenated, and peanut oils) we consume, the more pressure there is on the body to make cholesterol. The reason there is pressure to make cholesterol is that consuming these oils in abundance causes inflammation (by altering prostaglandin production from PG1 to PG2), and cholesterol is the basic building block for creating cortisone to "put out the fire." This is going to be news to you, but the more stress you are under, the more cholesterol your body makes, because cholesterol is the precursor to cortisone, which takes away inflammation.

Cholesterol has many important functions in the body. If it gets too low (such as 160 mg/dL, the low target sometimes promoted by doctors), it can have negative effects on the body. Cholesterol is a part of cell membrane formation. Health begins and ends at the cellular level. You don't want your cholesterol to be too low.

Cholesterol is used to make natural cortisone; one reason you may have pain is that you are taking certain medications to unnaturally lower your cholesterol. Cholesterol is used to make natural hormones for water retention and mineral absorption, and vitamin D for strong bones and immune support. Bile acids, which are very important for digestive function, are also derived from cholesterol. Cholesterol covers our skin, protecting it from dehydration and foreign invaders. Finally, cholesterol is used as an antioxidant. It is like a fireman in the body.

Cholesterol is neither good nor bad. It is necessary. Let me tell you a story. Let's say you are under stress and have been eating more sweet items than usual. Eating sweets creates a state of inflammation in the system. Our ingeniously designed bodies include adrenal glands, which make cortisone when inflammation needs to be subdued.

Let's take the scenario further. You are under stress and have been eating a lot of sweets as well as dead, processed foods. You don't feel good and visit your family healthcare provider, who suggests a blood test. You agree. Your LDL cholesterol (the one you have been told is BAD) comes back high, and your overall cholesterol is 220. You are given the "no meat and cheese" story, and you go home hoping not to go on another medication.

Let's break down the scenario a bit further. The sugar you consume interrupts normal metabolism in the body. Sugar depletes minerals, upsets the formation of pain-relieving fat hormones, and creates stress on the adrenal glands to make pain-relieving cortisone. This cycle continues for some time, years actually. Your body runs out of the resources needed to make cortisone; the good news is that your body has a backup plan, cholesterol.

Your adrenal glands tell the brain they need more cortisone. Your brain sends out an "e-mail," and cholesterol is promptly released from a number of sources. The cholesterol is being transported to help "put out the fire" of inflammation. You see, cholesterol is a precursor for cortisone. (Refer to the flow chart in Chapter 8; it all starts with cholesterol.) Since cholesterol is not water-soluble, it cannot move through blood on its own; it needs a means of transportation. We will call the vehicle that takes cholesterol to the fire the "LDL fire truck."

You continue consuming foods like sugar and trans fat, which cause more inflammation. Your body is under distress and you are tired, depressed, and in pain. Your blood sugar fluctuates; you have headaches, fibromyalgia, and on and on. You are alarmed! Your LDL cholesterol is going up, and you are afraid, so you start to take one of the most prescribed medications on the planet. Your cholesterol goes down, but you start having the side effects described on the sheet of paper that comes with the medication.

Here is what is happening. LDL cholesterol IS NOT THE BAD GUY! It is doing its job, putting out the fire. HDL is considered the good guy when it is up. The reason it is up is because it is taking the cholesterol back to the firehouse; the fire is out. Here is the question: What caused the fire (inflammation)?

I have had patients not eat eggs, red meat, and cheese for years, and guess what. They still had high cholesterol. Why? Because they were avoiding the WRONG FOODS while consuming sugar as well as fats that were designed to be better than lard and beef tallow. The foods people should be *avoiding* are the exact ones they have been told to *eat*; low fat is actually trans fat. Compounded by high levels of sugar used to enhance flavor, trans fat creates inflammation in the body. The low-fat, high-carbohydrate diet was created to lower cholesterol, based on the premise that there was no cholesterol in plant-sourced oils. Trans fat or partially hydrogenated oil is causing the fire. I discuss this in greater detail in my book *Dr. Bob's Trans Fat Survival Guide: Why No Fat, Low Fat, Trans Fat Is Killing You!*

I have had patients who did not eat eggs for 20 years but still ate sweets. Their cholesterol never went down until they got off the sweets and started eating Dr. Bob's ABCs (apples, beets, and carrots) every day. One apple has 22 grams of carbohydrates, so I encourage eating half of one a day, along with beets and carrots.

Eating apples can lower your cholesterol 13 percent, and eating beets can lower your cholesterol 40 percent. I see it every day in my practice. Cholesterol attaches itself to the beet fiber and is released in the colon. I am not talking about beet juice, but beet fiber. I prefer fresh, organic beets grated on a salad, or baked at 400 degrees Fahrenheit for one hour or until fork-tender.

To prepare, cut the beets into small pieces or wash them and keep them whole; sprinkle with balsamic vinegar, Celtic Sea Salt®, and olive or coconut oil. Bake at 400 degrees Fahrenheit. Cool the beets, put them in a sealed container, and freeze the extras. I normally cook 10 or more beets per week. I wear gloves to prevent red-stained hands, and I use a sharp knife. I eat several beet pieces on my mixed green salad every day. Additional beet and vegetable recipes are included in the Appendix.

Beets do have a side effect: They can turn your stool, or bowel movement, a deep red. Don't be alarmed; that is good. Beets will also help you have a firm, full bowel movement.

I do not suggest commercially pickled or canned beets. Use fresh beets from the market. I know from experience that if you minimize the sugar in your life and stop eating trans fat, you will see results in as little as three months.

WHAT YOU NEED TO KNOW TO AVOID PARTIALLY HYDROGENATED OIL, OR TRANS FAT!

Trans fat, or partially hydrogenated oil, is one of the leading challenges facing our society today. This man-made fat has permeated nearly every aspect of the modern food chain in the United States. It has wreaked havoc on the detoxifying organs. I know you have heard a lot about fats in the last 30 years. Please indulge me and continue reading. This information will make a difference in your overall health and that of your family.

In America, we have been so inundated with news about FAT that we are experiencing an epidemic of FAT phobia. Confusion is everywhere. FAT, or OIL, is not the ENEMY. The kind of oil people are choosing is the problem! You need to make wise selections.

Well-meaning freelance writers look for information to educate the public about staying thin while you eat. Food manufacturers are scurrying to find alternatives for the oils with which they fry and cook, as they try to maintain flavor, keep the government off their backs, and sustain profit margins for investors. Have you noticed that huge players in the food industry are announcing changes in their cooking oils? Do you know why they are switching? Better-educated consumers are demanding healthier ingredients. Education and access to information have changed the world in which we eat and live.

THE VILLAIN:
PARTIALLY HYDROGENATED OIL, OR TRANS FAT

Ready or not, here I come! I would like to take the next few minutes to explain to you the simple facts about partially hydrogenated fat...the villain of the day. It all started in 1873, when the first "batch" of partially hydrogenated oil was developed in Europe. (Research was being conducted to find a new source of wax for candles.) The American public had its first taste of mass-produced "oleomargarine" during World War II. I remember as a child squeezing a sealed plastic bag of white "goop" and then pressing a red button that released yellow dye to color the material to look like butter; we would spread it on our bread with jelly. Margarine is a little more sophisticated today; nonetheless, it is not a viable replacement for butter.

Partially hydrogenated oil, commonly called trans fat (and by the way, the double name confuses consumers), is made by heating vegetable oil at very high temperatures. The heating process continues as hydrogen is pumped into the container in the presence of a metal catalyst. The process is stopped right before the hydrogen is fully loaded—hence the name "partially hydrogenated." The exact final result of the process is not precisely known. Trans fat is one of the by-products of the process. Full hydrogenation would result in a solid substance. Partially hydrogenated fat is not solid at room temperature. By the way, you are not creating trans fat when you fry food at home unless you are cooking packaged foods or using a commercial source of trans fat (such as Crisco®). Frying olive oil at high temperatures does not translate to trans fat.

Vegetable oil does not have cholesterol in it; animal products do. People were told to avoid products made with animal tissue, e.g., lard, beef tallow, cheese, heavy dairy cream, and eggs. According to conventional medical thought, if the public stopped eating these foods, the heart attack problem would go away. What most do not realize is that the human body makes up to 75 percent of its cholesterol on an "as needed" basis. **Cholesterol is essential for our survival as a species; it is a precursor for sex hormones.**

The public was lead to believe that partially hydrogenated oil, or trans fat, was not fat because it did not have cholesterol. People who are unaware of the health dangers of trans fat today will tell you they avoid animal-sourced fat but will eat the low-fat, vegetable-sourced trans fat. When the low-fat/no-fat diet started, **the idea was that low-fat meant no CHOLESTEROL.** The low-fat diet was aimed at two groups:

♂ **People who were not supposed to eat a diet that led to heart disease**

♂ **People intending to lose weight**

All you have to do is look around to see that this plan has not worked. People are heavier now than ever before, and heart disease and heart attacks are the leading causes of death in the Western world. Americans have been on the LOW-FAT "kick" for nearly 40 YEARS, and they still have heart disease! Keep in mind that the low-fat diet is loaded with partially hydrogenated oil, or trans fat, with SUGAR added to enhance flavor. This DEADLY combination has not helped lower cholesterol like everyone thought it would. It actually raised cholesterol, and the portion of cholesterol it raised was the LDL, or "BAD," component. Compounding the problem, trans fat also lowered HDL, or "GOOD" cholesterol. Natural vegetable oil, not altered by man, will not raise cholesterol itself. What happens is that the twisted fat molecule of the once healthy oil causes a predicament at the cellular level. The body responds with a defense mechanism that raises cholesterol.

The medical community and food manufacturers were, and still are, beside themselves about the reports of LDL and HDL cholesterol levels. Someone did not do his or her homework. This is why we need long-term studies before it is proclaimed that items such as genetically modified foods, artificial sweeteners, and cloned animal products are safe.

Fake food will generally cause an inflammatory response at the cellular level. Trans fat raises cholesterol because it is one of the primary causes of inflammation. The body produces cholesterol to protect itself. Remember, cholesterol is being released to make components for decreasing inflammation—to put out the fire. The medical community is doing everything it can to artificially lower cholesterol. That is why we have "side effects" with cholesterol-lowering medication—the body can get confused when cholesterol is lowered artificially. (See the omega-3 diagram on page 260.) Trans fat interferes with inflammation-relieving PG1 and PG3 (prostaglandins).

Today, the restaurant business alone uses FIVE BILLION POUNDS of trans fat per year. EIGHT BILLION POUNDS are used by our society as a whole. That is a lot of FAT. The major seed producers are looking for new hybrid seeds for making oils that will not be TRANS FAT–based. These oils, by the way, will more than likely be from a genetically modified source. NOT GOOD!

Let's talk physiology; I promise it will be simple. TV advertisements attempt to lure the public with tasty morsels made with trans fat. What is the problem with trans fat? It tries to fool Mother Nature. We live and die at the cellular level. The cells in our body become perplexed when trans fat is hanging around in abundance. Following are only a few of the many complications that occur when trans fat raises LDL cholesterol:

♂ **Inflammation response**

♂ **Small holes in the cell membrane**

♂ **Correlation to low birth rate**

♂ Precipitation of childhood asthma

♂ Inhibition of essential fatty acid metabolism

♂ Alteration of enzyme reactions in the body

♂ Decrease of the red blood cells' response to insulin

There are small amounts of trans fat found in nature. Generally, the body will use these molecules for energy. When there is a large quantity of trans fat, the body will start incorporating it into cellular membranes. This is not good.

My experience with and study of trans fat started back in the 1970s. I want you to understand a few components of the dilemma created by this fake fat. When you eat a meal, your body takes the food and breaks it down. Various nutrients are needed to complete the sequence—items like B complex, vitamin B6, calcium, magnesium, zinc, enzymes, and others. All these ingredients are necessary for the body to do its job.

If one of the components is missing or in short supply, the body suffers. For example, vitamin B6 (see B6 in the omega-3 diagram) is commonly low in most people who eat on the run—either by choice or by eating anti-vitamins like sugar. When you don't have enough B6, you can develop carpal-tunnel or wrist-pain symptoms. The carpal-tunnel condition is caused (in most cases, excluding structural reasons) by a lack of vitamin B6. Without B6, the body does not create enough of a fat-tissue hormone called a prostaglandin. The prostaglandin in this case is created to take away inflammation. PAIN can result from this poor fat metabolism. So carpal-tunnel symptoms are caused by more than repetitive stress. Think about this: "Rosie the Riveter" was building planes and ships during World War II using manual tools and did not have carpal tunnel. She had a different diet than we do today. Her meals were not convenience foods loaded with trans fat.

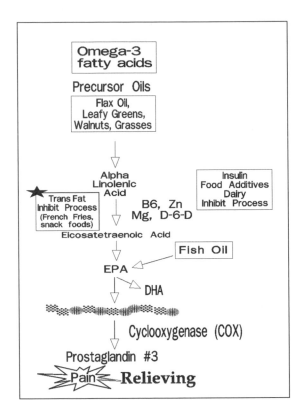

This next piece of information will be the most important for you. TRANS FAT interferes with the metabolic pathways that have to do with brain health (DHA in the diagram) and heart health (EPA in the diagram). **Trans fat sabotages the process.** You can also slow and stop the process with a lack of nutrients.

What you might not know is that trans fat has a half-life. As you may remember from biology and chemistry, uranium and other metals have half-lives of thousands and even millions or billions of years. Trans fat's half-life is 51 days, which is the reason convenience foods have a long shelf life. This means that if you eat a food containing trans fat, or partially hydrogenated fat, its negative effects will linger in you, with 25 percent of their potency, for at least 102 days. Now you can see how insidiously trans fat affects your health.

It is estimated that nearly 30 percent of America's youth between the ages of four and nineteen will eat at a fast-food restaurant on any given day. The most common food requested while dining out is chicken nuggets, followed by America's most popular vegetable... French fries. It is also reported that 30 percent of our family meals are eaten outside the home, and more meals than ever are being ordered for takeout. Some of you reading this have trans fat in your system, and it may be there for up to three more months; or maybe you are among those who are educated about trans fat and avoid it.

Trans fat is the leading cause of health problems today, because it has gone undetected for nearly 40 years and permeated nearly every aspect of our food chain. It cunningly slows and stops fat metabolism, and the public is just now finding out about it. Denmark outlawed trans fat years ago. There are major health-food chains that will not allow it in their stores, which should tell you something.

You need to be a label reader. In January 2006, the government required all foods to have the amount of trans fat indicated on the package. But there is a loophole: If a product has one-half gram or less of trans fat per SERVING, the manufacturer can legally say "0 grams trans fat." When you see "0" on the package, you should turn it over and examine the nutrition facts. If you see partially hydrogenated oils, gently put the package down.

I will give you an example of what eating "0 grams trans fat" might be like. Eat 15 potato chips (a typical serving) from a bag labeled "0 grams trans fat" and you think you are okay. What happens at number 16? BUSTED! One-fourth of a donut, one-half of a conventional peanut butter and jelly sandwich, one delicious chocolate chip cookie could put you over the TOP. Start looking for the words *partially hydrogenated fats*. They are in vitamins, candy, bread, cereal, novelty items...literally everywhere. You must become label savvy.

You will see more cities voting to get trans fat out of restaurants. There was a study released in the late 1990s that said if you ate more than one gram of trans fat a day, you would increase your chance of cardiovascular disease by 20 percent. This information was released over 10 years ago. Have you heard about it?

Let me close with this. We should want trans fat not only out of restaurants but also out of school lunches. Feeding kids food with trans fat leads to obesity. And from my research, the number one cause of ADHD is TRANS FAT. Join me; write letters to your school board, and raise your voice at school meetings. It's important for the health-educated public to support this grassroots drive to get rid of trans fat.

You are usually required to bring your life insurance policy up to date when you reach 50. I needed to upgrade my policy, and I've been doing exactly what I've told you to do in this book. I do not eat sweets; I do not drink alcohol or soda; I eat eggs and red meat (once a week); I exercise every day; and I eat half an apple daily and beets at lunch, with five or six medium carrots. The results from my insurance exam were so overwhelmingly healthy that they LOWERED—yes, you read it right—they LOWERED my premium. My cholesterol, blood sugar, blood pressure, heart rate, and EKG reading were all within the normal ranges. This can happen to you. You need to follow the natural principles you have been reading about in the book. My patients have the same results I do.

FACTS ABOUT FAT — ACTION STEPS

☐ Fat is necessary for life, so eat the right kinds of fat.

☐ I would avoid saturated fat sourced from animals and keep red meat to a minimum.

☐ Avoid all man-made, processed fats. These would include partially hydrogenated fat (trans fat) from any source.

☐ Become label savvy; I personally avoid soybean oil–based products.

☐ Use rice oil for high-temperature frying. I also suggest coconut oil; I know it's saturated, from a plant source, but it is considered okay. Butter, ghee, and high-oleic safflower and sunflower oils can be heated to high temperatures. When the oil is smoking, the temperature is too high.

☐ Sauté foods with olive oil. I prefer my patients to take one tablespoon of flax oil from an organic source per one hundred pounds of body weight daily. Some healthcare providers suggest marine sources of omega-3 fats. I am not opposed to that, but I have found from experience that you can obtain the results you are seeking by using plant-based flax oil and supplementing with whole-food zinc, magnesium, calcium, and whole-food B vitamins. These constituents help create the formation of long-chain fats needed for optimal health.

☐ You may want to try primrose oil, which is an omega-6 oil, but I have found it may be a bit more logical to use black currant seed oil. It supplies not only omega-6 oil but also omega-3 and omega-9 oils, covering more of your hormonal needs.

☐ Oil is necessary for hormone production. Avoid all man-made fats, especially new ones that will be developed to be "safe" and trans fat–free. Not sure what to take? Have your EFAs assessed (see Chapter 15).

☐ For more details on fats and the effects they can create in the body, including ADHD, Alzheimer's disease, and pain syndromes, read *Dr. Bob's Trans Fat Survival Guide: Why No Fat, Low Fat, Trans Fat Is Killing You!*

NOTES _____

_____

_____

_____

_____

_____

_____

PATIENT TESTIMONY:

When I first came to see Dr. Bob, I had cysts and a lot of pressure and discomfort around my period. I had been taking over-the-counter medications, such as Midol® and aspirin. After following his recommendations, I now consume very little sugar and fewer carbs, and I am trying to stay away from trans fat (but haven't mastered this yet). I now have no symptoms, not even cramps, and I'm not taking any medication!

The care and information provided by Dr. DeMaria have improved my life greatly. I have more energy, and I hardly get sick at all. Even when others get so sick they have to miss work, I don't get sick at all. Dr. Bob is great! He really knows his stuff and can help most of the medical problems we have today. A really great blessing and valuable asset!"

Rebecca Szilagyi

Study Finds Link Between Fries and Breast Cancer

A study examining the role childhood diet plays in breast cancer has found an association between eating French fries regularly during the preschool years and developing breast cancer as an adult.

Each weekly serving of French fries girls consumed between ages 3 and 5 increased their risk of developing breast cancer as adults by 27 percent, according to researchers at Brigham and Women's Hospital and the Harvard School of Public Health.

The association was not found with potatoes prepared in other ways.

The finding is the first of its kind and must be confirmed by other studies, said lead author Karin Michels, an associate professor at Harvard Medical School and clinical epidemiologist at Brigham and Women's Hospital in Boston.

"This is something nobody's really looked at before. It's really new," she said, adding, "It could be due to chance."

The finding of a correlation between French fries and breast cancer does not necessarily point to a cause-and-effect relationship between the two, however.

Michels speculated the French fries may be implicated in breast cancer because they are prepared in fats that are high in harmful trans-fatty acids and saturated fat.

The dietary survey examined the childhood eating habits of participants in the Harvard Nurses' Health Study. To obtain information about what adult women had eaten as preschoolers, the researchers asked the mothers of participants in the nurses' study to fill out questionnaires asking how often their daughters had eaten 30 different food items.

The researchers analyzed data gathered in 1993 from 582 participants with breast cancer and 1,569 women without breast cancer. The participants were born between 1921 and 1965, so their mothers were being asked to recall information from decades earlier.

Michels noted these recollections may have been unreliable, especially when made by mothers who already knew their daughters had breast cancer.

Consumption of whole milk was associated with a slightly decreased risk of breast cancer, though most of the milk consumed during those decades was whole milk, Michels said.

"Only one food so distinctly stood out as being associated with breast cancer risk," Michels said, and that was the French fries.

She said dietary influences may be more significant during early life than during adulthood, because the breast of a girl or infant is more susceptible to environmental influences than the breast of a mature woman.

Dr. Larry Norton, deputy physician in chief of the breast cancer program at Memorial Sloan-Kettering Cancer Center in New York, warned against overinterpreting the results.

"I wouldn't go out and change Americans' dietary habits on the basis of this, but it's certainly worth pursuing the hypothesis with additional research," he said.

Michels said her study doesn't prove that giving up French fries will protect against breast cancer.

But with child obesity rates rising, she said, "There are numerous reasons to avoid French fries."

Source: Roni Rabin, "Study Finds Link Between Fries and Breast Cancer," *Newsday* (August 18, 2005).

Chapter 23

Sweet Alternatives and the Glycemic Index

I would like to provide information on what you should be doing about sugar. I have come to the conclusion that addiction to sugar is a leading cause of many of the health challenges facing our society today. When you have a sugar habit, your body gets used to the substance as it would to a drug; eating sugar becomes like adding kindling to a fire that is constantly consuming as much wood as is thrown on it. Therefore, the more sugar you consume, the more you will desire. This is true for both men and women. This chapter will give you ideas for sweet substitutes and will save you from the vicious cycle created by consuming too much sugar.

Sugar is by far one of the most misunderstood factors affecting health in the Western world. Either people are in denial about their addiction to sugar or they are totally ignorant about how the body is paralyzed by its detrimental effects. Splenda® claims to be sourced from a natural product: sugar. The whole marketing campaign is based on the fact that Splenda® is naturally sourced, and the public has bought this hook, line, and sinker. Splenda® is basically chlorinated sugar. You are actually consuming herbicide sugar when you eat it. There is a battle going on between the "fake" sugars and Splenda® because the latter is advertising the fact that it can be heated; therefore, it is safe to bake and cook with it. In other words, Splenda® is being positioned as the safest product. However, I know that long-term use of Splenda®, aspartame, acesulfame potassium, and other sugar substitutes will produce severe toxic effects. I see the results in my practice daily.

In this chapter, I have included examples of ways to sweeten the foods and beverages you enjoy. I have also provided a list of products that are not helpful and should be avoided.

STAR SWEETENERS: THE BEST OF THE NATURALS

Become sugar-savvy! The term *natural*, as applied to sweeteners, can mean many things. The sweeteners recommended below will provide you with steady energy because they take a long time to digest. Natural choices offer rich flavors, vitamins, and minerals without the ups and downs produced by refined sugars.

Today's sugar substitutes were actually the natural sweeteners of days past, especially honey and maple syrup. You should stay away from all man-made (artificial) sweeteners and the "sugar alcohols" (with names ending in "ol"). In health-food stores, be alert for sugars disguised as "evaporated cane juice" or "cane juice crystals." These can still cause problems, regardless of what the health-food store manager tells you. My patients have seen huge improvements by changing their sugar choices.

Brown rice syrup. Your bloodstream absorbs this balanced syrup, high in maltose and complex carbohydrates, slowly and steadily. Brown rice syrup is a natural choice for baked goods and hot drinks. It adds subtle sweetness and a rich, butterscotch-like flavor. Enzymes are the magic ingredients for getting sweetness from starchy brown rice, but the actual process varies depending on the syrup manufacturer. "Malted" syrups use whole, sprouted barley to create a balanced sweetener. Choose these syrups to make tasty muffins and cakes. Cheaper, sweeter rice syrups use isolated enzymes and are a bit harder on blood-sugar levels. For a healthy treat, drizzle gently heated rice syrup over popcorn to make natural caramel corn! Store the syrup in a cool, dry place.

Barley malt syrup. This sweetener is made much like rice syrup, but it uses sprouted barley to turn grain starches into a complex sweetener that is digested slowly. Use barley malt syrup to add molasses-like flavor and light sweetness to beans, cookies, muffins, and cakes. Store the syrup in cool, dry place.

Stevia. This sweet South American herb has been used safely by many cultures for centuries. Extensive scientific studies back up these ancient claims to safety. However, the FDA has approved stevia only when labeled as a dietary supplement, not as a sweetener. Advocates consider stevia to be one of the healthiest sweeteners as well as a tonic for healing skin. Stevia is 150 to 400 times sweeter than white sugar, has no calories, and can actually regulate blood-sugar levels. Unrefined stevia has a molasses-like flavor; refined stevia (popular in Japan) has less flavor and fewer nutrients. I would avoid trade-named stevia products modified with additional ingredients; read the label before purchasing.

Fruit Sweet™. This blend of pear and pineapple juice concentrates contains fruit sugars, mostly fructose. Extremely neutral in flavor, it is the natural sweetener of choice by diabetics. The richness of Fruit Sweet™ helps reduce the fat in a recipe. Concentrated fruit juices taste sweeter than honey or any syrup or sugar, so less is needed. With 280 calories per 100 grams, concentrated fruit juices beat sugar's 385 calories per 100 grams. Besides having the nutritional advantage, these concentrates are humectants, keeping baked goods fresher for a longer period.

Whole fruit. For baking, try fruit purees, dried fruit, and cooked fruit sauces or butters. The less water remaining in a fruit, the more concentrated its flavor and sugar content. You'll find fiber and naturally balanced nutrients in whole fruits like apples, bananas, and apricots. To add mild sweetness and moisture to baked goods, mix in the magic of mashed winter squashes, sweet potatoes, or carrots!

Fructose. In whole foods, fructose provides balanced energy.

Honey. It takes one bee an entire lifetime to produce a single tablespoon of honey from flower nectar. But that small amount goes a long way! Honey is mostly made of glucose and fructose and is up to twice as sweet as white sugar. Honey enters the bloodstream rapidly. Look for raw honey, which still contains some vitamins, minerals, enzymes, and pollen. Honeys vary in color (according to their flower source) and range in strength from mild clover to strong orange blossom. A benefit of eating honey produced in your geographical region is that it may reduce hay fever and allergy symptoms by bolstering your natural immunity.

Maltose. The primary sugar in brown rice and barley malt syrups, maltose is a complex sugar that is digested slowly. It is the sugar with "staying power."

Maple syrup. It takes about 10 gallons of maple sap to produce 1 gallon of maple syrup. Like honey, a little goes a long way. Maple syrup is roughly 65 percent sucrose and contains small amounts of trace minerals. Maple syrup has a rich taste and is absorbed fairly quickly into the bloodstream. Select real maple syrup that has no added corn syrup. Also, look for syrups that come from organic producers who don't use formaldehyde to prolong sap flow. Grade A syrups come from the first tapping; they range in color from light to dark amber. Grade B syrups come from the last tapping; they have more minerals and a stronger flavor and color.

Date sugar. This sweetener is made from dried, ground dates; is light brown; and has a sugary texture. Date sugar retains many naturally occurring vitamins and minerals, is 65 percent sucrose, and has a fairly rapid effect on blood sugar. Use it for baking in place of brown sugar, but reduce your baking time or temperature in order to prevent premature browning. Store it in a cool, dry place.

Concentrated fruit juice. All concentrates are not created equal. Highly refined juice sweeteners are labeled "modified." These sweeteners, similar to white sugar, have lost both their fruit flavor and their nutrients. Better choices are fruit concentrates that have been evaporated in a vacuum. These retain rich fruit flavors and aromas along with many vitamins and minerals. Carefully read labels on cereal, cookie, jelly, and beverage containers, and then choose products with the highest percentage of real fruit juice. Beware of white grape juice concentrates that aren't organic; their pesticide residues can be high!

SWEETENERS TO AVOID

I would avoid any artificial sweetener. I do not encourage the use of any chemically altered product. Currently, Splenda® is being marketed as a viable product. Look at its bright yellow packet, which says, "Made from Sugar." Now, let me ask you something: Do you consider sugar nutritious? Of course not! I would also not put NutraSweet®, Equal®, or any other artificial product in my body. Why would you want to put additional stress on an already overworked liver? Let's look at some additional sugars, both natural and synthetic, that are to be avoided.

Brown sugar. Brown sugar is simply refined white sugar that is sprayed with molasses to make it appear more whole. **Turbinado sugar** gives the illusion of health but is just one step away from white sugar. Tubinado is made from 95 percent sucrose (table sugar). It skips only the final filtration stage of sugar refining, resulting in little difference in nutritional value.

Corn syrup. Found everywhere, corn syrup is used in everything from bouillon cubes to spaghetti sauce to some "natural" juices. Processed from cornstarch, corn syrup is almost as sweet as refined sugar and is absorbed quickly by your blood. Corn-derived sweeteners pose another problem: They often contain high residual levels of pesticides, which are common allergens. Corn syrup is a cheap and plentiful sweetener often used in soft drinks, candy, and baked goods. It is very similar to refined sugar in composition as well as effect.

Aspartame. A common synthetic sweetener, aspartame affects the nervous system and brain in a very negative way. Aspartame is made from two proteins, or amino acids, which give it its super sweetness. Aspartame has many harmful effects: behavioral changes in children, headaches, dizziness, epileptic-like seizures, and bulging of the eyes to name a few. Aspartame is an "excito-toxin," a substance that overstimulates neurons and causes them to die suddenly (as though they were excited to death). One of the last steps of aspartame metabolism is the production of formaldehyde. The next time you consume diet soda, consider that you are literally embalming yourself.

Sucrose. Found in white sugar and maple syrup, sucrose requires very little digestion and provides instant energy, followed by plummeting blood-sugar levels. It stresses the entire body system.

Glucose, also called **dextrose.** When combined with sucrose, glucose subjects your blood sugar to the same ups and downs. In whole-food form—in starches like beans and whole-grain breads, which are also rich in soluble fiber—glucose takes longer to digest, resulting in more balanced energy.

Sorbitol, mannitol, and xylitol. These are synthetic sugar alcohols. Although they can cause less of an insulin release by the pancreas than sugar, they cause many people gastric distress. You see these sugars listed as ingredients in foods, especially those labeled "sugar-free."

Unrefined cane juice. This is sugarcane in crystal form—nothing more, nothing less. Unrefined cane juice is brown and granulated, contains 85 to 96.5 percent sucrose, and retains all of sugarcane's vitamins, minerals, and other nutrients. Cane juice has a slightly stronger flavor and less intense sweetness than white sugar.

Crystalline fructose. This refined simple sugar has the same molecular structure as fruit sugar. It's almost twice as sweet as white sugar yet releases glucose into the bloodstream much more slowly. Extra sugar gets stored in your liver as glycogen instead of continuing to flood your bloodstream.

High-fructose corn syrup (HFCS). Called maize syrup or glucose-fructose syrup in the UK and glucose/fructose in Canada, HFCS comprises any of a group of corn syrups that has undergone enzymatic processing to convert its glucose into fructose and has then been mixed with pure corn syrup (100 percent glucose) to produce a desired sweetness (from Wikipedia). In the United States, HFCS is typically used as a sugar substitute and is ubiquitous in processed foods and beverages, including soft drinks, yogurt, industrial bread, cookies, salad dressing, and tomato soup. I have found that it may be one of the leading causes of obesity, as it interferes with the normal hungry-full feedback loop in the body.

SUGAR SUBSTITUTION

Amount Indicates the Equivalent of
1 Cup of White Sugar

Sweetener	Amount	Liquid Reduction	Suggested Use
Honey	½–⅔ cup	¼ cup	All-purpose
Maple syrup	½–¾ cup	¼ cup	Baking and desserts
Maple sugar	⅓–½ cup	None	Baking and candies
Barley malt syrup	1–1½ cups	½ cup	Breads and baking
Rice syrup	1–1⅓ cups	½ cup	Baking and cakes
Date sugar	⅔ cup	None	Breads and baking
Fruit juice concentrate	1 cup	⅓ cup	All-purpose
Stevia	1 tsp./cup of water	1 cup	Baking

(*Note:* If you have a serious blood-sugar regulation problem, such as diabetes or hypoglycemia, see your healthcare practitioner to determine the types and amounts of sweeteners your body can handle. It is best to choose foods with glycemic indices of 50 to 80. Foods in this range will give you the best chance to minimize exaggerated insulin responses.)

GLYCEMIC INDEX

The glycemic index measures the degrees to which different foods are able to raise blood glucose. The greater the blood-glucose level, the greater the insulin response. Therefore, we want to choose foods with low glycemic indices. (See the table starting on page 275.) There are many specific benefits of consuming foods with low glycemic indices:

1. Blood lipids are reduced in hypertriglyceridemic patients.
2. Insulin secretion is reduced.
3. Overall blood-glucose control improves in insulin-dependent and non-insulin-dependent diabetic subjects.

4. There is a reduction in abnormal blood-glucose, insulin, and amino-acid levels in patients with cirrhosis.

5. Urea excretion is reduced, presumably by increased nitrogen trapping by colonic bacteria.

6. Foods with low glycemic indices may enhance satiety.

7. Foods with low glycemic indices may increase athletic performance.

GLYCEMIC INDICES OF FOODS

FOOD	GLYCEMIC INDEX
BREADS	
Rye (crispbread)	95
Rye (wholemeal)	89
Rye (whole-grain, i.e., pumpernickel)	68
Wheat (white)	100
Wheat (wholemeal)	100
PASTA	
Macaroni (white, boiled 5 min.)	64
Spaghetti (brown, boiled 15 min.)	61
Spaghetti (white, boiled 15 min.)	67
Star pasta (white, boiled 5 min.)	54
CEREAL GRAINS	
Barley (pearled)	36
Buckwheat	78
Bulgur	65
Millet	103
Rice (brown)	81
Rice (instant, boiled 1 min.)	65
Rice (parboiled, boiled 5 min.)	54
Rice (parboiled, boiled 15 min.)	68
Rice (polished, boiled 5 min.)	58
Rice (polished, boiled 10–25 min.)	81
Rye kernels	47
Sweet corn	80
Wheat kernels	63

FOOD	GLYCEMIC INDEX
BREAKFAST CEREALS	
All-Bran®	74
Cornflakes	121
Muesli	96
Porridge oats	89
Puffed rice	132
Puffed wheat	110
Shredded wheat	97
Weetabix™	108
COOKIES	
Digestive	82
Oatmeal	78
Plain crackers (water biscuits)	100
"Rich tea"	80
Shortbread	88
ROOT VEGETABLES	
Potato (instant)	120
Potato (mashed)	98
Potato (new/white, boiled)	80
Potato (russet, baked)	118
Potato (sweet)	70
Yam	74
LEGUMES	
Baked beans (canned)	70
Bengal gram dal	12
Butter beans	46
Chickpeas (dried)	47
Chickpeas (canned)	60
Frozen peas	74
Garden peas (frozen)	65
Green peas (canned)	50
Green peas (dried)	65
Haricot beans (white, dried)	54
Kidney beans (dried)	43
Kidney beans (canned)	74
Lentils (green, dried)	36

FOOD	GLYCEMIC INDEX
Lentils (green, canned)	74
Lentils (red, dried)	38
Pinto beans (dried)	80
Pinto beans (canned)	38
Peanuts	15
Soya beans (dried)	20
Soya beans (canned)	22
FRUITS	
Apple	52
Apple juice	45
Banana	84
Grapes	62
Grapefruit	36
Orange	59
Orange juice	71
Peach	40
Pear	47
Plum	34
Raisins	93
SUGARS	
Fructose	26
Glucose	138
Honey	126
Lactose	57
Maltose	152
Sucrose	83
DAIRY PRODUCTS	
Custard	59
Ice cream	69
Skim milk	46
Whole milk	44
Yogurt	52
SNACK FOODS	
Corn chips	99
Potato chips	77

SWEET ALTERNATIVES AND THE GLYCEMIC INDEX — ACTION STEPS

☐ Avoid all artificial, man-made sweeteners.

☐ Chromium, up to nine tablets daily, will minimize sugar cravings.

☐ Reduce your amount of protein per serving if you crave sweets after eating larger amounts of protein. Consume more, smaller servings of protein to minimize this reaction.

☐ Gymnema, up to three tablets daily, minimizes the taste of sugar.

☐ Focus on local honey as a sweetener. The herb stevia can also be used. We use Fruit Sweet™ when we bake, which is infrequently.

☐ Read all labels. Evaporated cane juice, raw sugar, and organic crystals are still sugar.

NOTES _____

_____

_____

_____

_____

_____

_____

_____

_____

_____

_____

PATIENT TESTIMONY:

"When I first came to see Dr. DeMaria, I had been dealing with minor hot flashes that caused me to break out in sweats during the day. I also had a low thyroid and adult acne. I cut back on my sugar consumption (which was the most difficult) and started to take supplements for my thyroid. The information and care provided by Dr. Bob have improved my life. I have less pain and fewer breakouts on my face."

Maria Gilmore

Chapter 24

Achieving Your Normal Weight Naturally!

A ttaining one's optimal weight in today's fast-paced world appears eternally elusive. There always seems to be another book or magazine article suggesting that if you eat this food and/or avoid that one, your pounds will magically slip away, never to return. How many times have you been down that road?

Over my career, I have seen countless people in the same boat, gaining and losing hundreds of pounds. It does not have to get harder as you get older. I have helped lots of patients lose weight and keep it off. The key is to allow the body to heal itself; then watch the pounds melt away naturally. There is no magic bullet, just natural healthcare principles that must be followed.

Generally, a consistently obese body that does not respond long-term to selected food avoidance and portion control is an unhealthy system. The body will not allow fat to be released because the fat is being saved for a future time, or the system is so toxic that releasing fat results in a self-destructive response. I have had many patients tell me that they really watch what they eat, and have been disciplined, but the weight just stays. Is that you? So what is up?

The answer is multi-tiered:

1. **A foundation must be built on a solidly functioning hormonal, or endocrine, system.**

2. **The cleansing organs must be detoxified.**

3. **Toxic substances must be avoided.**

I am a student of "body watching"; people come in all shapes and sizes. There are various visible patterns of fat distribution on the bodies of people who have organs that are toxic, overloaded, and burned out.

Some carry their weight all over the body, which suggests thyroid-gland distress. These individuals may have cold hands and feet, high cholesterol, constipation, and some of the other body signals discussed in Chapter 7. They may have small, cherry-like nodules on their skin (cherry hemangiomas), suggesting estrogen saturation.

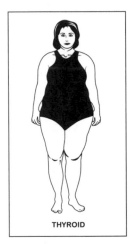

THYROID

Exposure to damaging chemicals used in food production and household goods is a common contributor to thyroid distress. Xenohormones, found in cleaning products, aerosols, lotions, fabrics, paints, and many other common domestic items, are a part of a toxic chain that interferes with normal hormone function. Elevated estrogen levels, whether natural or due to chemicals, impair thyroid function and congest the liver/gallbladder relationship, resulting in stagnant gallbladder bile flow.

When the thyroid is hampered in doing its work, you will see overall weight gain. That is why consuming conventionally sourced animal products containing synthetic estrogen to "fatten" the animal tissue has created an enormous challenge for unsuspecting consumers. Clean machines (such as your body) always work better with the least amount of outside chemicals.

Chlorine in the shower, fluorine in tap water, and bromine in a pool or hot tub create an extra toxic burden on the body and the liver/gallbladder detoxification system, as they compete with iodine receptors. Iodine deficiencies are common in our general dietary food patterns and compound the entire situation. The result is a full figure, or the thyroid body type.

Stress, whether emotional or physical, affects an organ in the body called the adrenal gland, as discussed previously. The adrenal gland supplies many critical hormones for our existence; one is called cortisol (cortisone).

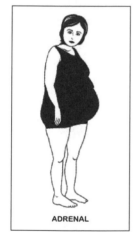

ADRENAL

When you are under stress, your cortisol levels are up, and your body tends to convert carbohydrates (cookies, pasta, grain snacks, doughnuts, etc.) to FAT. What is significant is that eating "naked sweets" (items that are strictly carbohydrates or refined-grain products with sugar added but no protein to slow down the burn process) will result in the release of cortisol in a negative feedback loop to stop the rampage of insulin that is simultaneously secreted by the pancreas. Patients who are stressed and eat a lot of carbohydrates and stimulants tend to carry more of their extra tissue as a "spare tire" around the waist—the adrenal pattern.

The intentional or unknowing consumption of toxic food and drink, including artificial sweeteners, taste enhancers, preservatives, and even prescription medications, can overload the very important liver detoxification system. Your liver has many job descriptions. A key function of the liver is to dispose of unwanted and unnecessary substances. Someone who has a huge, protruding belly with "Humpty Dumpty" beanpole legs generally has a liver that has expanded, is in a compromised state, and is currently not working to its full potential. Fat and fluid are hanging over the belt.

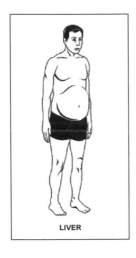

LIVER

A person with this body type will require real discipline, because addictive choices have created his or her downwardly spiraling state of health.

Another body shape, which occurs in females at any age after the secondary sexual characteristics appear, consists of tissue accumulation along the outer thighs and possibly on the buttocks. This shape, which reflects estrogen saturation, is called the gonadal or ovary type. Ovarian malfunction can precipitate this shape. When you do not have enough iodine, your ovaries will not make enough progesterone to balance estrogen. I have also noticed that patients who come into the office with "saddle bags" tend to have liver-congestion issues, which result in unprocessed estrogen. They may have skin eruptions including psoriasis, gallbladder symptoms aggravated by eating fatty or greasy foods, and even high liver enzymes. Liver function is further compromised by eating an overload of carbohydrates.

OVARY

The real challenge is that you can have a combination of body types due to hormonal miscues along with over-consumption of sweets, lack of exercise, and toxic reservoirs.

Let me describe a common picture. A female may have the gonadal pattern, with the initial layers of fat being laid down along the thighs; then, as the addiction to carbohydrates and sweets becomes ravenous, additional fat cells are deposited on and along the buttocks. The patient is now contending with a hormonally initiated addiction to sweets.

An area that is not often talked about is the fact that fat cells can create estrogen. This is a double-edged sword for the general population, because today we are dealing with unprecedented amounts of fake estrogens, or xenohormones, which mimic estrogen and stress the liver/gallbladder. Estrogen dominance creates havoc in the body and taxes the liver. You need the liver to process the hormones in the body. The alteration of this loop escalates the dilemma of fat accumulation.

An exhausted system, with hormonal depletion, organ congestion and toxification, and a general overall state of poor health, will not reduce excess fat until it is healthy. If you are struggling with excess fat, you need to become healthy and not start another fad diet; otherwise, you will be chasing a state that is not attainable. Now, you cannot get impatient, and you do not want to get caught up in the "moderation" style of eating. No cookies means NO cookies, even small ones. I don't care how healthy they are. The carbohydrates in them will throw a wrench into your system.

The answer to your problem starts with normalizing your body's hormonal system. If you do not restart that loop, you will not achieve your optimal health; therefore, you will not lose weight permanently.

The hypothalamus, the chief executive officer of the body, tells the rest of the body what to do. It connects the emotional and physical aspects of a person. I have seen from experience that it can take anywhere from six months to a year to refuel and restart the hormone loop. If you have had your gallbladder removed, it will take longer because the liver has been compromised, and the liver is the hormone recycle depot.

To build a foundation for pituitary function, I start with the following supplement protocol for supporting and restructuring the overall hormonal system (pituitary, thyroid, adrenals, and ovary or testes): I use glandular products to support brain and male and female hormone function, usually three of each product. I have also found

---

that most people who need to lose weight require a full-spectrum oil. That is why I like black currant oil. I encourage this support to be used for a minimum of three months.

I also suggest that you follow the Page Food Plan, outlined in Chapter 20, as a template for what to eat and what not to eat. Avoid any processed food item that has the potential to stress the Phase I and II liver-detoxification process. I would focus on eating cruciferous vegetables: broccoli, cabbage, cauliflower, Brussels sprouts, and kale. They are best consumed raw, steamed, or sautéed in olive or coconut oil. You should add a whole-food iodine product, starting with a minimum of three milligrams a day, if you are focusing on cruciferous vegetables. I would recommend that you fill out the "Symptom Survey" and "Toxicity Questionnaire" in the Appendix, to be used as a benchmark, and then fill them out again at the end of the program.

How do you know when you have a proper hormonal balance? Well, an objective approach would be to do a hair tissue mineral analysis and look at the selenium level, which tends to be low with a stressed pituitary. Check your TSH, T3, and T4 before you start the process; a low TSH is often associated with a stressed pituitary. We add a whole-food vitamin E, a minimum of three daily, to increase selenium levels. Also, if you start to see browning of your skin, this is a signal that your pituitary gland and liver do not have enough whole-food E. The liver has everything to do with skin lesions. Do not use synthetic vitamin E.

In our practice, we have access to a tool called the acoustic cardiogram. It translates sound energy, made by the closing of heart valves, into a mechanical graph. Various patterns can be observed. If we see minimal graph sounds, it indicates a stressed hormonal system. Refer to Chapter 15 for more details and for the location of a practitioner near you.

For one month, we have our patients go on a detoxification program focused on limited foods, with a colon cleanse and green food (food that is green). Green food is necessary for promoting whole-body purification. The plan for the month includes protein, Gastro-Fiber®, green food, and a colon cleanser.

Upon completing the one-month cleanse and having your hormones pointed in the right direction, I assess the needs of your major hormonal organs. Often, more than one hormonal organ needs help. Review Chapters 7 and 8, on thyroid and adrenal health, respectively. You need to follow the protocols in those chapters.

An important step is to rate the function of the hypothalamus and pituitary. These areas in the body are not generally monitored. A subtle way to stay on track is periodically to check your selenium level through hair analysis, and your serum TSH in the thyroid panel. Support your system with what you have learned. You may need to stay on the products discussed in this chapter because you may not be able to change your lifestyle and will need to continue to support all of your endocrine organs. The supplements I use have never caused any body signals of toxic accumulation. I have successfully used them since the early 1970s as a patient and as a natural health doctor.

Here are a couple of points. I generally have to supplement a patient's desire for sweet items. This is a HUGE challenge. Those "innocent" morsels have a cumulative effect that tends to settle in the region of the buttocks and thighs. We really encourage taking a whole-food chromium supplement (up to nine daily). Chromium helps cool the craving for sugar. Also, gymnema, up to three tablets a day, will diminish the taste of sweets. We also use a whole-food bile salt that helps take away the passion for sweets.

I would direct you to Chapter 6, on liver function, and Chapter 17, on cleansing, and suggest that you follow the protocols to clean your "machine." This is essential for long-term success in maintaining your ideal weight.

For long-term success, you will want to monitor your saliva pH. A patient who is acid will tend to be more toxic, with a greater burden on the whole system—which will postpone weight reduction. This may be an issue for some since it is easier to stay in an acid state, because normal cell metabolism, stress, and acid-ash foods create an acid condition.

The glycemic values of foods need to be considered for long-term weight management. I have included a simple glycemic chart starting on page 275. Focus on foods in the 50-to-80 range. As a side note, even though the foods you consume are in the mid-range, do not go overboard and eat a lot of them. They still have calories. I would avoid the foods in the higher range because they will stimulate insulin release, which is the last fire you want turned on if you want to stay at your ideal weight.

Taking flax oil, one tablespoon per one hundred pounds of body weight, and avoiding foods that cause inflammation (like sugar, dairy, and trans fat), will help your body stay in a healthier state. Inflammation that can be detected through a boggy or spongy wrist usually suggests that the intestines may be acting like a sieve, with undigested protein particles flowing through the intestinal lining. These create havoc with the immune system and cause the whole body to be on alert, holding onto water to keep the particles in solution. I recommend coconut oil as a cooking medium and as a butter replacement. Coconut oil creates normal hormone function, which helps burn additional fat in the body.

Trans fat, statistically, when it has been studied and monitored, will actually increase your weight over time. Test animals that are fed trans fat have up to a 7 percent increase in weight compared to other research participants ("Six Years of Fast-Food Fats Super-sizes Monkeys," *New Scientist*, June 2006). Therefore, the claims that the low-fat (trans-fat) diet is healthy and a way to lose weight are actually wrong.

By following the protocols you have learned throughout the book, your overall system will be working in harmony. Your challenge, as the maestro, is to control the desire for sugar, which releases insulin—which crescendos into cortisol release. By far, two of the most significant pieces of advice I can leave you with are **do not eat sugar** and **avoid foods that have chemicals added**. Your body has to process each of these chemicals and looks at the man-tampered ones as foreign invaders. You will have more challenges managing your weight if you eat synthetic ingredients.

I see so many people today who are extremely overweight, to the point that they can hardly walk, and I don't want you to become one or remain one. If you want to be successful, your focus is to do the following:

♂ **Eat less, eat right (fiber-based veggies and protein).**

♂ **Avoid trans fat, which in itself causes extra weight.**

♂ **Drink adequate water.**

♂ **Avoid all grains and alcohol (including wine).**

♂ **Maintain sufficient exercise and sleep patterns.**

♂ **Avoid stress and overcommitments.**

PATIENT TESTIMONY:

"I met Dr. Bob in 1984, after I fell on my buttocks on a slippery rock. My mother convinced me to go see Dr. Bob, and he has been monitoring and treating me ever since. Recently, my feet and legs were swelling and I was just miserable, so rather than go to my family physician who would only suggest more medication, I decided to discuss it with Dr. Bob. I made an appointment and brought all of my medications and supplements in and asked him what to do. Dr. Bob was pretty blunt in his approach, but he told me that if I didn't do something now, I wouldn't be around much longer to do anything at all.

Dr. Bob told me to use the Page Food Plan and explained which supplements I should take to get me and my congested liver back on track. Immediately, I started shopping for organic vegetables and meat to eat, doing liver cleanses two to three times per week, also a colonic and getting lymphatic massages. The change from the food that I was routinely consuming to fundamental organic foods has helped me to lose more than 33 pounds in less than 12 weeks. The best part of this story, though, is that I am not hungry. By eating smaller amounts of food more frequently, I really keep my hunger to a minimum. A lifestyle change like this is normally quite difficult, but I am hopeful that the Page Food Plan, chiropractic care, lymphatic massages, and herbal supplements will help me keep the weight off permanently while continuing to improve my health."

Terri L. Osborn

THE BODY TYPE QUIZ!

IDENTIFYING YOUR BODY TYPE

Before you take the quiz, your answers to several questions up front will quickly tell you if your liver and gallbladder are involved. If the answer to any of these questions is yes, you may want to read Chapter 6, on the liver, and focus on cleansing and on eating items according to the Page Food Plan.

Again, if you ANSWER YES TO ANY of the seven questions below, you need foods that support the liver. You would do best eating Dr. Bob's ABCs, and initiating castor-oil packs. You do not need to go through the quiz—you already have your answer. Taking a bile salt–based, whole-food product should be a part of your daily protocol with gallbladder removal.

☐ **Have you had your gallbladder removed?**

☐ **Do you have a history of gallstones?**

☐ **Can you not lose weight on high-protein diets (e.g., Atkins)?**

☐ **Do you dislike consuming lots of heavy, protein-type foods?**

☐ **Are you unable to digest fatty or greasy foods, especially at night?**

☐ **Do you have a history of liver problems?**

☐ **Do you have a protruding, distended belly (potbelly)?**

DIRECTIONS

Circle one letter (A, B, C, or D) for each question below.
If you are experiencing more than one symptom related to a
particular question, circle the one that is most prominent.
If you are experiencing none of the symptoms for a given
question, leave that question blank.

1. Do you...	A. crave sweets, breads, and pasta? B. crave salt (pretzels, cheese puffs, or salty peanuts) or chocolate? C. crave deep-fried foods or potato chips? D. crave ice cream, cream cheese, sour cream, or milk?
2. Are you...	A. often depressed or feeling hopeless? B. a worrier or often anxious and nervous? C. irritable, moody, or grouchy in the morning? D. moody or irritable at certain times of the month?
3. Do you...	A. feel better on fruits and berries? B. need coffee or stimulants to wake up? C. experience a tight feeling over your right, lower stomach area or rib cage? D. experience constipation during menstruation?
4. Do you have...	A. brittle nails with vertical ridges? B. facial hair as a female? C. pain/tightness in your right shoulder area? D. pain in your right or left lower back/hip area?
5. Do you have...	A. a weight problem more evenly distributed? B. a pendulous abdomen, meaning it is hanging, sagging, and loose? C. a protruding abdomen (potbelly)? D. excess fat on your thighs and hips (saddlebags) and a lower stomach bulge?
6. Do you have...	A. dry skin, especially on your hands and around your elbows? B. swollen ankles, such that socks leave creases on your ankles? C. flaky skin or dandruff on your eyebrows and scalp? D. cyclical menstrual hair loss?
7. Do you have...	A. indentations on both sides of your tongue where the tongue meets the teeth? B. atrophy (shrinkage) of your thigh muscles, with difficulty getting up from a seated position? C. dark yellow urine? D. hot flashes or a history of bad menstruation?

8. Do you have...	A. a loss of hair on the outer third of your eyebrows? B. dizziness when getting up too quickly? C. hot or swollen feet? D. cyclical menstrual brain fog?
9. Do you have...	A. to sleep with socks on at night because of feeling cold? B. chronic inflammation in the body? C. headaches or a heavy-feeling head in the morning? D. excessive menstrual bleeding?
10. Do you have...	A. puffiness around your eyes? B. an unusual feeling of being "out of breath" while climbing stairs? C. skin problems (psoriasis, eczema, brown spots)? D. low sex drive?
11. Are you or do you have...	A. excessive skin sagging under your arms? B. twitching under or on top of your left eyelid? C. not a morning person, and you feel more awake at night? D. weight gain one week before your menstrual period?
12. Do you...	A. have dry hair and hair loss? B. wake up in the middle of the night (2:00 to 3:00 a.m.)? C. have a deep crevice (the appearance of a deep crease) down the center of your tongue and/or a white film on your tongue? D. have an upper body that is thinner than your lower body?
13. Do you experience...	A. not being able to maintain curls in your hair after using a curling iron? B. cramps in your calves at night? C. more itching at night? D. water retention at certain times of the month?
14. Do you...	A. become excessively tired in the early evening (7:30 to 8:00 p.m.) and you are more awake in the early morning? B. have a more active bladder at night than during the day? C. have a yellow tint to the whites of your eyes? D. have a history of ovarian or breast cysts?
15. Do you have...	A. a lack of get-up-and-go (vitality)? B. calcium issues or deposits (bursitis, tendonitis, kidney stones, heal spurs, early cataracts)? C. major moodiness if you skip a meal? D. difficulty losing weight after pregnancy?
16. Do you have...	A. a history of being on low-calorie diets? B. low tolerance for stressful situations, getting easily irritable and on edge? C. stiffness and pain more in your right shoulder and right side of your neck? D. pain and tightness in one knee, which is worse during the menstrual cycle?

Count up the total for each letter:

Total A (Thyroid) _____   **Total B (Adrenal)** _____

Total C (Liver) _____   **Total D (Ovary)** _____

Weight loss is probably one of the biggest challenges facing our society today. I have seen wonderful results by focusing on improving the hypothalamus and pituitary foundation pillar of hormonal health. I consistently see patients who come into the office under stress, with signals of diminished pituitary function. Hair analysis, the symptom survey, and thyroid function tests (including TSH values) have been effective tools in helping me monitor and improve body function for my patients. We have had patients who never lost weight before see the weight melt away because supplementation and lifestyle modifications create normal functioning of the brain-to-body mechanism. The brain is capable of sending the messages that the body needs to function optimally.

NOTES _____

_____

_____

_____

_____

_____

_____

The basic information in this chapter has been taken from *The 7 Principles of Fat Burning: Get Healthy, Lose Weight and Keep It Off!*, by Eric E. Berg, DC.

PART V

CONCLUDING
THOUGHTS

Chapter 25

Finishing
the Puzzle

Way to go! This is the beginning of your journey. You can now end the chapter in your life of less-than-optimal hormonal health, by changing your paradigm. I suggest that you evaluate everything you have been exposed to in this book. You should have learned that your body needs to be fed the right whole foods. It desires to be hydrated with water from a pure source; to be exercised on a regular basis to maintain structural integrity; to have consistent, uninterrupted communication from brain cells to tissue cells; and to have the least possible exposure to outside toxins, whether from food, drink, water, or external applications to your body.

You have read a bunch of new information, and maybe some of it has stretched you a bit. You may even be angry. I have a lot of new patients who respond with anger when they learn the facts. They are angry because they have been given the wrong information and have allowed their precious organs to be removed. The knowledge you have gained will support the structures you have remaining. I do not want you to think I am suggesting that your body can recreate organs; of course, it cannot. I have had patients who thought their gallbladder would grow back. It will not. You need to support the liver if your gallbladder has been removed, so it will have the proper flow of bile (which should trickle at an uninterrupted rate).

Cells in the body have the ability to create what the body needs. Not all of this is clearly understood; science does not have the answer to everything. You may not function at the level you did prior to surgery, but I have had patients achieve some pretty amazing improvements in body signals by eating the right foods and detoxifying the remaining tissue.

Something I would like to touch on is the fact that if you had surgery, and your symptoms abated, you need to figure out why your system failed in the first place. You have to ask yourself, "Why did the organ respond in such a way?" For example, heavy menstrual flow more than likely suggests estrogen dominance. If you had ablation or a hysterectomy, you still have the potential to be in a state of estrogen saturation. As another example, if you had your gallbladder removed and did not change anything else, your liver is still producing thick, pasty bile. You need to restore a healthier environment in order for your body ultimately to work.

Do not be misled by well-meaning friends. I am serious about this. I have had many conversations with patients, family members, and friends who say that their associates and acquaintances think they have gone nuts. Others may not be able to figure out why you are now eating apples, beets, and carrots. These same critics don't think there is anything wrong with having a doughnut or pastry for breakfast. They cannot understand why you are now drinking water instead of "energy drinks." God forbid you should admit that you have decided to avoid liver-stressing alcohol.

You have read many sets of "Action Steps." I would start by assessing what you are eating. Focus on eating whole food, as I have said throughout the book. It's a mantra that you will be thankful you chose to live by.

Jan Roberts is a pharmacist and clinical nutritionist in Australia and New Zealand, and the author of several books. She says, in her article "Addressing Menopause Naturally," in the March 2007 issue of *To Your Health*, "Women will seek out the products that best support their own efforts and address their core or foundation health." What exactly is "core or foundation health," and what are these self-help efforts?

First of all, women should know that all of the hormones, neurotransmitters, endorphins, and other factors that can reduce menopausal symptoms depend on an adequate supply of vitamins, minerals, amino acids, and essential fatty acids. These building blocks come from, or have precursors in, the foods and drinks women consume. Unfortunately, most modern diets are unlikely to supply an adequate complement of these building blocks. That is why it is critical for you to make the changes necessary to guarantee long-term benefits. You need to seek out the items mentioned in the Page Food Plan (Chapter 20) and food transition guide (Chapter 21). The food is out there, but you will not find it in a cellophane package or at a fast-food or franchise restaurant.

The conventional medical community has not entirely correlated health issues to food yet. I want you to understand that a good portion of your health issues are directly related to what you have done to yourself. It is critical for you to change what you have done up to this point. This is a HUGE key to your long-term health.

I would not suggest that you go out and start eating a whole bunch of vitamins. Taking vitamins, especially synthetic ones, may create more of a challenge than your body can handle.

You do not want to go off your medication without having a consultation with a skilled healthcare provider who has the experience to walk you through restoration steps. You need to focus on feeding your adrenal glands, thyroid gland, ovaries, and liver the whole-food vitamins and minerals they need to function fully, at optimal levels.

I would also—and this will be a challenge but it can be done—avoid soy and wheat products. They both diminish zinc in your body.

Also, soy, when studied, most often comes from genetically modified sources and is processed so much that by the time it gets to
your plate, it is nearly useless nutritionally. I know this may be the
opposite of what you are hearing. However, for many years, everyone was told to use the low-fat, no-fat, trans-fat diet. Where did
that get everyone? Soy has a natural affinity to aluminum and has
antitrypsin characteristics. Wheat, with its gluten, causes the villi in
the intestine to stick together. This will limit mineral absorption and
alter the entire system.

Review the Food Transition Chart in Chapter 21, and the Page
Food Plan in Chapter 20. Identify what you are eating now that
would be best to change. Do not throw out any food in your house.
Use logic. If you have kids, go slowly.

Okay, you are on your way. Don't be anxious; give yourself some
time. Slowly start incorporating what you have learned. It will get
better, I promise. I have seen it happen so many times before. It is
naturally right...

NOTES _____

_____

_____

_____

_____

_____

_____

Chapter 26

Bonus Chapter: Balancing Male Hormones

In my practice, I also address issues concerning male health. I would like to very briefly discuss a few common male health concerns, which may help you, as a woman, understand what is going on with the men in your life. The balance of hormones in the male body is not as intricate as that in the female body. The primary concern for men relates to the cholesterol-originating chart in Chapter 8. Testosterone can be sourced from cholesterol like the other steroid hormones. Review the information I have presented about the adrenal glands, liver activity, and diet. When men have stress in their daily lives, they will have impaired adrenal function, with all the nutrients for cellular function being used to make cortisone to handle the stress and very little left over to make testosterone. Men, in the deficiency mode, lose their desire for sexual intimacy; that is, they can have a decreased libido. I see this commonly on the symptom survey form I use in my office when initiating a whole-body assessment. A lack of sexual desire coincides with a run-down endocrine, or hormonal, system. It is as if the spark plugs do not have any fuel to spark. The way the body is operating, the nutrients needed to encourage sexual arousal are being used for survival.

The most challenging patients I treat and educate are males between the ages of 25 and 45. These individuals still think they have the testosterone and ability of a 19-year-old, but in actuality, most have the body of a 55-year-old. These men are at the point in their lives where work can be very challenging. Many financial responsibilities arise, such as college tuition, a mortgage, and "toy" payments (e.g., for a boat, vacation house, or club fees).

The weekly diet journals recorded by my male patients are anything but nutritional. Eating on the run and going out with buddies for a night or a weekend do anything but promote a healthy waistline. Cholesterol runs high with this type of lifestyle; the serum readings are near the price of gasoline. Your man just does not feel well.

Work pressures and a fear of the unknown generate far too many demands on a man's physiology. Before he knows it, a man has prescriptions for blood pressure and cholesterol medications, a "mild" antidepressant, and a pill to promote an erection. Sound too far out? Not really. I have consultations like this consistently. This individual needs to eat the foods suggested in Chapter 20, about the Page Food Plan, as well as follow everything that you are doing. If not, he will suffer from a loss of sexual desire and poor overall health. There was an article in the *Wall Street Journal* on May 12–13, 2007, entitled, "Is Your Wife Pushing You to See a Doctor? Read This—and Go." The subtitle of the article contains some very important information: "Doctors say wives are in a unique position to persuade their husbands to seek medical care. Because erectile function is an important barometer of a man's health."

I want to describe the physiology of male hormones. I will attempt to keep it simple. Read slowly, and I know you will get a better idea of what is going on. Male hormones are called androgens. *Androgen* is the generic term for any natural or synthetic compound, usually a steroid hormone, that stimulates or controls the development and maintenance of masculine characteristics in vertebrates by binding to androgen receptors. This includes the activity of the accessory male sex organs and development of male secondary sex characteristics. Androgens, which were first discovered in 1936, are also called androgenic hormones, or testoids. Androgens are also the original anabolic steroids. In addition, they are the precursor of all estrogens, the female sex hormones. The primary and most well-known androgen is testosterone.

Testosterone is a steroid hormone from the androgen group. It is primarily secreted in the testes of males and the ovaries of females, although small amounts are secreted by the adrenal glands. Testosterone is the principal male sex hormone and an anabolic steroid. In both males and females, it plays key roles in health and well-being. Examples of the benefits of testosterone include enhanced libido, energy, and immune function, and protection against osteoporosis.

On average, the adult male body produces about 20 to 30 times the amount of testosterone that the adult female body does. The human hormone estrogen is produced in greater amounts by females, lesser amounts by males. Testosterone causes the appearance of masculine traits, e.g., deepening voice, pubic and facial hair, muscular build, etc. Like men, women rely on testosterone to maintain libido, bone density, and muscle mass throughout their lives. Men rely on estrogens to protect them from prostate cancer.

A subset of androgens is adrenal androgens, which include any of the steroids synthesized by the adrenal cortex (the outer portion of the adrenal gland). These function as weak steroids, or steroid precursors, and include dehydroepiandrosterone (DHEA). DHEA is a steroid hormone produced from cholesterol in the adrenal cortex. It is the primary precursor of the natural estrogen androstenedione (andro), an androgenic steroid produced by the testes, adrenal cortex, and ovaries. While androstenedione is converted metabolically to testosterone and other androgens, it is also the parent structure of estrone. Use of androstenedione as an athletic or body-building supplement has been banned by the International Olympic Committee as well as other sporting organizations.

From my continued observation, men would do best to limit their stress, which I know is easier said than done. I stopped doing most extracurricular activities when I was helping to raise our sons. I did not want to burn out my adrenal glands. Optimal health is about prioritizing. Men also need to minimize their consumption of sugar. Sugar, by far, is a leading cause of poor health.

Furthermore, as a family, we lived within our budget. Please remember this saying: "Your earning power does not ever satisfy your yearning desire." Try to minimize your consumption desire. You won't have to work so hard, which means less stress. Financial concerns are one of the leading causes of divorce in America. One of the purposes of this book was to prevent family issues, including divorce.

I want to share with you a few secret weapons so you can protect yourself and the men in your life. Men need iodine, just like women do. I personally supplement myself with up to 12 milligrams of iodine a day. If you have dry eyes, iodine may help. Men who have prostate swelling and/or elevated PSA readings will be pleasantly surprised when those levels go down over time with iodine. I encourage a regular supply of Celtic Sea Salt®, a great source of iodine. I always suggest some type of assessment to determine iodine function; good markers would include T3, T4, and TSH. Urine iodine levels are also helpful. I make recommendations based on test results.

Men and women need to check their torso, legs, and arms for small, raised, cherry-red, bead-like bumps, officially called "cherry hemangiomas." An abundance of these little bumps is a possible sign of estrogen saturation. When men have too much estrogen, they can have prostate issues. A leading factor that increases estrogen in the body is eating conventional versus organic meat. I know that budgets can be limited; however, organic meats are worth saving for.

Both men and women can be impacted by a deficiency of zinc. I generally see diminished senses of taste and smell in those who need zinc. Eating wheat and soy products will deplete zinc, as will sugar and stress. Memory loss, slow healing, white spots on the nails, and impaired insulin function can be precipitated by a zinc deficiency. Men need zinc for the prostate to function—this is critical. You may want to do the zinc taste test, described in Chapter 15, to identify any potential issue with zinc.

Men are impacted by blood sugar and adrenal levels, which are a part of the human hormonal system. The rules for thyroid function also apply to men. Men need to have a balance in all areas to function well, just as women do. The natural principles apply to both males and females. Before I give you some final tips, I want you to review the insightful information presented in this chapter so far.

Men experience andropause, sometimes called "male menopause," typically between the ages of 45 and 55. This information will give you some insight into the issues males contend with.

ANDROPAUSE

♂ Andropause is defined as the loss of androgen dominance in men.

♂ Andropause is caused by functional imbalances in the male hormone pathway wherein free testosterone declines 1 to 2 percent yearly while sex hormone–binding globulin gradually elevates, compensating for testosterone decline.

♂ Testosterone is made from cholesterol and plays an important role in supporting the thyroid and healthy triglycerides and cholesterol; statin drugs (used to lower cholesterol) are shown to reduce testosterone.

♂ Symptoms of andropause may include mood swings; depression; pessimism; asthenia; myasthenia; insulin resistance; hypertension; mid-body fat gain; dysglycemia; loss of libido; erectile dysfunction; osteoporosis; prostate/ urinary problems; and thin, dry skin.

ANDROPAUSE VS. MENOPAUSE

ANDROPAUSE	MENOPAUSE
☐ Testosterone reduction	☐ Estrogen reduction
☐ Body fat increase	☐ Body fat increase
☐ Overall health depletion	☐ Overall health depletion
☐ Osteoporosis increase	☐ Osteoporosis increase
☐ Cardiovascular disease increase	☐ Cardiovascular disease increase
☐ Prostate cancer increase	☐ Breast cancer increase

BALANCING MALE HORMONES — ACTION STEPS

☐ For optimal testosterone levels, reduce stress and eat no sugar.

☐ Men need to have their adrenal and thyroid function up to par to have optimal health.

☐ Focus on eating protein and veggies, versus carbohydrates and sweets (which stress adrenal function).

☐ Have hair analysis done; if it shows a zinc deficiency, treat accordingly. Avoid wheat and soy if your zinc levels are low.

☐ Taking a quality source of omega-3 oil, one tablespoon a day per one hundred pounds of body weight, is a good regimen to follow for optimal hormonal health.

☐ I commonly suggest a protocol for male patients that includes glandular support for the testes (for which I use an orchic glandular), pituitary, and adrenals. It is wise to take some type of liver support, flax oil, and iodine. I like all patients to be tested for vitamin D prior to taking a supplement. I also like our patients to take a full-spectrum oil like black currant seed capsules. It is good to take folic acid and B12, which help the creation of adequately sized red blood cells. I follow a protocol like this, which helps keep my endocrine system at a level of optimal health.

☐ I stopped consuming alcohol many years ago. I used to have a lot of cherry hemangiomas; I now have one or two. Men need to read Chapter 6, on the liver.

☐ You would do best to show this book to the men in your life so they will have a better understanding of women. Female hormones are quite an intense puzzle and need more than a magic pill for restoration. It is a team effort.

☐ I have observed that many men today have enlarged breast tissue, or "man breasts." This condition often is associated with the conversion of testosterone into estrogen. I use a specific product to assist the body in stopping this process. This enzyme-imbalance issue is quite common, even in adolescent males.

NOTES _____

_____

_____

_____

_____

_____

_____

_____

_____

Final
Thoughts

Okay, this is it! I pray the information you have learned from these pages has impacted your life and permitted you to become the captain of your own ship. The course that I have plotted for you may not seem easy at first, but trust me: Take baby steps, do not leave any out, and you will be on top of the world without unnecessary surgery. This book is good for the whole family. You will want to talk to both your male and female children and grandchildren. The game of life is very serious and has a lot of snares that can trap you into a false sense of security. Prescription medication has saved a lot of lives; I am not denying that, but it has also created a lot of permanent injury, including premature death. To get what you have never had before, you must do what you have never done before. Be brave; be the first one in your circle of friends and family to make a difference. It is a matter of life and death. The world is waiting, and time is quickly running out.

Be Blessed

Dr. Bob DeMaria
America's Drugless Doctor

APPENDIX

The following assessment is also available at
www.druglessdoctor.com.
When completing the assessment online,
you will receive a complete, computer-generated
report that is uncannily accurate and helps create
strategies for addressing common health challenges;
or you can follow the directions in step 8.

DIRECTIONS FOR THE
SYMPTOM SURVEY

1. Fill in the date and your name, age, surgeries, medications, and supplements.

2. Place an X in any and all boxes next to symptoms you have on a daily basis only.

3. Complete the Barnes Thyroid Test at the bottom of the third page (even if you do not have a thyroid problem).

4. Write down everything you eat/drink for one week. List any symptoms you may have at the bottom.

5. Have your blood pressure taken sitting, and then immediately standing. Record it.

6. Have your pulse taken sitting, and then standing. Record it.

7. Complete the Thyroid Patch Test.

8. You have a couple of options: You can take the form to your natural healthcare provider and/or make an appointment for a phone consultation with Dr. Bob or one of his associates to discuss your state of health. For details, visit www.druglessdoctor.com.

SYMPTOM SURVEY

NAME:_____AGE:_____DATE:_____

SURGERIES: _____

MEDICATIONS: _____

SUPPLEMENTS: _____

(If necessary, attach an additional sheet.)

Instructions:

Place an *X* by the symptoms that you notice on a daily basis.

GROUP ONE

❏ Acid foods upset	❏ Gag easily	❏ Appetite reduced
❏ Get chilled often	❏ Unable to relax, startle easily	❏ Cold sweats often
❏ "Lump" in throat	❏ Extremities cold, clammy	❏ Fever easily raised
❏ Dry mouth, eyes, nose	❏ Strong light irritates	❏ Neuralgia-like pains
❏ Pulse speeds after meal	❏ Urine amount reduced	❏ Staring, blink little
❏ Keyed up, fail to calm	❏ Heart pounds after retiring	❏ Sour stomach frequent
❏ Cuts heal slowly	❏ "Nervous" stomach	

GROUP TWO

❏ Joint stiffness after arising	❏ Always seem hungry, feel "lightheaded" often	❏ Constipation, diarrhea alternating
❏ Muscle, leg, toe cramps at night	❏ Digestion rapid	❏ "Slow starter"
❏ "Butterfly" stomach, cramps	❏ Vomiting frequent	❏ Get "chilled" infrequently
❏ Eyes or nose watery	❏ Hoarseness frequent	❏ Perspire easily
❏ Eyes blink often	❏ Breathing irregular	❏ Circulation poor. sensitive to cold
❏ Eyelids swollen, puffy	❏ Pulse slow, feels "irregular"	❏ Subject to colds, asthma, bronchitis
❏ Indigestion soon after meals	❏ Gagging reflex slow	
❏ Difficulty swallowing		

GROUP THREE

❏ Eat when nervous	❏ Heart palpitates if meals missed or delayed	❏ Crave candy or coffee in afternoons
❏ Excessive appetite	❏ Afternoon headaches	❏ Moods of depression, "blues," or melancholy
❏ Hungry between meals	❏ Overeating sweets upsets	❏ Abnormal craving for sweets or snacks
❏ Irritable before meals	❏ Awaken after few hours' sleep, hard to get back to sleep	❏ "Lightheaded" if meals delayed
❏ Get "shaky" if hungry		
❏ Fatigue, eating relieves		

GROUP FOUR

❏ Hands and feet go to sleep easily, numbness	❏ Get "drowsy" often	❏ Bruise easily, "black and blue" spots
❏ Sigh frequently, "air hunger"	❏ Swollen ankles, worse at night	❏ Tendency to anemia
❏ Aware of "breathing heavily"	❏ Muscle cramps, worse during exercise; get "charley horses"	❏ Nose bleeds frequent
❏ High altitude discomfort	❏ Shortness of breath on exertion	❏ Noises in head, or "ringing in ears"
❏ Open windows in closed room	❏ Dull pain in chest or radiating into left arm, worse on exertion	❏ Tension under the breastbone, or feeling of "tightness," worse on exertion
❏ Susceptible to colds and fevers	❏ Afternoon "yawner"	

GROUP FIVE

- Dizziness
- Dry skin
- Burning feet
- Blurred vision
- Itching skin and feet
- Excessive hair loss
- Frequent skin rashes
- Bitter, metallic taste in mouth in mornings
- Bowel movements painful or difficult

- Worrier, feel insecure
- Feeling queasy; headache over eyes
- Greasy foods upset
- Stools light-colored
- Skin peels on foot soles
- Pain between shoulder blades
- Use laxatives
- Stools alternate from soft to watery

- History of gallbladder attacks or gallstones
- Sneezing attacks
- Dreaming, nightmare-type bad dreams
- Bad breath (halitosis)
- Milk products cause distress
- Sensitive to hot weather
- Burning or itching anus
- Crave sweets

GROUP SIX

- Loss of taste for meat
- Lower bowel gas several hours after eating
- Burning stomach sensations, eating relieves

- Coated tongue
- Pass large amounts of foul-smelling gas
- Indigestion ½–1 hour after eating; may be up to 3–4 hours

- Mucous colitis or "irritable bowel"
- Gas shortly after eating
- Stomach "bloating" after eating

GROUP SEVEN

(A)
- Insomnia
- Nervousness
- Can't gain weight
- Intolerance to heat
- Highly emotional
- Flush easily
- Night sweats
- Thin, moist skin
- Inward trembling
- Heart palpitates
- Increased appetite without weight gain
- Pulse fast at rest
- Eyelids and face twitch
- Irritable and restless
- Can't work under pressure

(B)
- Increase in weight
- Decrease in appetite
- Fatigue easily
- Ringing in ears
- Sleepy during day
- Sensitive to cold
- Dry or scaly skin
- Constipation
- Mental sluggishness
- Hair coarse, falls out
- Headaches upon arising wear off during day

- Slow pulse, below 65
- Frequency of urination
- Impaired hearing
- Reduced initiative

(C)
- Failing memory
- Low blood pressure
- Increased sex drive
- Headaches, "splitting or rending" type
- Decreased sugar tolerance

(D)
- Abnormal thirst
- Bloating of abdomen
- Weight gain around hips or waist
- Sex drive reduced or lacking
- Tendency to ulcers, colitis
- Increased sugar tolerance
- Women: menstrual disorders
- Young girls: lack of menstrual function

(E)
- Dizziness
- Headaches
- Hot flashes
- Increased blood pressure
- Hair growth on face or body (female)
- Sugar in urine (not diabetes)
- Masculine tendencies (female)

- Hot flashes
- Increased blood pressure
- Hair growth on face or body (female)
- Sugar in urine (not diabetes)
- Masculine tendencies (female)

(F)
- Weakness, dizziness
- Chronic fatigue
- Low blood pressure
- Nails weak, ridged
- Tendency to hives
- Arthritic tendencies
- Perspiration increase
- Bowel disorders
- Poor circulation
- Swollen ankles
- Crave salt
- Brown spots or bronzing of skin
- Allergies, tendency to asthma
- Weakness after colds, influenza
- Exhaustion, muscular and nervous
- Respiratory disorders

GROUP EIGHT

❏ Apprehension	❏ Depression	❏ Nervousness
❏ Irritability	❏ Noise sensitivity	❏ Headache
❏ Morbid fears	❏ Acoustic hallucinations	❏ Insomnia
❏ Never seem to get well	❏ Tendency to cry without reason	❏ Anxiety
❏ Forgetfulness	❏ Hair is coarse and/or thinning	❏ Anorexia
❏ Indigestion	❏ Weakness	❏ Distraction
❏ Poor appetite	❏ Fatigue	❏ Confusion
❏ Craving for sweets	❏ Neuralgia	❏ Dizziness
❏ Muscular soreness	❏ Neuritis	❏ Instability

FEMALES ONLY / MALES ONLY

FEMALES ONLY		MALES ONLY
❏ Very easily fatigued	❏ Menses scanty or missed	❏ Feeling of incomplete bowel evacuation
❏ Premenstrual tension	❏ Acne, worse at menses	❏ Prostate trouble
❏ Painful menses	❏ Depression of long standing	❏ Urination difficult or dribbling
❏ Depressed feelings before menstruation		❏ Night urination frequent
❏ Menstruation excessive and prolonged		❏ Depression
❏ Painful breasts		❏ Pain on inside of legs or heels
❏ Menstruate too frequently		❏ Lack of energy
❏ Vaginal discharge		❏ Migrating aches and pains
❏ Hysterectomy/ovaries removed		❏ Tire too easily
❏ Menopausal hot flashes		❏ Avoid activity
		❏ Leg nervousness at night
		❏ Diminished sex drive

THYROID PATCH TEST

Purchase a small bottle of tincture of iodine and paint a 2 × 2 in. patch at the crease of your elbow or behind your knee. The iodine patch should be seen for 24 hours. If the iodine patch leaves, it is a sign that your body is utilizing and/or absorbing the iodine. Keep track of the hours that the iodine is visible.

_____ **hours**

BARNES THYROID TEST

This test was developed by Dr. Broda Barnes, MD, and is a measurement of the underarm temperature to determine hypothyroid and hyperthyroid states. The test is conducted by the patient in the morning before leaving bed—with the temperature being taken for 10 minutes. The test is invalidated if the patient expends any energy prior to taking the test—getting up for any reason, shaking down the thermometer, etc. It is important that the test be conducted for exactly 10 minutes, making the prior positioning of both the thermometer and a clock important.

PRE-MENSES FEMALES AND MENOPAUSAL FEMALES
Any two days during the month.

FEMALES HAVING MENSTRUAL CYCLES
The second and third days of flow OR any five days in a row.

MALES
Any two days during the month.

You can do the following test at home to see if you may have a functional low thyroid. Use an oral thermometer or a digital one. When you use a digital one, place the probe under your arm for five minutes, and then turn your machine on; continue on for an additional five minutes. When using a regular thermometer, shake down the night before.

DATE: _____ TEMPERATURE: _____

DATE: _____ TEMPERATURE: _____

DATE: _____ TEMPERATURE: _____

DATE: _____ TEMPERATURE: _____

BP SIT _____   BP STAND _____

PULSE SIT _____   PULSE STAND _____

SALIVA PH _____   BLOOD TYPE _____

Patient's Daily Diet Report

Patient's Name: _____

Dates: From _____ **To** _____

(Be *sure* to list all foods and beverages consumed each day of this Diet Report.)

	1st Day	2nd Day	3rd Day	4th Day	5th Day	6th Day	7th Day
Morning Meal							
Noon Meal							
Evening Meal							
Foods and Beverages Used at Other Times							
SYMPTOMS							

TOXICITY QUESTIONNAIRE

Section I: Symptoms

Rate each of the following based upon your health profile for the past 90 days.

Circle the corresponding number.	
0	Rarely or never experience the symptom
1	Occasionally experience the symptom; Effect is not severe
2	Occasionally experience the symptom; Effect is severe
3	Frequently experience the symptom; Effect is not severe
4	Frequently experience the symptom; Effect is severe

1. DIGESTIVE
a. Nausea and/or vomiting	0	1	2	3	4
b. Diarrhea	0	1	2	3	4
c. Constipation	0	1	2	3	4
d. Bloated feeling	0	1	2	3	4
e. Belching and/or passing gas	0	1	2	3	4
f. Heartburn	0	1	2	3	4

Total: _____

2. EARS
a. Itchy ears	0	1	2	3	4
b. Earaches, ear infections	0	1	2	3	4
c. Drainage from ear	0	1	2	3	4
d. Ringing in ears, hearing loss	0	1	2	3	4

Total: _____

3. EMOTIONS
a. Mood swings	0	1	2	3	4
b. Anxiety, fear, nervousness	0	1	2	3	4
c. Anger, irritability	0	1	2	3	4
d. Depression	0	1	2	3	4
e. Sense of despair	0	1	2	3	4
f. Apathy / lethargy	0	1	2	3	4

Total: _____

4. ENERGY / ACTIVITY
a. Fatigue / sluggishness	0	1	2	3	4
b. Hyperactivity	0	1	2	3	4
c. Restlessness	0	1	2	3	4
d. Insomnia	0	1	2	3	4
e. Startled awake at night	0	1	2	3	4

Total: _____

5. EYES
a. Watery, itchy eyes	0	1	2	3	4
b. Swollen, reddened or sticky eyelids	0	1	2	3	4
c. Dark circles under eyes	0	1	2	3	4
d. Blurred / tunnel vision	0	1	2	3	4

Total: _____

6. HEAD
a. Headaches	0	1	2	3	4
b. Faintness	0	1	2	3	4
c. Dizziness	0	1	2	3	4
d. Pressure	0	1	2	3	4

Total: _____

7. LUNGS
a. Chest congestion	0	1	2	3	4
b. Asthma, Bronchitis	0	1	2	3	4
c. Shortness of breath	0	1	2	3	4
d. Difficulty breathing	0	1	2	3	4

Total: _____

8. MIND
a. Poor memory	0	1	2	3	4
b. Confusion	0	1	2	3	4
c. Poor concentration	0	1	2	3	4
d. Poor coordination	0	1	2	3	4
e. Difficulty making decisions	0	1	2	3	4
f. Stuttering, stammering	0	1	2	3	4
g. Slurred speech	0	1	2	3	4
h. Learning disabilities	0	1	2	3	4

Total: _____

Section I: Symptoms

(Continued)

9. MOUTH / THROAT

a. Chronic coughing	0	1	2	3	4
b. Gagging, frequent need to clear throat	0	1	2	3	4
c. Swollen or discolored tongue, gums, lips	0	1	2	3	4
d. Canker sores	0	1	2	3	4

Total: _____

10. NOSE

a. Stuffy nose	0	1	2	3	4
b. Sinus problems	0	1	2	3	4
c. Hay fever	0	1	2	3	4
d. Sneezing attacks	0	1	2	3	4
e. Excessive mucous	0	1	2	3	4

Total: _____

11. SKIN

a. Acne	0	1	2	3	4
b. Hives, rashes, dry skin	0	1	2	3	4
c. Hair loss	0	1	2	3	4
d. Flushing	0	1	2	3	4
e. Excessive sweating	0	1	2	3	4

Total: _____

12. HEART

a. Skipped heartbeats	0	1	2	3	4
b. Rapid heartbeats	0	1	2	3	4
c. Chest pain	0	1	2	3	4

Total: _____

13. JOINTS / MUSCLES

a. Pain or aches in joints	0	1	2	3	4
b. Rheumatoid arthritis	0	1	2	3	4
c. Osteoarthritis	0	1	2	3	4
d. Stiffness, limited movement	0	1	2	3	4
e. Pain, aches in muscles	0	1	2	3	4
f. Recurrent back aches	0	1	2	3	4
g. Feeling of weakness or tiredness	0	1	2	3	4

Total: _____

14. WEIGHT

a. Binge eating / drinking	0	1	2	3	4
b. Craving certain foods	0	1	2	3	4
c. Excessive weight	0	1	2	3	4
d. Compulsive eating	0	1	2	3	4
e. Water retention	0	1	2	3	4
f. Underweight	0	1	2	3	4

Total: _____

15. OTHER

a. Frequent illness	0	1	2	3	4
b. Frequent or urgent urination	0	1	2	3	4
c. Leaky bladder	0	1	2	3	4
d. Genital itch, discharge	0	1	2	3	4

Total: _____

Section I Total: _____

TOXICITY QUESTIONNAIRE

Section II: Risk of Exposure

Rate each of the following situations based upon your environmental profile for the past 120 days.

16.	Circle the corresponding number for questions 16a – 16f below.				
0 Never	**1** Rarely	**2** Monthly	**3** Weekly	**4** Daily	

a. How often are strong chemicals used in your home? (disinfectants, bleaches, oven & drain cleaners, furniture polish, floor wax, window cleaners, etc.)	0 1 2 3 4
b. How often are pesticides used in your home?	0 1 2 3 4
c. How often do you have your home treated for insects?	0 1 2 3 4
d. How often are you exposed to dust, overstuffed furniture, tobacco smoke, mothballs, incense, or varnish in your home or office?	0 1 2 3 4
e. How often are you exposed to nail polish, perfume, hair spray, and other cosmetics?	0 1 2 3 4
f. How often are you exposed to diesel fumes, exhaust fumes, or gasoline fumes?	0 1 2 3 4
	Total: _____

17.	Circle the corresponding number for questions 17a – 17b below.			
0 No	**1** Mild Change	**2** Moderate Change	**3** Drastic Change	

a. Have you noticed any negative change in your health since you moved into your home or apartment?	0 1 2 3
b. Have you noticed any negative change in your health since you started your new job?	0 1 2 3
	Total: _____

18.	Answer "Yes" or "No" and circle the corresponding number for questions 18a – 18d below.	No	Yes
a. Do you have a water purification system in your home?		2	0
b. Do you have any indoor pets?		0	2
c. Do you have an air purification system in your home?		2	0
d. Are you a dentist, painter, farm worker, or construction worker?		0	2
	Total: _____		

Section II Total:	_____

GRAND TOTAL (Section I & Section II)	_____

Add up the numbers to arrive at a total for each section, and then add the totals for each section to arrive at the grand total. If any individual section total is 6 or more, or the Grand Total is 40 or more, you may benefit from a Clinical Purification™ program.

Adapted with permission from Dr. Gina L. Nick, author of *Clinical Purification™: A Complete Treatment and Reference Manual*. Healthcare professionals may obtain complete copies of this book at a professional discount from Standard Process Order Department at 1-800-558-8740. Patients may purchase the book through retail outlets.

ALKALINE-ASH AND ACID-ASH FOOD GROUPS

A	B	C	D	E	F
Most Alkaline	**Alkaline**	**Lowest Alkaline**	**Lowest Acid**	**Acid**	**Most Acid**
Stevia	Maple Syrup, Rice Syrup	Raw Honey, Raw Sugar	Processed Honey, Molasses	White Sugar, Brown Sugar	NutraSweet®, Equal®, Sweet'N Low®
Lemons, Watermelon, Limes, Grapefruit, Mangoes	Dates/Figs, Melons, Grapes, Kiwi, Berries, Apples, Pears, Raisins	Oranges, Bananas, Cherries, Pineapple, Peaches, Avocados	Plums, Papaya, Processed Fruit Juices	Sour Cherries, Rhubarb	Blueberries, Cranberries, Prunes
Asparagus, Onions, Vegetable Juices, Parsley, Raw Spinach, Broccoli, Garlic	Okra, Squash, Green Beans, Beets, Celery, Lettuce, Zucchini, Sweet Potato	Carrots, Tomatoes, Fresh Corn, Mushrooms, Cabbage, Peas, Potato Skins, Olives	Spinach, Kidney Beans, String Beans	Potatoes, Pinto Beans, Navy Beans, Lima Beans	Soybean, Carob
	Almonds	Chestnuts	Pumpkin Seeds, Sunflower Seeds	Pecans, Cashews	Peanuts, Walnuts
Olive Oil	Flax Oil	Canola Oil	Corn Oil		
		Amaranth, Miller, Wild Rice, Quinoa	Sprouted Wheat Bread, Spelt, Brown Rice	White Rice, Corn, Buckwheat, Oats, Rye	Wheat, White Flour, Pastries, Pasta
			Venison, Cold-Water Fish	Turkey, Chicken, Lamb	Pork, Beef, Shellfish
	Breast Milk	Goat Milk, Goat Cheese, Whey	Eggs, Butter/ Yogurt, Buttermilk, Cottage Cheese	Soy Cheese, Raw Milk, Soy Milk	Cheese, Homogenized Milk, Ice Cream
Lemon Water, Herb Teas	Green Tea	Ginger Tea	Tea	Coffee	Beer, Soft Drinks

RECIPES

Beet and Vegetable Recipes

What's great about beets:

✓ One-half cup of cooked beets has a mere 37 calories.

✓ One-half cup of cooked beets has 17 percent of the recommended daily intake (RDI) for folate, plus vitamin C, potassium, and iron.

✓ Beets give you the cancer-fighting antioxidant beta-carotene, plus two grams of healthy fiber.

✓ Beets are naturally sweet but have only seven grams of sugar per half-cup serving.

Buying tips:

✓ Look for firm beets with smooth skin. Smaller ones are usually more tender than larger ones.

✓ Beets range in color from deep golden yellow to crimson and can even be white.

✓ The lighter the color, the more mellow the flavor. The Chioggia beet is nicknamed "candy cane" because its core is striped with red and white circles.

✓ Beets are often sold with their nutritious greens attached. Avoid wilted greens, and sauté them like their relative Swiss chard.

Storing basics:

✓ Cut off the greens, leaving about one inch of stem. Place in a plastic bag and refrigerate for up to two weeks.

Cooking 101:

✓ Keep the skins on during cooking; this helps retain moisture and nutrients. To remove the skins—and prevent staining—rub the cooked beets with a paper towel or run them under cold water while wearing rubber gloves.

✓ No time to cook? Raw beets can be peeled, grated, and tossed with a light vinaigrette for a quick, healthy salad. Spark up the flavor with grated gingerroot or sesame oil.

Did you know?

✓ It's not an old wives' tale: Urine may turn reddish after you eat beets. This reaction, called beeturia, is harmless.

Oven-roasted beets:

✓ To prepare, rub with olive oil, sprinkle with salt and pepper, and place in a roasting pan. Bake at 375 degrees Fahrenheit for approximately 45 minutes, or until a knife can easily go through the center of the beet. Remove the skins. Slice and serve warm, plain, or tossed with butter and vinegar. Or chill the cooked beet slices and layer on top of greens. Dress with vinaigrette, and sprinkle with toasted nuts and blue or goat cheese.

Shredded Beets with Celery and Dates

Preparation time: about 10 minutes

Makes about 4 cups, or 8 accompaniment servings

Ingredients: 1 pound beets, peeled; 3 stalks celery, thinly sliced; ½ cup pitted, dried dates, chopped; 3 tablespoons fresh lemon juice; salt and coarsely ground black pepper

Cut beets into quarters. In a food processor with the shredding blade attached, shred beets; transfer to a large bowl. Stir in celery, dates, lemon juice, and ¼ teaspoon each of salt and pepper. If not serving right away, cover and refrigerate up to four hours.

Each serving: About 50 calories, 1 gram protein, 13 grams carbohydrates, 0 grams total fat, 2 grams fiber, 0 milligrams cholesterol, 110 milligrams sodium.

Red Cabbage Spaghetti with Golden Raisins

Preparation time: about 10 minutes

Cooking time: about 25 minutes

Makes about 8 cups, or 6 accompaniment servings

Ingredients: Salt; 1 small head red cabbage (about 1½ pounds); 1 tablespoon olive oil; 1 small onion, chopped; 1 clove garlic, crushed with a press; 1 cup apple juice; ½ cup golden raisins; pinch ground cloves; 8 ounces thin spaghetti (rice pasta)

1. Heat large, covered saucepot of cold water and 2 teaspoons salt to boiling over high heat.

2. Meanwhile, discard any tough outer leaves from cabbage. Cut cabbage into quarters; cut core from each quarter. Thinly slice cabbage.

3. In a 12-inch skillet, heat oil over medium heat. Add onion and cook about 8 minutes or until tender, stirring occasionally. Add garlic and cook 1 minute, stirring. Stir in cabbage, apple juice, raisins, cloves, and ½ teaspoon salt. Cover and cook about 15 minutes or until cabbage is tender, stirring occasionally.

4. About 5 minutes before cabbage is done, add pasta to boiling water and cook as label directs.

5. Reserve ¼ cup pasta cooking water; drain pasta. Stir pasta into cabbage mixture in skillet; add cooking water if mixture seems dry.

Each serving: About 255 calories, 7 grams protein, 50 grams carbohydrates, 3 grams total fat (0 grams saturated), 4 grams fiber, 0 milligrams cholesterol, 275 milligrams sodium.

Broccoli Gratin

Preparation time: about 10 minutes

Cooking/broiling time: about 20 minutes

Makes about 4 cups, or 8 accompaniment servings

Ingredients: 1 pound broccoli florets; 1 pound Yukon Gold potatoes, peeled and cut into 1-inch chunks; 2 cups water; pinch ground nutmeg; ¾ cup freshly grated Parmesan cheese (about 2½ ounces); salt and coarsely ground black pepper

1. In a 4-quart saucepan, place broccoli, potatoes, and water. On high heat, cover and heat until boiling. Then reduce heat to medium-low and cook, covered, 17 to 20 minutes, or until potatoes and broccoli are very tender, stirring once halfway through cooking.

2. Meanwhile, preheat the broiler and set the oven rack 6 inches from the source of heat.

3. Drain vegetables in a colander set over a large bowl, reserving ¼ cup vegetable cooking liquid. Return vegetables to saucepan. With a potato masher or slotted spoon, coarsely mash vegetables, adding some reserved cooking liquid if mixture seems dry. Stir in nutmeg, ¼ cup Parmesan, ½ teaspoon salt, and ¼ teaspoon pepper.

4. In a shallow, broiler-safe 1- to 1½-quart baking dish, spread vegetable mixture; sprinkle with remaining Parmesan. Place dish in oven and broil 2 to 3 minutes or until Parmesan is browned.

Each serving: About 95 calories, 6 grams protein, 13 grams carbohydrates, 3 grams total fat (2 grams saturated), 2 grams fiber, 6 milligrams cholesterol, 305 milligrams sodium.

Lemon Cilantro Eggplant Dip

Preparation time: about 10 minutes, plus chilling

Roasting time: about 45 minutes

Makes about 2 cups dip

Ingredients: 2 eggplants (1 pound each), each halved lengthwise; 4 cloves garlic, unpeeled; 3 tablespoons tahini (sesame puree); 3 tablespoons fresh lemon juice; salt; ¼ cup loosely packed fresh cilantro; chopped toasted or grilled pita wedges; carrot and cucumber sticks and red or yellow pepper slices

1. Preheat oven to 450° F. Line a 15½ × 10½ in. jelly roll pan with nonstick foil (or use regular foil and spray with nonstick cooking spray). Place eggplant halves, skin-side up, in foiled-lined pan. Wrap garlic in foil and place in pan with eggplant. Roast vegetables 45 to 50 minutes or until eggplant is very tender and skin is shriveled and browned. Unwrap garlic. Cook eggplant and garlic until easy to handle.

2. When cool, scoop the eggplant flesh into a food processor with the knife blade attached. Squeeze out the garlic pulp from each clove and add to food processor with tahini, lemon juice, and ¾ teaspoon salt; pulse to coarsely chop. Spoon dip into serving bowl; stir in cilantro. Cover and refrigerate at least 2 hours. Serve dip with pita and vegetables.

Each tablespoon: About 10 calories, 0 grams protein, 2 grams carbohydrates, 0 grams total fat, 1 gram fiber, 0 milligrams cholesterol, 55 milligrams sodium.

Sesame Ginger Brussels Sprouts

Preparation time: about 15 minutes

Cooking time: about 15 minutes

Makes about 4 cups, or 8 accompaniment servings

Ingredients: 2 containers (10 ounces each) Brussels sprouts; 2 tablespoons tamari (which is available wheat-free); 2 teaspoons grated, peeled fresh ginger; 1 teaspoon Asian sesame oil; 1 table-spoon olive oil; 1 large onion (about 12 ounces), cut in half and thinly sliced; 2 tablespoons water

1. Trim stems and any yellow leaves from Brussels sprouts. Cut each sprout lengthwise into quarters. In a cup, stir together tamari, grated ginger, and sesame oil.

2. Meanwhile, in a nonstick 12-inch skillet, heat olive oil over medium heat until hot. Add onion and cook about 5 minutes or until the onion begins to soften, stirring occasionally.

3. Increase heat to medium-high; add Brussels sprouts and water; cover and cook about 5 minutes or until sprouts are beginning to soften and brown, stirring once. Remove cover from skillet and cook about 5 minutes longer or until sprouts are tender-crisp, stirring frequently. Remove skillet from heat; stir in tamari mixture.

Each serving: About 65 calories, 3 grams protein, 10 grams carbohydrates, 3 grams total fat (0 grams saturated), 3 grams fiber, 0 milligrams cholesterol, 165 milligrams sodium.

Strawberry Spinach Salad

Preparation time: about 5 minutes

Makes about 12 cups, or 6 accompaniment servings

Ingredients: 1 pound strawberries, hulled and sliced; 2 tablespoons plus 1 teaspoon white balsamic vinegar; 1 tablespoon olive oil; salt and coarsely ground black pepper; 2 bags (5 to 6 ounces each) baby spinach; 3 ounces goat cheese, such as Montrachet, crumbled (¾ cup); ¼ cup sliced almonds, toasted (see note)

1. In a blender, puree ¾ cup strawberries with vinegar, olive oil, ¼ teaspoon salt, and ⅛ teaspoon pepper. Transfer vinaigrette to a large serving bowl.

2. Add spinach and remaining strawberries to bowl and toss to coat with dressing. Crumble goat cheese over the top of the salad and sprinkle with toasted almonds.

Each serving: About 115 calories, 6 grams protein, 7 grams carbohydrates, 8 grams total fat (3 grams saturated), 7 grams fiber, 7 milligrams cholesterol, 215 milligrams sodium.

Note: To toast sliced almonds, place in a small skillet and cook over medium heat 2 to 3 minutes or until golden, stirring occasionally. Transfer to a plate to cool.

MAKE IT QUICK

Oven-Roasted Brussels Sprouts

Trim and halve Brussels sprouts from two 10-ounce containers; toss in a jelly roll pan with 1 tablespoon olive oil. Roast in a preheated 450° F oven 20 to 25 minutes or until tender and browned, stirring once or twice. Toss with 2 tablespoons seasoned rice vinegar and pepper to taste. Serves 4.

Each serving: About 95 calories, 4 grams protein, 14 grams carbohydrates, 4 grams total fat (0.8 gram saturated), 5 grams fiber, 0 milligrams cholesterol, 295 milligrams sodium.

Basil and Balsamic Beets

In a 13 × 9 in. roasting pan, toss 2 pounds beets with 1 tablespoon olive oil. Roast in a preheated 450° F oven 1 hour or until tender. Cool beets; peel and discard skins. Dice beets; toss with 2 tablespoons each chopped fresh basil and balsamic vinegar, 1 tablespoon honey, and ¼ teaspoon salt. Serves 4.

Each serving: About 115 calories, 2 grams protein, 19 grams carbohydrates, 4 grams total fat (0.5 gram saturated), 4 grams fiber, 0 milligrams cholesterol, 260 milligrams sodium.

Grilled Eggplant with Feta and Fresh Mint

Cut one large eggplant (about 1½ pounds) into ½-inch-thick slices; brush each slice with 2 tablespoons olive oil. Place on a hot, ridged grill pan over medium-high heat; cook eggplant slices 4 to 5 minutes per side or until tender. Transfer to a platter. Sprinkle with ¼ cup feta cheese and 2 tablespoons chopped fresh mint, and drizzle with fresh lemon juice. Garnish with lemon wedges. Serves 4.

Each serving: About 105 calories, 3 grams protein, 9 grams carbohydrates, 7 grams total fat (2 grams saturated), 4 grams fiber, 8 milligrams cholesterol, 110 milligrams sodium.

WORKS CITED

Berg, Eric. *The 7 Principles of Fat Burning*. Alexandria: KB Publishing, 2010.

Davis, Martha, Elizabeth Robbins Eshelman, and Matthew McKay. *The Relaxation and Stress Reduction Workbook*. Oakland: New Harbinger Publications, Inc., 2008.

DeMaria, Robert. *Dr. Bob's Guide to Stop ADHD in 18 Days*. Elyria: Drugless Doctor LLC, 2010.

DeMaria, Robert. *Dr. Bob's Trans Fat Survival Guide*. Elyria: Drugless Healthcare Solutions, 2005.

Erasmus, Udo. *Fats That Heal, Fats That Kill*. Burnaby, BC: Alive Books, 1993.

Gittleman, Ann Louise. *Why Am I Always So Tired?*. New York: HarperCollins Publishers, 1999.

Lepore, Donald. *The Ultimate Healing System*. Salt Lake City: Woodland Publishing, 1998.

Madeira, John. *Setting Things Straight*. Self-published, 2006.

Sharma, Hari, and Rama K. Mishra. *The Answer to Cancer*. New York: SelectBooks, 2002.

Tips, Jack. *The Healing Triad: Your Liver...Your Lifeline*. Austin: Apple-a-Day Press, 1998.

Wilson, James. *Adrenal Fatigue*. Petaluma: Smart Publications, 2001.

PRODUCT INFORMATION

There are many companies that create excellent products. I have personally used and recommended the items mentioned in the book with consistent success. You may already have a preferred source of supplements. I would encourage you to use what you have found to be successful; but if you are like so many who come into my office with boxes and bags of partially used bottles and have experienced minimal or no improvement, maybe it is time to seek other options.

If this is your first time thinking about implementing a drugless, natural strategy to achieve optimal health, I suggest that before you spend your time and money, you find a knowledgeable, experienced drugless healthcare provider to assist you in navigating all the possibilities. For those of you who have been pursuing natural care for some time and have either reached a plateau or are not getting the response you expect, do not give up; you would be wise to pursue another provider or contact me to help you. I intentionally did not list a specific protocol for the conditions and body signals discussed because you and your physiology are as unique as your fingerprint, requiring individual treatment.

You can locate many items, such as castor-oil packs and pH paper, at your local health-food or natural-food store. I have recommended products from the companies listed on the next page with great success. The source and quality of the items you utilize do make quite a difference.

If you are unable to locate the products, you can call 1-888-922-5672 or visit www.druglessdoctor.com.

I recommend the following nutritional manufacturers:

✓ **Biotics Research**

✓ **Omega Nutrition**

✓ **The Grain & Salt Society (Selina Naturally)**

CONSULTATIONS AND SERVICES

I am frequently asked about conditions for which individuals are not receiving answers. I would suggest that you exhaust your local community of healthcare providers. If you are not able to find answers, you can have a phone consultation with me or one of my associates. Patients also travel to our clinic. You can visit my website at www.druglessdoctor.com for details. Procedures including hair analysis, saliva testing, and other screens can be completed long-distance. You would follow the same procedure as you would for a consultation, since these services would need to be sent to the appropriate lab.

SEMINARS, WORKSHOPS, WELLNESS EVENTS, BUSINESSES, CHURCHES, ORGANIZATIONS

I am available on a limited basis to travel to your location. There are attendance minimums. I generally need to schedule six months to one year in advance, so if you are thinking about having a special event, please contact me early, at 1-888-922-5672 or drbob@ druglessdoctor.com.

Index

bromine, 84
bronzing of left cheek, 179
brown rice syrup, 268, 269
brown sugar, 271
B vitamin, 23, 33, 34, 70

C

caffeine, 94, 145
calcium carbonate, 175
calcium citrate, 218
calcium-D glucarate, 41
calcium lactate, 218
calcium levels, 85, 86, 104, 115, 116, 175, 263
cancer, 2, 3, 21, 39, 58, 62, 73, 188, 192, 234
cane juice crystals, 268
carbohydrates, 32, 234, 245, 246
    refined, 232
carcinogens, 2, 3, 41
carpal tunnel syndrome, 259
castor oil, 200–201
    massage, 201
    topical applications, 202
castor-oil pack, 199, 201, 202, 203, 204
    benefits, 204
cat stretch, 125
causes of hormonal imbalances, 26
cellular metabolism, 12
Celtic Sea Salt®, 82, 98, 110, 111, 149, 166, 219, 243, 254, 304
Center for Science in the Public Interest (CSPI), 220
cervix, 15
chemotherapy treatment, 63
cherry hemangiomas, 282, 304, 307
chiropractor, 50, 114, 137, 178, 197
chlorinated water, 111
chlorine, 84, 86, 110, 283
cholesterol, 16, 26, 36, 71, 90, 91, 96, 251, 257, 258
cholesterol-lowering medication, 258
chromium, 115, 182, 243, 278
chronic fatigue, 22
cleansing protocols, 70–74, 199–215
clinical testing, 177
coconut oil, 288
coffee enema, 72, 73, 210–214
    preparation, 211
cold sores, 179
colon, 70
    functions, 191
    problems, 204
colonic irrigation, 70, 205, 208, 287
complex carbohydrates, 146
concentrated fruit juice, 271
conjugated estrogens, 19
constipation, 17, 26, 48, 70, 71, 83, 204

convenience foods, 14, 78
copper, 25, 48
coral calcium, 175
corn syrup, 272
coronary artery spasm, 23
corpus luteum, 16, 46
cortex, 91
cortisol, 16, 17, 32, 84, 90, 91, 148, 172, 283
    elevated, 107
cortisone, 16, 36, 95, 252, 283
    production, 91
crystalline fructose, 273
cyclooxygenase (COX), 260
cystic breasts, 48

D

dairy, 39, 58, 221, 236, 288
date sugar, 270, 271
Davis, Martha, 148
depression, 17, 21, 22, 33, 37, 47, 48, 54, 71, 305
detoxification, 74, 282, 287
dextrose, 272
DHEA (dehydroepiandrosterone), 16, 50, 90, 98, 172, 303
    symptoms of deficiency, 53, 54
    symptoms of excess in females, 54
DHT (dihydrotestosterone), 90
dietary changes, 142, 187–198
dietary support, 146
digestive aids with calcium, 175
dihydrotesterone (DHT), 90
diindolylmethane (DIM), 41
dioxins, 39
distilled drinking water, 175
DNA damage, 21
doorjamb push-up, 125
Dr. Bob's ABCs (apples, beets, and carrots), 41, 64, 178, 254
Dr. Bob's Trans Fat Survival Guide: Why No Fat, Low Fat, Trans Fat Is Killing You!, 254, 263
dry mouth, 71
dry skin, 37, 83, 202, 305
dysglycemia, 305
dysplasia, 6, 131, 202

E

edema, 20, 23
electrolytes, 12
endocrine glands, 6, 12, 32, 301
endocrine system, 12
    glands comprising, 13
    imbalances and deficiencies, 14
endometrial cancer, 21
endometriosis, 21, 48, 131, 196
enzymes, 13, 259
Equal®, 271

proteins, 32, 57, 173
protomorphogens, 82
proton-pump inhibitors, 223
Provera®(medroxyprogesterone acetate), 22
psoriasis, 71
psycho-sensitive medications, 78
pulmonary embolism, 21, 23
pyruvic acidosis, 172

R

Rabin, Roni, 266
radiation treatment, 63
raw sugar cane, 235, 278
red wine, 237
*Relaxation and Stress Reduction Workbook,
The,* 148
relaxation exercises, 147, 149
reproductive system, 12
respiratory infections, 204
retracted testicles, 39
rice syrup, 274
ricinoleic acid, 200
Roberts, Jan, 298
rotational subluxation, 183

S

sacroiliac joint, 177
saliva hormone test, 172
saliva pH test, 170
saliva progesterone and estrogen test, 96,
98, 136
saliva test, 172, 197, 288
saliva zinc test, 170
salt, cravings, 26, 44, 92
saturated fats, 250, 262
secondary sex characteristics, 91
sedentary lifestyle, 94
selenium, 81, 149, 182, 287
serum globulin level, 116
serum levels, 83
sex hormone–binding globulin (SHBG), 22
sex hormones, 17, 24, 90, 91, 257
Sharma, Dr. Hari, 63, 190
simple carbohydrates, 145
skin rashes, 23, 70, 71
skin tabs, 179
sleepiness, 48, 83, 92
smoking, 93
sodium chloride, 81, 180
sodium lauryl sulfate, 91, 132
sodium retention, 82
sorbitol, 272
soy, 41, 78, 79, 139, 146, 149, 193, 217,
220, 299, 300, 305, 306
    avoidance, 142
    phytoestrogenic effects, 146

soy milk, 236
Soy Online Service, 146, 221
spider veins, 34, 62, 179
spinal adjustment, 123
spinal alignment, 123, 141, 146
spinal cord, 120
spinal misalignment, 122
spinal subluxation, 137
Splenda®, 267, 268, 271
steroid, 20, 36, 50, 90, 301
steroid androgen hormone, 54
steroid system, 18–19
sterols, 19
stevia, 269, 274, 278
stimulants, 94
stress, 16, 17, 26, 84, 92, 93, 115, 144,
147, 289, 306
stroke, 23
subluxation, 122, 146, 182
sucrose, 271, 272
sugar, 26, 33, 82, 97, 136, 149, 179, 221,
224, 232, 259, 267, 288
    avoidance, 142
    cravings, 92
    metabolism, 91
sugar alcohol, 268, 272
sugar substitutes, 267–273
sugar substitution, 274
sunglasses, 14, 26
supplements, 5, 86, 137, 217–221
sweetener alternatives, 267–273
sweeteners, 235, 267–273, 278
    to avoid, 273
Swiss balls, 227
synthetic estrogen, 16, 18, 19
    side effects, 18
Synthroid®, 82

T

T3 (triiodothyronine), 49, 80, 83, 84, 136, 173,
220, 226, 286, 304
    testing, 197
T4 (thyroxine), 49, 80, 83, 84, 136, 173, 220,
226, 286, 304
    testing, 197
table salt, 81
table sugar, 271
testes, 13, 50, 285, 306
testoids, 91, 302
testosterone, 22, 50, 54, 90, 91, 92, 172,
301, 303, 305, 306
    in females, 55
    symptoms of deficiency in females, 55
    symptoms of excess in females, 55
therapeutic massage treatments, 61
threonine, 219
thymus gland, 13, 201

thyroid evaluation, 115
thyroid function tests, 294
thyroid gland, 5, 6, 13, 17, 139, 282, 285,
  305, 306
    fueling, 77–88
    functions, 79, 80
    low-functioning, 112
    parts, 80
thyroid medications, 223
thyroid panel of tests, 116, 136, 137, 184
thyroid-releasing hormone (TRH), 81
thyroid-stimulating hormone (TSH), 80
thyroxine (T4), 32, 80
Tietze syndrome, 149
Tips, Jack, 67
tonsils, 57, 64
toxins, 70, 94, 135
To Your Health, 299
trachea, 80
trans fat, 26, 93, 134, 144, 154, 187, 258,
  260, 261, 288, 289
    avoidance, 255
TRH (thyrotropin-releasing hormone), 81
triglyceride fatty acid, 200
triglycerides, 234
triiodothyronine (T3), 80
TSH (thyroid-stimulating hormone), 49, 80, 83,
  225, 226, 286, 294, 304
    testing, 197
turbinado sugar, 271
turmeric, 73, 74
twin-scale measuring, 176, 177
tyrosine, 80, 84

U

Ultimate Healing System, The, 110, 219
unrefined cane juice, 273
urinary issues, 83
urine analysis, 177
urine iodine loading test, 86, 173
uterus, 12, 15

V

vagina, 15
vaginal dryness, 37
vaginal infections, 204
varicose veins, 34, 62, 179
vegetable juice, 73
vegetable oil, 256
vegetables, 233
venous thromboembolism, 21
vitamin D, 91, 111, 173
vitamin K, 70

W

walking, 167
Wall Street Journal (WSJ), 104, 302
water, 60, 64, 74, 134, 165, 171, 236, 237,
  289, 297
    chlorinated, 111
water retention, 37, 47
weight gain, 20, 22, 37, 47, 71, 83, 234
weight loss, 294
*What Your Doctor May Not Tell You About
  Premenopause*, 42
wheat and grains, 234, 235, 299, 305, 306
whey, 219
white blood cells, 44
White, Dr. Stuart, 42
whole-food B vitamins, 32, 41, 98, 136, 263
whole foods, 64, 79
whole-food-sourced iodine, 136
whole-food supplements, 146, 147
whole-food vitamin E, 179
whole-food zinc, 263
whole fruit, 269, 270
Why Am I Always So Tired?, 146, 193, 219
Wilson, James, 175
windpipe, 80

X

xenohormones, 16, 26, 38, 50, 282, 285
    common sources, 38
    disorders related to, 39
    steps to avoid exposure, 39, 40
x-ray assessment, 182
x-ray mammography, 185
xylitol, 272

Y

yeast infection, 172
yogurt, 217

Z

zinc, 38, 48, 192, 259, 263, 299, 304, 305
zinc deficiency, 179, 191, 192, 306
zinc sulfate, 170

Special Appearances
Radio, TV &
Corporate Events

Dr. DeMaria is available on a limited basis to speak at your next Corporate Event or Convention. His energetic speaking style will inspire, educate, and motivate your employees to greater levels of health, wealth, and personal confidence. Dr. Bob's enthusiam for life is **contagious!**

To schedule or inquire please call:

1.888.922.5672

or email: drbob@druglessdoctor.com

Books by Dr. Bob

Dr. Bob's Drugless Guide to Detoxification

This may be the most toxic time in history. Daily headlines report the negative conditions of our water, food, and air. The "green movement" is popularly creating a mind-set to secure a safe, cleaner environment, but little is said about the circumstances our bodies need to contend with. This book is a logical plan that establishes true wellness in your body from the inside out. Dr. Bob shares clinically proven, time-tested protocols that can be followed in the comfort of your own home—no need to travel to expensive clinics or follow strict and stressful diet plans.

You will learn what to purchase at your own grocery store to maintain a healthy body; how to be empowered to make wise choices and not be dependent on medications; how to avert possible surgical intervention to remove an exhausted, dysfunctional organ; and what to eat and what to avoid to create an optimally functioning cellular environment!

Dr. Bob's Drugless Guide to Balancing Female Hormones

The time-tested information in this book is designed to create a state of optimal health in the female hormonal system. Dr. Bob's insight into cellular function will empower the reader to make wise choices for nourishing and detoxifying the body with items that can be easily incorporated into a day-to-day routine. You will learn that a clear and clean lymphatic system is important and that a functioning liver is vital for balance. Nutrients like iodine and proper oil help create the foundation needed to progress into hormonal maturity without annoying body signals. You will be exposed to the procedures that Dr. Bob has used in his career to transition his patients to feeling great without medication.

Dr. Bob's Guide to Stop ADHD in 18 Days

A Drugless Family Guide to Optimal Health

SEE IF YOU CAN PASS THE ADHD TEST ON PAGE XXII. Anyone can successfully overcome ADHD and hyperactivity without drugs. This book details how to get your children and family off medications and detrimental junk foods filled with trans-fatty acid, dairy products, sugar, and preservatives, so that they can have optimal, natural health. This is a simple, effective, step-by-step plan that includes taking FLAX OIL and modifying your diet and vitamin/mineral intake. The protocol will improve your nervous system function and help you overcome behavioral and learning problems. It will improve insomnia, mood swings, and irritability. The result will be that your body is healing itself naturally. Participants in the pilot program saw improvement in only 18 days. NATURALLY!

Dr. Bob's Trans Fat Survival Guide:

Why No Fat, Low Fat, Trans Fat Is KILLING YOU!

This book explains the dangers of trans fat, commonly called hydrogenated or partially hydrogenated fat, as well as how to recognize this fat in everyday foods by properly reading nutritional labels. Along with trans fat, you will learn about the different types of fats; which ones are beneficial; and which ones should be used for cooking, baking, or eating. Not to leave the reader hanging with questions on how to eliminate dangerous fats and take on a healthier approach to life, there are several sections dealing with how to make those changes, transitioning healthier foods into one's eating plan. This book will encourage and empower you to make better choices and learn to live an optimally healthy life.